GALLERY

'Ne'er quiet beach stone or shell lay upon'

For Taeko Seki

Published 2017 by Waverley Books, an imprint of
The Gresham Publishing Company Ltd.,
Academy Park, Building 4000, Gower Street,
Glasgow, G51 1PR, Scotland, UK

Text copyright © William Hardie 2017
Photographs copyright © 2017 William Hardie and/or used
by arrangement and permission of the copyright holders.

A catalogue entry for this book is available from the British Library.

ISBN 978-1-84934-455-5

Printed and bound in the EU.

GALLERY

A Life in Art

William Hardie

WAVERLEY
BOOKS

Acknowledgements

My first debt is to Taeko Seki, who believed from start to finish that this book should be written. The late Barry Holmes was the first editor of the work. Carol Foreman helped me make my notes more coherent. Fiona Robertson was my secretary at the gallery. And without the unfailing support of my wife Gillian it could not have happened. To all the collectors, artists, and museums mentioned I am especially grateful.

W.H.

Credits

p.13	'I am a tadpole ... '	William Hardie
p.21	*Margaret*	William Hardie
p.42	'Sire he lives ... '	John Mason Neale
p.51	'The book is ... '	William Butler Yeats
p.52	'And a strange song ... '	Fiona Macleod
p.79	'Praxitella, aloof ... '	William Hardie
p.119	'Fearless approach ... '	Robert Graves
pp.157–9	*Timelessness*	
	Ancestor Worship	
	The Wrythen Newel	
	Autograph	
	Trapeze	William Hardie

Contents

1   Girl In A Paisley Shawl   7

2   Painting My Room   15

3   *Et Ego In Academia*   23

4   Albert Square   33

5   Portrait Of The Artist As A Young Man   49

6   The Third Man   61

7   Nineteen Eighty-Four   75

8   *Annus Mirabilis*   93

9   The Go-Between   103

10 My Camcorder's Been To Hollywood . . .   123

11 . . . And Conholt Park   135

12 At The Edge Of The Wood   145

13 Kimono   161

14 Room With A View   175

Postscript   185

Index   187

Picture Acknowledgements   192

Over twenty years my gallery staged nearly a hundred exhibitions of paintings. Earlier, as a museum keeper of art and then working in Christie's, I was looking at art from other perspectives. As a student I was reliant on the printed page but the experience of art was no less vivid for that. This book is a promenade through a *musée imaginaire* of some of these encounters.

1   Girl In A Paisley Shawl

Shamrockbank was my grandparents' house in Dumbarton on the River Clyde, west of Glasgow. You would hardly guess it today, but the town has a long history. Dumbarton Castle on the high basalt rock is the vestige of a royal past. This was the citadel of the Scots. The two-handed sword said to have belonged to William Wallace was once kept there. Dumbarton Rock and its Castle stand at the confluence of the Clyde with the River Leven which flows through the town from the bonnie banks of Loch Lomond.

Less martial is Dunglass Castle, built next to the Clyde shore eastward. With its minimal fortifications (the odd gun-loop here and there, a yett at the front entrance) and a walled garden containing a giant obelisk to Henry Bell, Dunglass is more fortified manor house than castle. Here in his younger days Charles Rennie Mackintosh, the Scottish architect, designer and artist, designed a decoration for one of the rooms and drew wild flowers in the glebe. Nearby at Bowling is the westernmost basin of the Forth and Clyde Canal, along which goods could be carried through the centre of Glasgow and to the port of Grangemouth on the Forth. Today rail and the switchback road are the connection to the bright lights of the city.

Old prints suggest that two centuries ago Dumbarton's dominant features were two tall cone-shaped glass-making kilns, which would have used potash from seaweed gathered mostly by women and burnt on the shore. 'Burning Kelp' is the subject of many a nineteenth-century Scottish painting; it ranks with 'Gathering Mussels' as a favourite subject, replaced by 'Gathering Mushrooms', a more fey semi-nocturnal activity recorded by the Glasgow School. The glass-making kilns are long-forgotten, but the famous Denny shipyard and Ballantine's whisky distillery were there until recently. 'The Artisans' was the name of the row of dwellings and workshops on the townside eastern bank of the Leven where many trades including some with links to the sea – carpentry, chandlery – would have clustered, all now obliterated by the improvers. At Singer they once made sewing machines for the world, at Alexandria, Turkey Red carpets, and at Babcox & Wilcox, airframes; all now gone. The novelist Tobias Smollett attended Dumbarton Academy and so two hundred years later did I, until I was seven years old.

Across the Leven bridge lies the other Dumbarton, where Shamrockbank and similar Victorian villas nestle into a leafy hillside with a panoramic view of the Clyde. This stretch of the river has seen newly built ships bound for the oceans of the world: from Henry Bell's *Comet*, the first seagoing steamship, and the *Cutty Sark*, built at Denny's yard in the town, to the *Queen Mary* and *Queen Elizabeth*, made in John Brown's shipyard. Although the Clyde is wide at that point, the shipping channel, then constantly dredged, is narrow. These icons of shipbuilding loomed large in the view from Shamrockbank and often came up in conversation. They were part of the view the town had of itself. Later I actually met Dr John Brown (later Sir) who had helped design the *Queens*. This was in the early 1980s when he looked like an elderly doctor of medicine who had touched immortality.

Every night the Belfast ferry would pass, lights ablaze, on its journey from the Broomielaw in the centre of Glasgow to Ulster. In the 1950s there was still enough river traffic to make it possible, just, to imagine the great days of the upstream shipyards and of the bustling wharves of the Broomielaw in Glasgow. To imagine the transatlantic tobacco, sugar and cotton traffic in the days of sail was a more difficult feat. At its peak in 1771 forty million pounds' worth of tobacco was shipped from Chesapeake Bay to the Clyde. James Boswell records departures for the Hebrides. Later, the great square-riggers would leave from Greenock down-river with their charge of emigrants to America and Canada.

William McTaggart's *The Sailing of the Emigrant Ship* captures more of the hope than the pathos of emigration, as well as a sense of sea and sunlight. Another painting on this theme, Thomas Faed's airless *The Last of the Clan*, stresses loss and separation from loved ones; dread of the present and the future, are there for all to see. These were the two faces of emigration, the creation of a better life or an enforced rupture from family and country. My family stayed where they were, at home.

Seascape and landscape imply transits, passages, journeys, roads to somewhere else. A house is a repository of memory, what has been rather than what might have been. Houses stand for permanence, what remains. At least they do for me, perhaps because as a family we have not been flighty or nomadic, tending to be of fixed abode at the same address for long stretches of time, and in an odd instance even returning. My paternal grandmother was orphaned as a child and was brought up by relatives, Sir and Lady Somebody-or-other, who at one stage, as my parents only discovered later, lived in the selfsame house in Manse Road, Bearsden, which we were later to occupy decades later as a family from 1957. As a weekend retreat they found and restored two railway cottages opposite the old Steele Road Smithy in which my paternal grandfather William Hardie had served his apprenticeship as a blacksmith before 1900. When we moved to Broughty Ferry a long time ago, we brought into the new house a painting illustrated in a book by the outgoing owner of the house, William Montgomerie. Margaret Morris and J.D. (John Duncan) Fergusson had been guests there, and we were visited by another artist, Peter Blake, who had just finished the *Sergeant Pepper* album cover. In the snowy winter of 1973 on my first evening in Toronto, I had dinner with Gladys and Willie Ralston, in the very same building where I met Kathleen Daly Pepper twenty years later. She was an artist who was married to the Group of Seven painter George Pepper and had a white handbag signed by Pablo Picasso. The art world too is small.

William Robertson, my maternal grandfather, was a builder and joiner in Dumbarton's College Street. He had a patent to his name as an inventor. He always carried a folding ruler in a tailor-made pocket in his suits, but although every inch the self-made man, he was also a fond grandfather, endlessly devising new delights for us children, just as he lavished much care on the large garden and his collection of paintings. Shamrockbank, his pride and joy, remains, as it was then, a square stone villa with a brass-studded outer door of oak behind which is a vestibule or porch, with flagstones and a glass-panelled door engraved 'Shamrockbank' leading to the hall and its tessellated floor. It sits on the north bank of the Clyde surrounded by gardens and a wood. Apple, pear and cherry trees planted for blossom as well as fruit stood beside espaliers of red- and blackcurrant. There was one young apple tree with which I think I was in love, Xerxes-like. I wanted it to be my tree. Each year it produced two or three beautiful apples with a red skin, perfect shape and white flesh – but this fruit was bitter. There were peonies, dahlias, chrysanthemums, roses, honeysuckle and, as everywhere on Scotland's west coast, rhododendrons (an importation from Nepal) and a rockery beyond the lawn with its rustic summer house. The kitchen garden was planted with vegetables, peas, summer fruit; and sweet peas for scent. As children we enjoyed the infinite possibilities of the outdoors and the predictable pleasures of the house, like a sprinkling of glucose powder on porridge in the morning, or the huge old mangle in action in the laundry with its flagstone floor. A tiny television appeared in time for the Queen's Coronation in 1953.

Our immediate neighbours might have been drafted in by an estate agent wishing to impress. Below the garden towards the shore was the Victorian pile of Methlan Park, with its Italianate tower and cypresses and a hothouse for its garden. To the right beyond the wood was an overgrown private road which continued beyond the estate wall of Helenslee House to the shore. Helenslee had belonged to the Denny shipbuilding family before it became Keil School; I visited it much later with Elizabeth Denny, but even in her company it was difficult to imagine in its less ascetic days. My grandfather did not keep a cellar, wine did not exist, and the household whisky was kept for medicinal purposes, being applied to midge bites. Presumably austerity had always reigned in the picturesque Carmelite Monastery in its tree-shrouded setting above Shamrockbank. Did they have pictures?

Mr Grant, a neighbour who was a director of Hiram Walker's whisky distillery in the town, often came with his sister Miss Grant to play cards of an evening. My mother played a good hand of bridge – a legacy from the long winter evenings round the fire at Shamrockbank. In 1939 she married my father who was training at Catterick in Yorkshire prior to an Army commission. The young couple lived in married quarters in Beverley, and I was born in Yorkshire. My father left for service in France, returning via Dunkirk. During much of the rest of the war, he was in India and Ceylon. He attended the Staff College of the Indian Army at Quetta (now in northern Pakistan) and stayed on for six months after the end of the war helping with the repatriation of prisoners. I wish I had asked him about the Dunkirk evacuation and about the India of the last years of the Raj. He loved India and brought back a small collection of shells and two Indian *kukri* but got rid of them as they were not the kind of things to have in a house with young children about.

During these years we lived in Chapelton Gardens in Dumbarton, one of a row of bungalows built by my grandfather. Uncle Jack Robertson, Aunt Rhoda and my cousins lived in another cottage, and the brother and sister Norman and Totie – her real name was Dorothy – Burnett in yet another. It was cosy; but I can remember sandbags, barrage balloons, and talk of an unexploded incendiary bomb removed from the roof at Shamrockbank. Both banks of the river received regular night visits from Luftwaffe raiders as they flew up-river at the limit of their range to attack the shipyards. Several bombs and numerous incendiaries came close – this was after all the Clyde, and near enough Denny's, John Brown's and the Clydebank shipyards to attract ordnance from German bombers. My grand-aunt's family were bombed out of their house close to the river. Fortunately there was nobody home at the time.

Shamrockbank was sold a long time ago, but I still remember where all the paintings (decorative pictures by the Glasgow School of painters) were hung in the house. Opposite the 'press' or shallow cupboard, behind whose door my grandfather recorded our heights – measured by his trademark ruler – was *The Girl in a Paisley Shawl* painted in 1917 by the Kirkcudbright artist Edward Atkinson Hornel. The girl in the painting seems to be about ten or eleven years of age; she is executing a dance or perhaps just striking an attitude with her voluminous multicoloured shawl. I met her in the flesh fifty years after Hornel painted her, interviewing her in Kirkcudbright as one of the two Mackenzie sisters who were his only models, for an article on the artist. The girls were often posed for photographs in the studio in Kirkcudbright. Miss Mackenzie in her interview with me described the artist as 'an awful man' – a term used in Scotland of a rogue who commands approval and disapproval in equal measure. Today his fondness for juvenile female subjects is deprecated. I found, however, that readers of my piece in 1968 were more exercised by the fact that Hornel used photography which was not considered quite the done thing despite its having fascinated artists from Degas to Hockney. Recently the pendulum of taste has swung in favour of Jack Vettriano, an artist who has had enormous success by using someone else's photographs to compose paintings of which the louche subject matter is the whole point.

The painting by Hornel was always 'Moira's picture' and is so inscribed on the back, in my grandfather's hand. She was the youngest of the family, probably not yet in her teens when the picture was bought. It is easily supposed that her fond father saw similarities between the young performer in the painting and the actress-to-be who was his darling daughter. She went on to minor stardom in the Citizen's Theatre in Glasgow where she met Stanley Baxter, whom she married. I often stayed with her in London in the house in Islington (a dainty terrace), in the rather grand Shepherd's Hill in Highgate, the chic flat in North Grove, and in the little Arts and Crafts house (another terrace) in East Finchley designed by Sir William Webb.

In the Shamrockbank dining room there was one of David Gauld's green-and-blue paintings of a summer *Landscape with Calves* (the artist's winter scenes were less colourful), a Stuart Park displaying *Red and White Roses* as luxury objects in an opulent carved giltwood frame, an early little D.Y. Cameron, *Cottage in Glencoe*, and an Impressionistic Gemmell Hutchison, *Young Mariners* (children with a toy sailboat), as well as a fine interior with a young mother and children by Jan Snoeck, one of the Hague School of artists then popular among Scottish collectors. The drawing room upstairs was reserved for special occasions; there was an upright piano which my mother and grandmother would play occasionally, and three watercolours by Russell Flint, one of them of *The Toft at Elie* where we would spend summer holidays by the seaside. Elsewhere there were watercolours of Scottish highland landscapes by D.Y. Cameron. These rooms were delicately lighted. There was a weighted centre electrolier in the dining room whose height could be adjusted above the dining table, shaded with fringed orange silk which cast a glowing circle of light. The drawing room had standard lamps with large shades which in the evening diffused light softly through the room. Lighting was a minor art form not neglected by our ancestors.

When we moved in 1947 to Shawlands in Glasgow's south side we visited Shamrockbank nearly every weekend. Post-war rationing was still in force and few travelled abroad then. From that time I have still a pocket atlas of the world with a four-leafed clover on the flyleaf inscribed in my own immature hand 'this brings good luck'. The little book was a treasure. I've always loved maps. I also loved, apparently, the sound of breaking glass: there were the smashed windows of a newly built wooden shed in the Borders and the disintegrated passenger window of a City Bakeries' van – a moving target – to prove it. It was a phase I was going through.

On my father's side of the family, my Hardie grandparents lived in a second-floor tenement in Cathcart in the south side of Glasgow. The kitchen had an old-fashioned range and their piano was in the sitting room. There was no garden, but my grandfather had an allotment on Cathkin Braes where he grew vegetables, and from there he would have a fine view over the city to the distant Campsie Hills in the north, and Ayrshire to the south. This was exactly the kind of Glasgow allotment that was nursery to the early botanical drawing skills of Charles Rennie Mackintosh who also lived in a Glasgow tenement with no garden. His *Cabbages in an Orchard* might have been observed in his father's allotment. My mother was very fond of Grandpa Hardie, who would walk over to visit us when we lived in Shawlands, nothing daunted by the five-mile round trip. He sought his fortune in Glasgow and rose 'respected from the highest to the lowest' to be in charge of the heat treatment plant at Weir's, engineers of marine pumps for the world's ships. This was another side of mighty Glasgow, the world of the blast furnaces that produced the steel from which were made the graceful vessels that would glide oceanwards past Shamrockbank and carry locomotives, Singer sewing machines and whisky to all corners of the globe. Glasgow steel production had reached a million tons by 1900. Fifty years later, 'Dixon's Blazes' from the Glasgow steel mills were still a red glow in the night sky fifteen miles away from the tranquil setting of Shamrockbank.

As it completes a trio of occupations – a trade, industry and finally the land – but mostly because he lived in an altogether grander house, I will introduce a third member of that generation. My great-uncle Hardie (whom I never knew) was a tenant farmer at Stonegarthside Hall near Newcastleton on the border with England. My father went there for summer holidays as a boy. He would go by train to Kershopefoot Station and walk through the fields up to Stonegarthside. My mother too would take the train as a schoolgirl from Glasgow to Lockerbie for her summer holidays. Did their paths ever cross on those journeys as children? I remember pheasant sandwiches prepared for us boys by my mother. Rail travel was still a whole adventure in those distant days.

We may now briefly observe the present author at a tender age:

> I am a tadpole not long born
> With legs so short and a tail so long
> My alarum clock is the wild bird's song
> That wakens me up in the dewy morn.

Written when I was about nine, a little older than Dr Johnson when he allegedly wrote 'Master Duck', this quatrain was at first rejected by the editor of the Glasgow High School magazine but accepted when I cannily re-offered it for publication the following year.

At about the same time I remember the school orchestra rehearsing the overture to *Swan Lake* while we smaller fry listened. Whether this inspired these autobiographical lines or not I forget: but the poem is obviously not only about a tadpole with a penchant for rhyme. I was spellbound, transfixed by Tchaikovsky's ravishing music. In those days, music was not on tap as it is today, and to encounter it in performance was a kind of divine revelation. I became a member of the school orchestra (back row of the third violins) for its 1953 Coronation performance of a piece called 'Processional' written for the occasion by the head of music, Harry McGill. The part was mostly semibreves but still taxing for the ten-year-old beginner. I have a good ear but little manual dexterity. The same is true of drawing, despite the efforts of Grandpa Robertson who always had a sketch pad to hand when we went on car runs together. With his love of painting, he cherished an idea that I would become an artist.

Music 'wakened me up' first. Pictures were still in the background. If the clarinet in *Swan Lake* was the 'alarum clock', the collection of paintings at Shamrockbank was a dawn, perhaps even a 'dewy morn'. When the debating, chess, music and other societies were formed in my year, I suggested the Museum Club to which we brought things that interested us. I think it closed its imaginary portals when I left the city of Glasgow for the town of Ipswich a year later.

2   Painting My Room

In 1953 my father was called by Shell to Ipswich, where we lived for four years in a large house that once belonged to the cartoonist Giles, whose doodles still enlivened the telephone corner. Our life in Suffolk soon settled into a congenial pattern. It was all new: thatched houses, flintstone churches and East Anglian voices, sweetcorn and marrows as well as tiny lizards in a garden part enclosed by open fields. I soon acclimatized to the Tudor-inspired red-brick Ipswich School, straw boaters worn in summer, and assimilating my accent to theirs (perhaps more to my own ears than to theirs). I also enjoyed success on the running track – notably the 440 yards at Holt in Norfolk – as well as in the English literature courses on Chaucer and Thomas Hardy, whose Wessex novels I could somehow picture happening in rural Suffolk. Flatford Mill, which had been painted by Constable, was only a lengthy bicycle ride away from our house on Henley Road along which we cycled to school every day. Much later I would see David Thomson's painting by Constable of this subject in his house in Toronto.

Nobody was more surprised than I, not having tried my hand at anything like it before, when I wrote a short piece describing the painting *Christ of St John of the Cross*, newly acquired by Glasgow Corporation from the artist Salvador Dali. I remember the prize, a volume of Shakespeare, of course, but even more do I remember winning it and applauding myself by way of a joke. This modest contribution to the Dali literature dates my earliest interest in the history of art to 1956. Some twenty-five years later I was to negotiate the sale of Dali's study for the *Christ* to Kelvingrove Art Gallery and

Museum. The study bore scant resemblance to the large finished work and seemed to be more a parody of it, like Picasso's famous numerals-instead-of-figures 'take' on Diego Velázquez's *Las Meniñas*. Later still, in 1993, when we had a stand at the Los Angeles Art Fair, we were approached by a short, wiry man in his seventies: 'Are you guys from Glasgow?' This gentleman explained that in his youth he had been a Hollywood stunt man and because of his well-defined physique had been hired by Salvador Dali as the model for the figure of Christ in the famous painting.

Coffee was the cultural aphrodisiac of the 1950s, our absinthe, and it could be had at its blackest from a small, bohemian clique of boarders at Ipswich School, the chief of whom was Martin Harris. He was soon to enrol in St Martin's School of Art in London at the age of sixteen and he it was who introduced me to Methuen's *A Dictionary of Modern Painting*. With its many illustrations and essays by excellent writers, this became the daily companion of my impending year out, and to it and that time I owe much the greater part of what I know today of twentieth-century art. I had also become hooked on jazz. Colin Scott was among the jazz *cognoscenti* of the school. He had a pure taste for New Orleans jazz from the Red Hot Peppers to the Hot Five and the Hot Seven. On the other hand Carl Delvert, a Swedish boy who was boarding at the school, was collecting all kinds of intriguing West Coast things I affected to scorn because they were usually by white musicians, jazz being black music by definition.

A musical marriage was made in heaven when, a hundred years ago in New Orleans, black musicians met European instruments and began to appropriate them to the blues. Over several generations, exponents of brass, reeds, keyboard and percussion have taken their instruments to undreamt-of levels of expressiveness. The musicians play the instruments, not the other way round; the jazz players 'inhabit' their horns. The very sight of Louis Armstrong lifting his trumpet and fingering the valves before playing tells you immediately: you'd better be ready for this! The instrument was in the hands of a master. Even the great jazz pianists like Art Tatum, Earl Hines, Fats Waller, Jelly Roll Morton, Teddy Wilson, Erroll Garner and Bud Powell, play piano with their own 'voice', as well as their own style of phrasing. They give the piano a sound as unique to the player as a fingerprint. From the incandescent tone and huge vibrato of the young Armstrong in short solos of colossal intensity, to Lester Young's laconic distillations of the blues over several choruses, a whole new music was created by these musicians whose work we were privileged to catch on the wing.

Then I was diagnosed with a form of bovine tuberculosis. True to its name, this condition is most commonly found in cattle and its symptoms I would call ruminative rather than disabling. It wasn't painful, although carrying some risks if not treated with streptomycin by daily injection and a daily dose of something nasty called PAS. I am not entirely sure to this day whether the whole episode was not some form of puberty-related hypochondria. I had to convalesce for a year (which would prove that the matter was not taken lightly even by me), and had X-ray checks for several years more.

After the initial blow about the change of lifestyle – missing my friends and not allowed on the running track – I took stock. My science and maths had begun to lag well behind my English. It was a relief not to have to worry about them for a while. Worse, I was becoming disruptive in the way the backward can be. I was the ringleader of a game involving – when the physics master's back was turned – throwing in the air the wooden cube, ball, pyramid, cone, egg and triangle to catchers several yards away. All of which was highly entertaining, until one day I had had enough and deliberately made an uncatchable throw. It reverberated for a while on the parquet floor of the physics lab as a wooden egg does. That I was lightly punished suggested to me that Mr Grimwade saw I wanted to be caught. By that time my science was a lost cause anyway. But to my two new interests, jazz and modern art, I was happy to devote all the time in the world. *A Dictionary of Modern Painting* and Panassié's *Dictionary of Jazz* were seldom out of my sight. The two books were windows through which I could review a great sweep of modern music and painting.

My room was repainted: white woodwork, apple green surrounds, old gold side wall facing an olive green side wall, deep crimson back wall and crimson carpet. Here I read about the exploits of Buddy Bolden, Joe 'King' Oliver, and Jelly Roll Morton. I listened to their records including Louis Armstrong's 1947 New York Town Hall concert, Sidney Bechet and Tommy Ladnier, Kid Ory, Jimmie Noone and Johnny Dodds and graduating from New Orleans via the mainstream masters like Art Tatum, Roy Eldridge and Lester Young on *Jazz Giants 56* to the West Coast players like Clifford Brown and Gerry Mulligan. At the beginning I confess that my first favourite big band was that of Stan Kenton: all that dissonance was very fifties. In art as well, one only has to remember Graham Sutherland's palette with its acid greens and acrid oranges, but as I had no pictures, the room took on the colours of the time.

There was also the American Forces Network radio from Germany, with electrifying solos by the Jazz at the Philharmonic players emerging through the static. People liked either 'traditional' or 'modern' jazz, rarely both. I once took an EP record of Clifford Brown and his All Stars to the new espresso bar in town. 'What is that cacophony?' demanded an indignant duffle coat. In summer 1957 I saw the Gerry Mulligan Quartet (Mulligan, Bob Brookmeyer, Red Callendar and Chico Hamilton) at the newly minted Royal Festival Hall in London, the masterpiece of Sir Leslie Martin. With their shimmering instruments in that futuristic auditorium, they and their music seemed to come from another world. Back in Ipswich I saw Ken Collier's band and people jiving including a guy with two ladies. The trumpeter had been to New Orleans and must have been amongst the first to make the long journey. Iachimo's visit to the court of Cymbeline seems less epic.

When writing this list of 'all the greats who played in my bedroom' I absentmindedly wrote the names 'Jane, Penny, Laurence, Margaret, Carolyn', a Freudian-looking error which pastes in names of maidens who, like the jazz players, were never anywhere near my bedroom except in my thoughts. But by this time I had got over my apple tree. I wasn't immune to such musical candyfloss as Eddie Calvert's 'Cherry Pink and Apple Blossom White', the kettledrummer Eric Delaney's 'Si Si', as well as Gene Vincent's 'Be Bop a Lula' and Frankie Lymon's 'Why Do Fools Fall in Love'. Like the music itself, I was a long way from the sophistication of later masterworks by Fats Domino, the Four Tops, the Four Seasons and the Everley Brothers. Pop was turning into seriously marvellous music in those far-off days, and it had to start somewhere. It came of age with 'Heartbreak Hotel', probably. Humphrey Lyttelton's 'Bad Penny Blues' (an acknowledged influence on the Beatles' 'Lady Madonna'), an acetate version, was often on the turntable. It is hard to believe that we were less than ten years away from the arrival of the Beatles. Even as the McCartney–Lennon songbook was beginning to be written, I was still nodding sagely to the current idea that there were no more melodies to be invented.

A final Shell move brought us back to Glasgow in 1957, to Bearsden in the north, which was where I lived with my parents and four brothers until after university. The *fin-de-siècle* illustrator Jessie Marion King had been a daughter of the eponymous manse in Manse Road where we lived; the watercolourist Gordon Thomas lived in the house opposite us (I see that I am still trying to rebut Margaret Durant's assertion that

Bearsden was a cultural desert). Glasgow Academy was a stern institution of learning but I did my best not to disappoint everyone too much. I was barred from games on grounds of health, but as my mind was teeming with music this did not seem very important, and was even an advantage. Classical music in the form of Classics Club recordings of Josef Haydn and Johann Sebastian Bach now vied with jazz in my discovery of the perpetual wonders of music. Lord Reith, founder of the BBC and old boy of the Academy, presented me with the Sixth Form English Prize. In the photograph he is standing in the centre of the prizewinners like Gulliver among the Lilliputians. He was immensely tall. My contemporaries at the Academy included the historians Norman Stone and Neil MacGregor (destined to be director of the British Museum from 2002 to 2015 and whom I hardly knew). I read recently that he cites the same Dali picture as the starting point of his own career. Also Niall Ferguson, whom I did not know at all as he was younger than I.

It wasn't until we lived in Glasgow again that it was possible to see the jazz immortals in the flesh. For the aficionado, and because they occupied so many of my daydreams then and even today, here is a list of some of the American legends whom I saw in concert in Glasgow: Louis Armstrong twice (at the Glasgow Odeon and again at Ibrox Stadium), Duke Ellington, Roy Eldridge, Dizzy Gillespie, Woody Herman, Max Roach, the Modern Jazz Quartet, Dave Brubeck, Ella Fitzgerald, J.J. Johnson and Kai Winding, Sarah Vaughan, and Count Basie. I still have a lingering feeling that I heard Duke Ellington twice, but that may be because Duke had changed into another suit – from cream to dark blue I think – for the second set which he introduced with a trademark line: 'The members of the orchestra would like you to know that they do love you – madly.' I once spoke to Buddy Tate, a former Basie tenor sax, whom I recognized at the carousel in Belfast airport when I was in Ulster to buy two paintings by Anne Redpath. I have a cigarette box that belonged to the pianist Walter Bishop Jr, given to me by his widow Keiko Bishop in New York. Walter Bishop was in the original Charlie Parker Quintet, and is on a recording I've had since I was fifteen. I just missed meeting Walter Bishop, but I did meet Ronnie McLean at the Blue Note jazz club in Tokyo, through Taeko Seki who had played *koto* with them both. The slightest contact was precious.

Improvisation began with melody but left it far behind and composition was to me the melodies of the past. 1959 was the year of Mozart's *The Abduction from the*

Seraglio at the Edinburgh Festival and the beginning of a fascination with his music and personality.

In art too, I began to experience the real thing. In the same year the Moltzau Collection was on show in Edinburgh, probably my first encounter with Pablo Picasso, Georges Braque, Henri Matisse and André Derain, apart from the examples in the MacInnes Collection at Kelvingrove. In that fine, long, sunny summer a group of young Glasgow artists held an outdoor exhibition of paintings on the railings of the Botanical Gardens: Carole Gibbons, Douglas Abercrombie and Alasdair Gray. When I got home I remember announcing 'I know what art is'. I was like the Englishman in the Fauconnier novel *Malaisie* who was improbably but unshakeably certain that Jean Jaurès was the greatest Frenchman who ever lived, although nobody else really knew who Jaurès was. What one *knows* is what defines us to ourselves, I can see that now.

In Hamburg in 1959 while staying with Bernd Brüggemann and his mother (whose husband had been killed on the Crimean front in World War II), I spent an afternoon in the Kupferstichkabinett going through their solanders of prints by Paul Klee. Also in Hamburg I bought a little book by Hans Hess, *Dank in Farben*, describing the same collection of Expressionist art that I was to stumble across in reality in Glasgow thirty years later. I then translated the book's commentary into English. In Flensburg – or perhaps it was Lübeck – one day I came across a delicious small exhibition of watercolours by Braque. I've looked for a record of it in the Braque literature in vain; it's almost as if I dreamt it.

I had a girlfriend called Hope who looked like Juliette Greco. Not doing anything sensible like learning how to be musicians, we were would-be existentialists whose favourite film was Alain Resnais's *L'Année Dernière à Marienbad*. We loved the Modern Jazz Quartet, Ernest Hemingway and Billie Holiday – and had no notion of what we wanted to do ourselves.

Hope eventually had a dress shop called *Hopes* with vintage clothes and uniforms, and married Alan Singleton. Alan's family were patrons of the avant-garde as owners of the Cosmo Cinema, Glasgow's best Art Deco building. They had a very good collection of Scottish Colourists. Later Alan would occasionally deal in antiques, but his approach wasn't very commercial. One day he was irritated beyond endurance by a client who insisted on haggling. Alan's response was to drop the studio-pottery bowl under discussion onto the pavement where it broke into smithereens, with the comment 'OK, have it'. Right *on*.

Later, at university, my friend James Knight, a gifted mathematician in whose memory when he died at the age of twenty-five the university struck a medal, was my rival for the attention of the charming Margaret Durant. Like me, she was in thrall to Lawrence Durrell's *The Alexandria Quartet*, eagerly awaiting the publication of each new volume: *Justine* in red, *Balthazar* in ochre, *Mountolive* in green, and *Clea* in a pale blue cover. *The Greengage Summer* was her other favourite reading. She was convinced that we were too middle-class to be creative; perhaps she had a point, although James Knight's poetry impressed me. Naturally we competed in writing poems to her. I wrote this 'rhyme-scheme':

Margaret

These small white flowers
In the dark room
Await your hand
And the day

Middle May:
Roses will, and
Still I, reach bloom.
Lush petals! hours
Of life yet

The poem was written when I was at Shamrockbank one weekend, and accompanied by lily-of-the-valley from the garden. I think the world-weary tone had something to do with the changes wrought by time on the familiar place now my grandfather was no longer there. When Uncle Stewart – my mother's elder brother – died in 1977 the house was finally sold and *The Girl in a Paisley Shawl* went to Moira in London.

3   *Et Ego In Academia*

I said goodbye to Margaret when I left for a year as an *assistant d'anglais* at the Lycée Mistral in Avignon. Parting was such bitter sorrow, the farewell party had gone too well and too long, and the train that took me to a sterner destiny might have steamed out of *Brief Encounter*, except that it was early morning. Then the Golden Arrow took me from London to Paris and the express train on to Avignon for nine months as *assistant d'anglais* at the Lycée Mistral.

The mortifications of exile lasted fully twelve hours, mostly of dreamless sleep. I woke to a blue Provençal sky, the smells of coffee and new-baked bread, and the chirping of cicadas. Life was wonderful again. I was only twenty-one.

My teaching duties turned out to be light to the point of defying gravity. I wrote verses in Avignon including *scroll, pampre, acroter* for a Glasgow University poetry competition. It was 'commended', which was more than fair because it was unfinished. I had taken a room in a hotel, but I only succeeded in rounding off as opposed to finishing the poem. It was a response to the classical decoration of wave (*scroll*), vine (*pampre*) and wheatsheaf (*acroter*) motifs on the Roman architecture of Provence and carved fragments in the Musée Lapidaire of Avignon. I had become interested in the idea that classical ornament derived from living forms. Much later I saw a farmer in Kefallonia dig out a perfect Greek key pattern instead of straight furrows in laying out a vegetable patch, the crop growing in the raised earth while water could run in the surrounding channels. To my satisfaction at least, this proved that the meandering pattern known as 'Greek key' began life as an irrigation plan. It is unlikely that it happened the other way round. Perhaps every Greek farmer knows this.

I saw Nîmes, with its perfect little Roman temple, the *Maison Carrée*, the amphitheatre, and the mighty aqueduct of the Pont du Gard connecting the Uzès spring to Nîmes. I also went to St Rémy and the Roman excavations of Glanum near Arles and the small mental hospital where Van Gogh had convalesced. My guide, Pamela Rachet, and I were the only visitors that day, and we were shown the little room in which Vincent had painted, complete with his boots and a rush-seated chair, in 1885. Pamela had written and illustrated a book about her life married to the top nurseryman of Provence; she had one of the first swimming pools there. Van Gogh would otherwise have recognized the Provence of his day. From 1885 to 1963 it was hardly changed. But Romanian seedsmen now have the business that was once the domain of Rachet Frères.

In the charming, dusty Musée Calvet in Avignon there was a group of works by Claude Lorrain's French follower the local artist Joseph Vernet, and in the Papal Palace the altarpiece by the mysterious Enguerrand Charonton. Later in the year I went to Banyuls-sur-Mer, Collioure and Port-Vendres near the Spanish frontier, where Mackintosh lived at the end of his life. At that time I had probably never heard of Mackintosh, although I did know about the connection of Henri Matisse and André Derain with the *Côte Vermeille*. I was struck with the idea that the 'wild' colours of the Fauve landscapes of this coast were almost realist: the landscape is vermilion red.

In the spring of 1963 I went to Athens on the Orient Express. My companion was Jimmy Knight, who started his journey in Glasgow; our meeting point was a station on the Swiss border. Although first and foremost a mathematician, James was also learned in botany and well versed in Homer. He had recently been to Athens and needed no persuasion to return. As the train wound through former Yugoslavia, we saw churches and mosques side-by-side in apparent harmony, with no hint of the horrors to come.

In the same compartment was a Scottish girl who turned out to be the daughter of the British ambassador to Greece. We were invited to dinner with the ambassador at the embassy. I caught myself speaking with an American accent throughout the evening: ah, what it is to be young and hoping to impress! The British Embassy was in a street in Athens renamed in honour of four EOKA terrorists who had been hanged by the British. (Later, in 1970 the colonels who were in power dominated Athens airport in the shape of huge banner portraits.) At night as we arrived, the floodlit white Parthenon atop the Acropolis was never to be forgotten; there is no preparation for architecture so moving. We also went to Corinth, the antiquities at Delphi and the Ancient Theatre of Epidaurus. Then back by train I went to Avignon, through the Rhône Valley with almond trees now coming into bloom.

Messieurs Brosseau, Grare, Fabre and Lefèbre, all English teachers, were hospitable, and their mesdames, and so were my younger friends Paul Cuchet and Christian Berdin. Perhaps not quite as hospitable as Monique tried to be. Or as the great phallus painted on a stray wall told me again one hot, solitary day, I was not quite alone in Avignon. I fell in love with a girl called Georgette, meeting her at a party in Marseilles. But I was twenty-one and why be an ill-foreboder, to paraphrase Burns. Why fret at a chance of felicity missed so early.

I saw Jean-Louis Barrault in the Roman Theatre of Orange. He was Hamlet and afterwards I had fox for dinner in a restaurant that, like the one we went to when we could afford it in Avignon, was still offering lovely old Provençal cooking. It was a beautiful night of open-air theatre, and the play was performed in front of '*le plus beau mur de mon royaume*' as Louis XIV called the Roman wall which is now the backdrop of the Theatre of Orange.

A diary entry, back again in Glasgow, records that in 1964 Nathalie Sarraute, one of the doyennes of contemporary French novelists, appeared in our Common Room. Introduced to her as representing the University French Club, I was tongue-tied in the presence of the literary lioness, who was small, grey and a paragon of the French novel. Reading her for the first time recently I did wonder why her prose, French at its most elegantly economical, hadn't been required reading for those of us attempting to learn the language. French and German literature and language were the main components of my degree. It was a luxury to be reading French poetry when all around were embarked on vocational courses that would lead somewhere. Reading European classics reminded us of one of the oldest uses of education: the enjoyment of literature. Perhaps the other faculties were enjoying the laughter of the gods as much we were, but I doubt it. Different gods perhaps.

The Modern Languages building was brand-new and filled with reproductions of great paintings, an idea owed to Professor Alan Boase, who instigated links between the French department and the new-fledged subject of History of Art, not then available as a degree, only as a subsidiary subject. Roger Brunyate's course on the *Quattrocento* was – to use the overused word – another revelation. Since then I have revered the works of the early Italian Renaissance as devotedly as a latter-day Pre-Raphaelite. An option in French Art and Architecture was available to us linguists, directed by Hamish Miles. This too was an inspiration. The half-dozen students taking the course read papers to each other. Mine was on Claude Lorrain. (Claude remains perhaps my favourite artist of all.)

I was learning that the masters of painting reflect the world with as much imagination and observation as the greatest writers and that their work can convey a uniquely immediate delight. I also discovered that I enjoyed lecturing, with the novice's tendency to overrun the allotted time. Later I became a visiting lecturer in the French department of Dundee University, lecturing a small class of honours option students in seventeenth- and nineteenth-century French art and architecture, following the pattern of Hamish Miles's honours course at Glasgow University.

My first job on graduating was with Euclid, ostensibly as a management trainee but effectively to help interpret for French or German clients. Euclid made large earth-moving machines and I had to translate technical courses for service mechanics. My French and German weren't up to the specialized vocabulary for case-hardened scraper teeth, planetary gears, loader buckets, ten-speed transmissions, heavy-duty hydraulics, rolling resistances, traffic efficiencies in open-cast mining and the like. I could appreciate their importance, even their beauty, but they didn't grab me. Quite soon Euclid indicated that perhaps I would like to consider looking elsewhere and were kind enough to present me with a farewell tankard inscribed 'July 1966'.

After this false start I went immediately to Andrew McLaren Young, head of the History of Fine Art department at Glasgow University, who mentioned the possibility of a job as research assistant in his department at the start of the new academic year. But this would take time to organize. In the meantime I had bought with £350 left me by my grandfather a converted Dragon from my brother Archie, who had taught me how to sail it. I decided to use the time to set off with various companions on a cruise in the sloop *Ngaisah* round the Morven and Bute shores for six weeks while the university pondered my future. The Western Isles are all-absorbing: ghosting out of Tighnabruaich or Craobh at first light, lying at anchor in the tidal stream of Loch Aline, the drama of the Midsummer Night Race round the Isle of Bute, broad-reaching south through Scalpay Sound off Skye, ashore at Tobermory (where I found a pole vaulter's pole for a halyard stuck at the diamond) which has a town clock with a double chime, like a Dutch clock. Even fitting-out was a pleasure although once I had to return pronto from Kilcreggan boatyard when I realized I was supposed to be viewing the collection of James Meldrum in his Glasgow flat that day. He had inherited paintings by Charles Rennie Mackintosh and Mackintosh's friend the painter John Quinton Pringle. His wife Eva's portrait by Philip de László was also in the house. She was Hungarian and the niece of the composer Zoltán Kodály.

Summer was nearly over when the university was able to decide whether I had a future with it. Happily, the answer was affirmative. I rejoiced to be back in the fold. This would be my first job in the field of art. I was now twenty-five. Time to be settling down.

During my time in the Fine Art department, then in Bute Gardens at Glasgow University, Margaret Macdonald and I sat at opposite sides of a partners' desk in the Whistler Room transcribing the huge James Abbott McNeill Whistler correspondence into card index form. Although not a natural Whistlerian, I enjoyed Whistler's personality and his writings and *bons mots* as reported by his ardent biographers Joseph and Elizabeth Pennell, but I was never likely to ascend to the empyrean of a chair in Whistler studies as she has done.

At the same time, the letters that were of wider interest (like the correspondence with Édouard Manet, Henri Fantin-Latour, Gustave Courbet, and Sergei Diaghilev – discussing an exhibition of the Glasgow School for St Petersburg) twinkled like stars in a tenebrous Whistler nocturne. Whistler was a good metropolitan counter to my own research into the provincial doings of the Scottish School (provincial in the political sense). One day Andrew McLaren Young introduced me to A.J. McNeill Reid, whose father, Alexander Reid, had been painted by Van Gogh. Reid senior had founded the very important London firm of Reid & Lefevre, who were as close as any gallery in Britain to the fountainhead of art in Paris. His advocacy of Edgar Degas is well known and reflected in the splendid pieces in the Burrell Collection. Perhaps no Glasgow collection echoes Reid's influence better than the exquisite McInnes Collection now at Kelvingrove, with its choice examples of Cézanne, Braque, Matisse, Gauguin, Picasso, Jean-Édouard Vuillard, Juan Gris and others of the Post-Impressionist School.

'The Glasgow Boys' was the title of a pioneering show for which the Scottish Arts Council (SAC) put me in charge of choosing works by E.A. Hornel and others. I found a delicious small painting, *Girl and Tree*, in the collection of Vice-Admiral Sir James and Lady Troup. Fascinating in itself, the picture was also interesting evidence of the mutual support system that existed between the Glasgow painters in their early years: Sir James Troup's father had been a relative of James Guthrie, a leading member of the early School, and had clearly bought the picture as a gesture of solidarity. The work on Hornel led to a two-part article for *The Scottish Art Review* which was my debut as an art historian. Later the trustees bought a very good early work by Hornel from me, the *Portrait of the Kirkcudbright Bellringer Winefield Nellens* (1886), and I wrote the valuation for Broughton House.

Dr Tom Honeyman, the doyen of art matters in Scotland, despite being older than I by fifty years, and perhaps seeing in me the tyro he had been once, was kind. We became friends. He had uniquely wide interests in the theatre as well as in art, and as a former director of Reid & Lefevre in London he had met almost everybody in the art world, from Albert Barnes to Salvador Dali. And in what other private collection in Glasgow could one find works by Louis Marcoussis, Alexander Calder and Dali? He had also once owned the great early Camille Pissarro now in the National Gallery of Scotland (NGS) from his Reid & Lefevre days, and the portrait of Mrs Honeyman commissioned from Wyndham Lewis during their time in London, as well as works by the little masters of the Euston Road School.

It was due to Tom Honeyman that, much later, I had access to key works by Stanley Cursiter, Vuillard, and Christopher R.W. Nevinson, as well as being asked by several members of the Honeyman family to help with the Wyndham Lewis portrait, the little Dali study already mentioned, a fine Ivon Hitchens, and several works by the Scottish Colourists. As dealers Tom Honeyman and Ian MacNicol had influenced their own generation of collectors and through them I met Alexander Kennedy and Edward Nisbet and saw their Glasgow School pictures.

Another outstanding collection at that time belonged to George Smith, a retired bachelor who resembled Vincent Van Gogh and had something of Vincent's saintly character. George Smith's collection of the work of Charles Rennie Mackintosh, entirely assembled on a modest salary and diligent attendance at Glasgow auctions, was kept in his terraced house in Cathcart. My first attempt to visit failed because I had left his address behind, and quickly found that 'George Smith, Cathcart' was insufficient to distinguish him from the other Smiths in the directory. He forgave this solecism, and I saw him there several times, my imagination fired by his passion for Mackintosh's work. Perhaps the most important piece in the collection was the Square Table. After bidding successfully for it, he found in its drawer a note explaining its provenance, which added considerably to its value.

On a later visit to George Smith I remember once airing my theory about the Mackintosh 'jazz age' geometrical flower paintings of the war years circa 1916, of which I owned one example. I had noticed that the eye saw a pattern different from what Mackintosh had actually drawn. Stylized flowerheads rendered by concentric lobed circles of alternating red and blue would re-form themselves *in the eye* as intersecting arcs, not the circles that were actually on the sheet of paper. This reminded me of Op Art in the hands of Bridget Riley. George Smith's house was the ideal place to test the theory, as he had three examples of these rare works by Mackintosh. They were not on display, but were fetched from under a bed, and propped up on the floor. To our delight, they 'worked': their geometry produced an illusion of arcs rather than circles. That the circles were designed to produce the illusion of a different pattern seemed proven. George Smith left his entire collection of Mackintosh, with a few very fine Scottish paintings, to the Hunterian Art Gallery.

In that part-stimulating and part-somnolent time (I'm afraid I would occasionally fall asleep at my desk) as a research assistant in the History of Fine Art department at Bute Gardens, Andrew McLaren Young was organizing an Edinburgh Festival exhibition to mark the centenary of the birth of Charles Rennie Mackintosh in 1968. All the excitement in the department seemed to be coming from the work on Mackintosh. The Print Room was full of solanders containing the University's collection of Mackintosh works on paper. I saw glimpses of them on occasion, and Mackintosh furniture seemed to keep emerging from storage in out-of-the way cupboards. Averil McIlwraith, a *Vogue* 'girl of the year' who was a brilliant illustrator, had been engaged in the design of the Mackintosh exhibition. Her gentle personality contrasted with the more fiery Henry Hellier, who was also working on the design and whom Andrew would have to dissuade from over-designing an exhibition which was never going to be lacking in strong design.

Having recently curated a major Whistler exhibition at the Freer in Washington D.C., Andrew was equally ambitious for the Mackintosh Centenary, which would go on from Edinburgh to the Victoria and Albert Museum and thus reach a large audience new to Mackintosh. Glasgow University's Mackintosh Collection, which is (like its Whistler Collection) of world class, was supplemented with works from Kelvingrove and the School of Art in Glasgow, as well as from Tom Howarth and other private collectors who were now a disappearing breed.

It was the opportunity of a lifetime and a huge task in those days of inadequate or non-existent collection catalogues and primitive storage or conservation. At the private view, in the course of a tribute to other Mackintosh scholars including Robert Macleod, whose book on Mackintosh had just appeared, Andrew was heckled by Cordelia Oliver, critic of *The Guardian*. Nobody seemed to know quite what this was all about, but it was in keeping with the fraught atmosphere surrounding the exhibition's preparation. Afterwards he ordered his customary dry Martini and fell asleep over lunch, exhausted from his labours which were, indeed, a far cry from the pedantic footling of much art-historical scholarship today.

Thus was a great exhibition born, an assembly of virtually unknown pieces brilliantly displayed. The Mackintosh revival began from that moment, and fifty years later shows no sign of lessening momentum. Still in a state of ignorance, I was dazzled, as everyone was. There was still so much to grasp and the first edition of my *Scottish Painting*, in which I included Mackintosh not because I understood him but because he simply could not be ignored, fails to grapple with his complexity. Mackintosh's thought processes link disparate ideas and disciplines in a way that makes it difficult to discuss his architecture or his applied design without referring to visual imagery in other media in which he was also, effortlessly, a master. Perhaps it is a problem of the right medium. In many ways the best, and certainly the most vivid account of Mackintosh and his work is still the documentary film made by Murray Grigor for the BBC in 1968.

Although the work I was being paid to do was purely concerned with the Whistler Archive, I took soundings with Andrew McLaren Young on writing a thesis on the Glasgow School of painters for a Ph.D. 'Don't waste your time on a thesis that nobody will read, write a book' was his succinct advice. Accordingly I began to plan a book which initially was to focus on the Glasgow School, but expanded as I became interested in the wider field of Scottish art. The research goal was to discover whether the dynamic nation of Scotland had produced any painting that could bear comparison with the modern French School whose work had obvious, classic supremacy. What interested me most was the avant-garde, however sporadic or short-lived: I was much less interested in those who developed a retardatory style, no matter how stylish. The book took about ten years from start to finish mainly because of the need to gather the pictorial evidence, the missing pieces of the jigsaw puzzle. It was published by Studio Vista in 1976 in London as *Scottish Painting 1837–1939*. (The second edition was twice as large and brought the narrative up to the present day.)

Academia has provided a sanctuary for reflection and study on topics which interest me but which I'd probably never get round to as a full-time academic. And so, if the job was humble, it was at least the start of my work on the Glasgow School. To see other painters than Whistler and to meet the collectors and dealers was salutary. Glasgow under McLaren Young was never likely to be ivory-towered. If the paintings were the chief documents, it was the task of the would-be art historian to unearth them. Andrew McLaren Young was quite positive about this – unlike the art historian I later sat beside at dinner in New York, for whom it was all a waste of time. The task of the art historian was to draw society and the artist in it, but she overlooked the fact that pictures interested me more than who had painted them. Had art history been social history I would have had less interest in it.

4   Albert Square

Dundee, like the winner of a game of musical chairs, occupies a south-facing elevation overlooking the River Tay's broad estuary. I had only once seen it distantly from the Fife shore, before the medieval town centre (the Nethergate) was destroyed with only the stern old tower of St Mary's left standing. The Fortingall yew, the William Sanger paintings at Kenmore, the Monymusk reliquary and the seventeenth-century fishing harbours of Fife were nearby, but they were not even in the same county. The poet Robert Burns was entertained at Breadalbane Castle. I once netted a trout at Killin, caught by my Uncle Jack, and when I went back there in 1985 it was to value the Tiffany window in the parish church. If Dundee was a mystery, the landscape that enwrapped it was an enigma.

Approached from the west on my first visit on 21 December 1967 Dundee looked excitingly modern. I became the first-ever keeper of art with Dundee Corporation on the strength of my eighteen-month résumé and a glowing reference from Andrew McLaren Young except for his mention of my 'appallingly hesitant manner'. I found it eight or nine years later, when as acting director I was looking through other records. The urge to know is sometimes better resisted.

Albert Square is an anthology of Victorian and Edwardian architecture. The Albert Institute housed the Dundee City Museum, Art Galleries and Library in a magnificent and charming Gothic Revival group, built on its own island in the middle of the square. Dominated by a beautiful double staircase to the old library, the Albert

Institute has a miniature Gothic undercroft which was the architect's trial run for the quadrangles of Glasgow University. Culturally, educationally and commercially this is the centre of the city. The Dundee symbolist artist John Duncan had his studio in the square until 1900 and the newspaper offices of D.C. Thomson are to the west beside the classical portico of Dundee High School.

I started my new job as keeper of art in January 1968. The River Tay was frozen at Broughty Ferry where I had digs near the castle and the little harbour, with an uninterrupted view over to Fife. The James Guthrie Orchar Collection was still housed in the custom-built gallery a few streets away. I would drive the fifteen-minute journey to the City Art Gallery in the Daimler Dart. As one of my fellow lodgers was manager of a building society in Reform Street, I soon found a flat at the upper end of Baxter Park Terrace with a view of the turrets of Morgan Academy, the tall trees, and the distant Tay. My office (which remains the largest I've ever had) with its fossil marble mantelpiece and working gas fire looked over to a statue of Queen Victoria (back view) and the Italianate Gothic Chamber of Commerce. The working day began at 8.30 a.m. The Art department was small: me, and technical support in the shape of Mr Whitton the assistant keeper and the art assistant, Miss Brymer. We got on well immediately, and soon knew our own jobs and did them with enthusiasm. 'Happy memories' as Mr Whitton writes in his annual Christmas card. Only once was there a brief divergence of views, when the new keeper proposed the need to re-catalogue the entire collection item by item. The labels for the pictures on display were, as Lord Crawford wrote to me, 'bleak and barren' because the pictures had hardly been studied. The 1926 catalogue was out of date and the collection urgently needed research and a new catalogue.

There were five very grand and handsome Victorian galleries to fill. A programme of exhibitions was needed to hold the attention of visitors, and research for my book on Scottish painting and the exhibition subjects could nourish each other. The most obvious and immediate way to provide a stream of temporary exhibitions was to turn to the field of contemporary art, which could be supplemented by historical shows that would be more study-intensive.

The new catalogue was duly published in 1973 during the centenary of Dundee City Art Gallery. The vast majority of the works held in Dundee's municipal collection are, from the cataloguer's point of view, very good beginner's fare because they are overridingly Victorian or modern pictures, with an emphasis on Scottish artists. Within this academically accessible category, there are few pitfalls, but signatures, inscriptions, dates and labels have to be examined with forensic care as each is potentially the bearer of an important piece of information about a picture – its title perhaps, who has owned it, even a letter or a note written by the artist and still tucked snugly inside the stretcher.

Were our Old Master paintings what they were claimed to be? Here I felt less secure and sought help from experts. On several occasions I took the overnight sleeper to London with a portfolio of Italian drawings under my arm, bound for the British Museum and the experienced eyes of that formidable team Philip Pouncey and John Gere of the Prints and Drawings department. Under the watchful regard of W.L. van de Watering at the Netherlands Rijksbureau voor Kunsthistorische Documentatie, I spent a week at The Hague making photographic comparisons with our interesting Dutch pictures from the Duncan Bequest and other sources. That a few of our pictures had been listed by such experts from the past as G.F. Waagen and Hofstede de Groot provided a link with a wider world of scholarship. In the Rijksbureau they brought their visitors a cup of tea mid-morning and again at 3 p.m. I wonder if this civilized custom survives.

On one or two occasions, by no means often, my boss, James D. Boyd, and I went together to see important local collections. One such visit was to the Duke of Fife's house where we thought His Grace's manners slightly lacking: he took us on a guided tour asking our opinions about everything, clutching a massive gin and tonic thoughtfully provided by his butler, while we went without. We visited Brigadier Naughton's house to discuss the Camperdown Collections. The family still owned the precociously assured Wilkie family portrait of Naughton ancestors, *William Chalmers Bethune and his Family*, now in the National Portrait Gallery in Edinburgh, a rare example of the greatest of all Scottish artists still in his native Fife, and still owned by the commissioning family after nearly 180 years. Early on we went to Balcarres House, where there was to be a small exhibition of early books from the famous Library. Lord Crawford was to introduce them to delegates from the British Academy Dundee meeting and we were there to lend display cases for the purpose. Exhibits from the shelves (some originally from Rubens's house in Antwerp) were annotated in Lord Crawford's distinguished but indecipherable hand.

On the strength of that visit I offered to catalogue the pictures at Balcarres in my spare time. I would go to Balcarres at weekends, leaving Gillie at home with the children. Such an arrangement was probably unsustainable. I was probably naive in thinking I could contribute anything useful to a collection well known to the most eminent of scholars from Bernard Berenson and Ellis Waterhouse to Lord Clark, with whom Balniel (later Lord Crawford) had arranged a famous exhibition of Italian art in Burlington House in 1933. I did make one useful discovery – a manuscript list in the Tate Gallery Archive giving details of the pictures hanging in the former Crawford town house in Edinburgh.

At Balcarres House I was able to study at close quarters a collection of marvellous quality containing masterpieces of Italian and Dutch art, as well as supremely fine portraits by Allan Ramsay, Sir Joshua Reynolds and Thomas Gainsborough. The Italian pictures were then all in the hall, chief among them a crucifixion scene by Duccio di Buoninsegna which later sold for £1m. Because the early Italian painters used a gold ground, this room seemed to glitter with gold.

It was a stimulating background against which to be cataloguing the less important, but still interesting Old Master pictures at Dundee. In 1969 with Magda Salvesen of the Scottish Arts Council, I organized an exhibition of Rembrandt etchings at the gallery. Lord Crawford lamented the sale of the family Rembrandt *Portrait of the Artist's Son Titus* to the Rijksmuseum, where there was a rather larger tercentennial exhibition than ours, but generously gave me the air fare to go to Amsterdam to see the show. On my return I went to visit Francis Cadell's nephew John Cadell and his family, which included a budding actor Simon Cadell, in their house in Highgate.

My improving acquaintance with Dutch painting from visits to Balcarres was beneficial in Dundee. One evening I was alone in the brightly lit Gallery V (probably after an evening class) where our best Dutch pictures were displayed, and found myself able to discover their signatures for the first time. The paintings by Gillis de Hondecoeter, Jan Both, Abraham van Beyeren, and Johann Amandus Wink (German painter of the Antwerp school) revealed themselves as signed works that night, all within half an hour. My eye, finally, was 'in'.

The Duncan Bequest of 1878 was the first and remains the most important of the benefactions received by Dundee. George Duncan and his wife were a glamorous young couple, to judge from the lovely portraits of them in the Dundee Art Gallery by Robert Scott Lauder. They lived in The Vine, the finest house in Dundee, a perfect Greek Revival ashlar mansion in Roseangle, with a view of the River Tay. From here George Duncan would have been able to watch the vessels of his Dundee Perth and London Shipping Company as they plied this reach of the river between Perth and Dundee. It is the nucleus of fine, mostly Dutch paintings from the Duncan Bequest that lends weight to the Dundee collection.

There was nearly a rival when in the early 1960s William Boyd of Broughty Ferry was contemplating giving his Post-Impressionist collection to the city. The Committee, however, fell out with Boyd who sold the collection and endowed a Chair of Dentistry in the new Dundee University, so much more practical than a Van Gogh or a Picasso.

Colin Thompson, Hugh Macandrew and Keith Andrews at the National Gallery of Scotland were all generous with time and suggestions regarding the private owners from whose collections our pictures had come. Provenance is important not just for the sake of the individual picture; it also provides a better idea of the taste of the owner. For example, the large painting at Dundee by Joseph Crawhall was owned by W.A. Coats, the thread tycoon from Paisley, who bought many works from Crawhall. It comes as something of a shock to identify him as the owner of a masterpiece of altogether greater calibre, *Christ in the House of Martha and Mary* by Johannes Vermeer, now in the National Gallery of Scotland. So the catalogue included indices of collectors, as well as portraits and a concordance which demonstrated that the 1926 catalogue was not forgotten.

A large show called 'Art Across The Tay' offered a cross-section of artists working in the north-east of Scotland, as much for the benefit of the new keeper as anyone else. I introduced Andrew McLaren Young, who opened the show, by saying that as head of the Fine Art department at Glasgow University he had sent acolytes to other departments, like Birmingham (Dennis Farr), St Andrews (John Steer), Leicester and the Barber Institute (Hamish Miles), Aberdeen (David Irwin), and Oxford (Martin Kemp) 'like a shower of sparks'. Andrew countered by saying I must be the 'spark' in Dundee. 'Art Across the Tay' had begun as a showcase for the talents of Robert Leishman and his friends, but I widened it to include everybody of any eminence who was painting in the region. Bob Leishman gave way with his customary good humour.

More fractious was my relationship with Dundee Art Society, who invited lectures from me nonetheless. They were accustomed to taking over the entire City Galleries for a month-long selling show of members' work every year. I thought this wasn't appropriate, especially when they had their own gallery premises in Dundee. I had written to them explaining this and offering two galleries instead of five. There was a meeting at which James McIntosh Patrick said that getting work accepted for Dundee Art Society's exhibition would be harder than being hung at the Royal Scottish Academy (RSA), which as a matter of fact was probably true as he and several other members of the Art Society were *hors concours* at the RSA. As I thought my views were sufficiently well known I did not speak – a mistake. For this, a lady member called me a coward. She apologized later. But it was like being sent a white feather.

At the 'Glasgow Boys' exhibition in 1968 I met the Glasgow painter Donald Bain during the private view at Kelvingrove, beginning a friendship that continued until the artist's death twelve years later. Donald Bain's work as a pastellist had recently been the subject of an exhibition in the Print Room of Glasgow University's Fine Art department. The university possesses a large early oil by him showing a cow in a field. As he and Andrew were standing in front of the painting one day Donald was heard to say 'Aye, Andrew, if ye were a bull ye'd be giein' it a lick.' He was neither modest nor a diplomat. But who else in Glasgow could talk of having met Matisse, Christian Dior and Frank Sinatra? Donald was perhaps not a great painter, but he was a *real* painter who produced a handful of great pictures.

In Dundee I organized a retrospective exhibition of Bain's work in 1969 from which Douglas Hall bought the large early *The Children of Lyr* for the Scottish National Gallery of Modern Art (SNGMA). For the city collection, Dundee acquired a Provençal work by Bain, a view of St-Paul-de-Vence, for the city collection. At around the same time I began to collect his work, which embodied an interesting Francophile taste and knowledge of the work of such Paris figures as Filippo de Pisis and Constant Permeke. My first one was a tiny drawing in white chalk and blue and green wash. It was of the sea at Cagnes in France; it caught the light and I propped it up beside my bed so that it would be the first thing I saw in the morning. Perth Art Gallery bought *Ossian*, a brave purchase. Margaret Morris Fergusson attended the private view and with Donald and Eunice Bain was our guest of honour at a dinner at the Angus Hotel in Dundee. Years later, I organized a posthumous exhibition of Bain's work for the

University of Strathclyde in Glasgow which allowed me to part-publish the artist's letters to J.D. Fergusson, with their vivid account of Bain's struggle to forge a career as an *artiste peintre*, as he always termed himself, to support his family and to achieve recognition.

Margaret Morris, Fergusson's wife, who had famously once been kissed by John Galsworthy in the back of a London taxi, had an eternally young aura. She was kind but a little intimidating. She later gave me lunch in her Manchester Square flat overlooking the Wallace Collection in London. I haven't found the date of this in the diaries. The omelette I do remember. Without any prompting she told me that although a vegetarian she supported abortion and could eat eggs. Meg's deep, throaty foghorn of a *grande dame* of the theatre was not something I noticed until I heard Stanley Baxter 'do' her voice. Ever the professional, Baxter looked somewhat askance at the amateurs of her Celtic Ballet. He was Bottom in *A Midsummer Night's Dream* by the Margaret Morris Players, for which the sets were designed by Donald Bain. Meg, who with J.D. Fergusson had loyally supported Donald Bain, wrote to me 'to thank you for your encouragement of Donald, he really is a sincere artist and a worker.' Paintings by the Glasgow painters Carole Gibbons and Alan Fletcher also arrived in the Dundee Collection.

Andrew McLaren Young extolled the vitality of the Duncan of Jordanstone College of Art, where Alberto Morrocco, David McClure and Jack Knox were in the Painting department. Contemporary shows, as indeed contemporary purchases, could set precedents or seem invidious but Dundee was a city of painters – and we were young. Many friendships were formed and we went to the houses of Alberto Morrocco, Peter Collins, Jack Knox, James Howie, Robert Cargill, James Morrison and the illustrator Dave Chapman, and the architects Sinclair Gauldie, John Clark and Richard Russell, who designed the Falkirk Wheel. Dundee bought pictures by some of the artists. James McIntosh Patrick (who later lent me his black suit for a principal's dinner at the University) was throughout my time in Dundee a stimulating presence. Once he unceremoniously took down an exhibition I had just hung with great care (by artist, chronologically) and completely rehung it; it looked much better his way. His walled garden at Magdalen Yard Road was luxuriant, with clematis running through the trees, and his collection of pictures included *The Birth of Venus* (now in the National Gallery of Scotland) by his future brother-in-law Edward Baird.

The show 'Seven Painters in Dundee' was the first of several to tour with Scottish Arts Council support. It was also one of the last with a Dundee link. The belief was that we would interest the town if we could concentrate on what was happening outside it. But George Dutch Davidson (who was not contemporary) and John Johnstone (who was) were some of the local painters whose work we were proud to show. As to acquisitions, Clara Young commented: 'For the first time ... here was an individual who pursued a policy of collecting contemporary Scottish Art.' But Young adds, 'Hardie's most notable achievements were in the area of twentieth-century collecting' and she singled out works purchased from Stanley Cursiter, William Johnstone and William McCance. The two paintings by J.D. Fergusson and the Joseph Crawhall were already there on long loan and perhaps don't count, but I was pleased with three other finds: the elaborate early Thomas Faed panel; a beautiful Stanley Spencer of *Love Letters* to add to the existing one, *A Corner of Cookham*; and a late, very Impressionistic *Portrait of May* by the Bridgeton painter John Quinton Pringle. Dundee Council will have been repaid with interest by the values of all these works today.

James McIntosh Patrick's large retrospective was occupying the galleries on my first visit, but Professor Young spoke about the painter's son Andrew McIntosh Patrick who was a director and would become managing director of the Fine Art Society in London. In Dundee was another luminary whom I should meet without delay – John Walton FRS, an eminent botanist who was the son of E.A. Walton, the Glasgow School painter. He owned several Mackintosh flower studies, although as Andrew hoped they would be left to Glasgow I was to 'keep my hands off them'. Professor Walton gave me information about his painter father, and told me that he used to use the botanical watercolours by Charles Rennie Mackintosh in his collection for teaching purposes in his classes at Glasgow University's Botany department. I later published the story (which I recently saw doubted in the Charles Rennie Mackintosh Society's *Journal*).

Andrew McLaren Young had collaborated with the architecture historian David Walker on the architectural handbook *Glasgow at a Glance*. Walker was co-author of a much-praised monograph on *The Architecture of Glasgow* and was still living in Dundee. He remains my oldest friend. With Kenneth Roberts the landscape painter we would meet in each other's houses to talk about art. Ken's wife Alison Roberts is descended from the family of the little master of Forfar, J.W. Herald, whose beautiful work I was seeing for the first time. I fondly thought of us as a Dundee School of Scottish art history as David's *Architecture of Glasgow* and my *Scottish Painting* were both in preparation at this time. As I was discovering, exhibitions went behind the surface of things in a way not always possible with solitary acquisitions.

When Andrew McIntosh Patrick was planning a survey exhibition on the Glasgow School at the Fine Art Society in London, he asked me to select the show and write the catalogue. Selecting it was a pleasure because between us we knew the whereabouts of all the Glasgow School paintings we wanted. More difficult would be the introduction. The more I thought about it and about the need for swathes of background history for such a little-known subject, the more I was daunted. Andrew McIntosh Patrick was a model of patience and from him I learned a hands-on approach: to dovetail text that was separate but belonged together, use the scissors!

The exhibition in New Bond Street in 1970 was the first in London since the Glasgow painters had exhibited at the Grosvenor Gallery in 1890. Then they had gone on to show in Munich's Glaspalast, to great critical acclaim. Over the next decade or more their work was seen all over Europe, North America and Australia, and Diaghilev was behind an exhibition of their work in St Petersburg. Their pictures were bought by collections public and private wherever they exhibited. No Scottish painters since Sir David Wilkie had received this measure of international attention in their lifetime.

The reason for their success was that they were a collective breath of fresh air at a moment when European painting had seen Impressionism become repetitive and formulaic, and the masterpieces of Van Gogh and Gauguin were still hardly known. Picasso was still a very young painter living in Barcelona (which was one of the European cities where the Glasgow artists' work was seen). In this vacuum the French-trained Arthur Melville, the realists William Kennedy, James Paterson and Joseph Crawhall , the more rugged homegrown painterliness of James Guthrie and William York Macgregor, and the decorative panache of E.A. Hornel and George Henry seemed attractively, daringly modern.

A comment by Hamish Miles on our London presentation of the Glasgow School in 1970 was that it 'would not be entirely convincing to someone not familiar with the subject' I think the same was true of its predecessor, the big Kelvingrove exhibition of

41

1968 for which I had selected paintings by Hornel. The truth is that all these exhibitions have been (like Roger Billcliffe's book on *The Glasgow Boys*) conscientiously inclusive, and thus have included mediocre material. What would convert the most hardened critic is a highly selective presentation, still generous in scale, but giving prominence to the realists of the early 1880s followed by some of the very original works emanating from the second, decorative phase of the Glasgow School from the later 1880s to 1900. Look at their range! The first phase would be represented by masterpieces like William Kennedy's *The Deserter*, William York Macgregor's *The Vegetable Stall*, Guthrie's *In the Orchard* as well as his more familiar pieces, with E.A. Walton and Joseph Crawhall. The decorative later phase would include almost any oils by Arthur Melville from his 1892 Spanish tour and some of his pyrotechnical watercolours, cubistic flowers by Stuart Park from around 1888/1890, *St Agnes* by David Gauld and *Good King Wenceslaus* by Alexander Roche, two marvellous works linked by a verse of 'Good King Wenceslaus':

> Sire he lives a good league hence
> Underneath the mountain
> Hard against the forest fence
> By Saint Agnes fountain.

The atmospheric evocations of Kirkcudbright and Japan by Henry and Hornel would be essential too. One of the Japanese works titled *Romance* shows two of the kimono-clad girls who were Hornel's playmates during his eighteen-month stay in Japan, with *yatate* and *kiseru*, and in the background a ship under sail in the moonlight. Another, perhaps the most beautiful of them all, belonged to the Glasgow dealer Ian MacNicol. I long believed that it represented two Japanese girls in kimono with fans in a garden with an orange tree. In fact these are girls playing battledore and shuttlecock at *o-shogatsu* (New Year), as Japanese girls still do. The boys fly kites. And it's not an orange tree, it's persimmon (*kaki*).

The Glasgow School created its own poetry and its own aesthetic. Widely appreciated by their contemporaries, they deserve a wider audience today. It is noteworthy that in the last thirty years Glasgow Art Galleries and Museums and the National Gallery of Scotland, mistaking the local for the provincial, have shown little enthusiasm for the Scottish School under curators more interested in the arcana of the German avant-garde or Italian drawings. Denys Sutton wrote in May 1970 in the *Financial Times*:

'The achievement of the Glasgow School is that its artists were in touch with modern movements but not at the expense of their own individualities ... surely there is much to be said for regionalism.'

It was an early insight into the life of the professional art dealer, when Andrew McIntosh Patrick wrote to me in March 1970: 'We have to take it all down and hang another show next week. Glory be and what a life!'

At the end of 1969 my director at Dundee had received a visit from Tom Honeyman. I was invited to join their meeting and told that the purpose of Tom Honeyman's visit was to secure loans of paintings by Scottish Colourists for an exhibition of their work, which would tour to the Scottish Arts Council's galleries in Glasgow's Blythswood Square and Edinburgh's Charlotte Square, and to other takers still to be decided on. Honeyman explained that although he was responsible for the selection of the show and Ailsa Tanner would write the bibliography, he wanted an introduction written by someone with a fresh perspective. Would I undertake the job? But of course. I wanted to identify the artistic personalities of these artists, who were then an acknowledged but still little-studied force in the history of Scottish art. In some of their work each of them can resemble their colleagues, at least superficially: this is especially true of Samuel John Peploe and Fergusson early on, and later of Francis Cadell and Peploe.

There was an oddity in the composition of a show that was to include Peploe, Leslie Hunter and Cadell but not Fergusson. There was really no excuse for this and the pretext that Honeyman would avoid the trouble of having to deal with Fergusson's widow Margaret Morris, while plausible, was scarcely respectable. These reservations grew unstoppably while I was thinking about the work, and surfaced in my text sufficiently to draw a letter from Meg: ' ... at last I have seen the Cat[alogue] of the 3 [triple underline] Colourists show! ... I want to tell you how much I appreciate your many mentions of Fergus, & of course ... your whole article is excellent... '

Honeyman was strictly correct; the exhibition was about 'Three Scottish Colourists' not 'The Three Scottish Colourists', and it was produced when Fergusson was still living and did not include him for that reason. It was an example of Honeyman's generosity that he wrote that in spite of everything he and I had 'delivered the goods'. In September of 1970 I received a letter from Professor Sir Ivor Batchelor. He had kindly entertained me with dinner when I had admired his fine collection of British drawings including important examples by David Wilkie and the Pre-Raphaelites, now in the British Museum. He wrote: 'I have greatly enjoyed your recent essays in the *Catalogues* of the 'Glasgow School' and 'Three Scottish Colourists' exhibitions. They combine sensitivity, erudition and a freshness and sharpness of focus which are immensely stimulating and which raise the standards of discussion of art in Scotland. No one else is doing work of this quality.' Nice.

During the course of researching the Honeyman papers, I found two significant comments. One was by the widow of S.J. Peploe who asserted in the family papers shown me by their son Denis Peploe that the Glasgow dealer Alexander Reid had known Gauguin as well as Van Gogh who famously painted his portrait. Since Reid was close to Glasgow painters such as George Henry whose *A Galloway Landscape* has always struck viewers by its affinity to Gauguin, this seemed to offer a more credible milieu for the Scottish work. Also in the Honeyman papers there was an account by the Scottish artist E.A. Taylor when he was living in Paris with his wife Jessie Marion King. Taylor wrote regarding the influence of the Paris artist Auguste Chabaud on the Scottish Colourists. This was interesting because it proved what was already visible from their work, that, not having the benefit of hindsight from which to choose their stylistic models in the ferment of Paris, the Scottish artists admired, as much as Cézanne, Matisse and Picasso, a painter – Auguste Chabaud – who now seems to us minor. It also explained the origin of the black outlines, characteristic of Chabaud, to which Fergusson and Peploe in particular resorted when painting edges.

In France three decades later, Donald Bain admired Matisse and Picasso (whose portrait he sketched several times at St-Paul-de-Vence) but *in practice* his work shows an equal interest in Constant Permeke's northern, expressionistic style, which suited his own temperament. This is confirmed by mentions of Permeke in Bain's letters from France. At different times the painters Georges Rouault, Christopher R.W. Nevinson, Albert Marquet, Paul Klee, Adolph Gottlieb and Alberto Burri strongly influenced William MacTaggart, William McCance, Alexander Graham Munro, Tom Pow, Charles Pulsford and Robert Cargill for a brief but intense period. In such cases it has nothing to do with copying. The artist is trying to understand the alchemy he has seen in the craft of other artists.

The exhibition had a successful tour, and I gave a lecture on it to a packed house (an indication of the growing interest in their work) at the Lady Artists' Club in Blythswood Square, Glasgow. I myself was now able to disentangle the four – not three – personalities among the Scottish Colourists, with Peploe the most intense and self-limiting, Hunter the most lyrical, Cadell the most brilliant, and Fergusson the most experimental. I had worked with Honeyman and his friends the Harrisons and the Services who had been the main supporters of the Colourists in Scotland. The final paragraph was so difficult to write that it delayed my text for a week and was finished on the train crossing the Forth Railway Bridge to a final meeting with the publishers. It is as close as I have come to defining the spirit of modern Scottish painting.

'There can be no doubt that the 'three Scottish Colourists', during some two decades from about 1910 to about 1931, produced a number of masterpieces. If these paintings derive more of their substance from Cézanne and Matisse, rather than from the radical group of French painters associated with Picasso, this does not diminish the originality of Peploe, Hunter and Cadell. An absence of theory need not imply an absence of logic. The best paintings by these Scottish painters are eminently logical, but their logic is determined by the material, the paint itself. This painterliness, this insistence on the quality of paint and the beauties proper to it, is their greatest strength. It is also the source of their considerable influence on subsequent Scottish painting.'

Since 1970 the values of these artists have climbed steeply year on year as the Scottish Colourists have become household names, enjoying much greater recognition today than they ever did in their own lifetimes. Their bright colours, beautiful painting (*belle peinture*) and agreeable subject matter have made them favourites with a public which loves them. And why should it not?

My next project explored a different vacuum in the history of Scottish art. In the mid-nineteenth century, at roughly the same time as the Impressionists in Paris, a generation of artists trained in Edinburgh had enjoyed unprecedented success in Edinburgh and in London. The Edinburgh side of the story was relatively well understood; in particular, William McTaggart's work and career had never gone out of favour. What was much less visible, partly because it was made for a London market, was the work of the no less successful but now ignored artists of this group who had made their careers beyond Scotland, chief among them Sir William Quiller Orchardson. We knew that no less a critic than Degas had expressed admiration of a painting by Orchardson. I noticed that the Forbes Collection's *Solitude* by Orchardson, which we borrowed from New York, looked a little like the work of Toulouse-Lautrec and placed a study for the picture on the cover of the catalogue. Why did Degas like Orchardson? The Scottish Arts Council decided to back the project, and Magda Salvesen and I were again working together. I warned her 'Don't run away and get married until this is finished' – advice she ignored when she ran away to live with Jon Schueler in New York, but not until the project was well under way.

Magda suggested that I should adopt a cataloguing system she had learned from Alan Bowness, her tutor at the Courtauld Institute, which simply entailed describing what one saw on the canvas. So often we leap to interpretation without really *looking* first. This advice worked particularly well with Orchardson, because all the details are there for a reason connected with the main theme. And as a Victorian, the artist took the historical accuracy of his period pictures very seriously. I asked Simon Jervis of the V&A for advice on the period furniture, and the costume historian James Laver commented on details of dress. The result I think was a much more interesting catalogue. Here is an example:

> 'A ballroom, with only one couple dancing (centre) the lady with her back
> to us. Left, a seated pianist is accompanying a violinist (whose head only
> is finished). To the right of the piano, a large azalea in flower. Right, a
> couple leave arm-in-arm; the lady little more than a blank on the canvas,
> except for her head and shoulders.'
>
> *(The Last Dance)*

James Laver told me that his interest in costume began when as keeper of paintings at the V&A he had realized that costume, which changes constantly according to fashion, was an invaluable tool in the dating of pictures.

Very large paintings by Orchardson were brought to Edinburgh at fabulous expense, including the famous *The First Cloud* from the National Gallery of Australia. Two of the paintings were the enormous *Napoleon on Board the Bellerophon* and *Napoleon at St Helena 1816*, the former from the National Maritime Museum. As I directed the 'hang' of this very big exhibition in the Royal Scottish Academy's Diploma Galleries, which it filled, I was conscious of feelings of megalomania which the dictator would have understood. One could read the huge banners erected on the RSA from Waverley Station and from the West End. It toured to several galleries including, of course, Dundee. The Clark connection was prominent as Lord Clark loaned quite possibly Orchardson's most poignant picture, *The Last Dance*, from Saltwood Castle, and his daughter Colette perhaps the most beautiful, *On the Lagoon*, a view of Venice from the water by moonlight.

What resulted from the exhibition was an appreciation of Orchardson's refinement in still life, which could approach that of Fantin-Latour, with a beautiful touch and sense of tonal values. If these qualities sometimes seemed at odds with his often melodramatic subjects, that was part of the pact with the devil of commercial reproduction which sustained so many Victorian academicians. We had answered the questions set by our own examination, and better understood the artist's real quality. The gulf between Scottish and French painting appeared if anything wider than ever, but that mattered less than we had thought. The show was a crowd-pleaser.

The paintings and their characters populated the galleries like visitors from an earlier age. But their merits were also clearer, if less French. Today the preference for pure painting favours McTaggart's style over Orchardson's, but in terms of his invention, as a draughtsman, and for his delicate brushwork, Orchardson was revered by his younger brother-artists in Scotland to whom he was a living legend. But the girl from Glasgow who danced at the *Folies-Bergères* in the 1890s remained the closest discoverable Scottish link to the milieu of Toulouse-Lautrec. Ivor Batchelor was less enthusiastic about the Orchardson and William Johnstone exhibitions. Rather than the upward trajectory his first letter celebrated, his second denigrated both Orchardson and Johnstone. And I was just getting started!

We have since had several paintings by William Johnstone and two near-abstracts come especially to mind. They had originally been a single wood panel but were sawn into two equal halves on completion because they made two perfectly balanced compositions, although the saw is not usually thought of as a painter's implement. It's more a sculptor's perhaps.

5 Portrait Of The Artist As A Young Man

There is something mysterious about Dundee, as there is about all old cities. It has a confiding sense of intimacy in the dark winters, and summer brings on a peculiar restlessness of the soul in the little-changing Angus countryside. A timeless landscape can affect the beholder with a sense of his own impermanence. The better I knew them, the more the city and county gave me the feeling that there was more behind the surface. Angus was the country of the Picts, one of the earliest aboriginal tribes of Scotland; an example of their ogham writing was found in a field near Inchyra. The carved stones and burial hoards of a millennium ago seem to employ symbols of early Christianity. The tiny museum at Meigle contained 'the greatest assemblage of sculpture of the Dark Ages' according to the HMSO guide. The castles of the Mearns and Angus of four centuries ago – Claypotts, Inverquharity, Powrie, Murroes, Huntly, Megginch, Invermark and Glamis further north – glimpsed part-hidden at the end of a long drive surrounded by tall trees or attached seamlessly to a farmhouse of the same local stone, are less imposing than those of Deeside, but no less beguiling. The panel painting of the *Crucifixion* at St Marnock's Church in Foulis Easter (not far from Dundee) is the most complete pre-Reformation example of its kind extant in Scotland.

There is a Dundee novel *Witch's Blood* about medieval Dundee by William Blain (whom I met), and Sir Andrew Ogilvy-Wedderburn once told me the tale of a necklace of black beads which came unstrung during a reel at a hunt ball. Supposed to be of jet, they were sent to be restrung and the jeweller in London identified the beads, not as jet, but as Russian black pearls. *Life on the Dniva* was written by a local lady from Broughty Ferry; a link with the Netherlands, the Baltic and Russia was natural, given Dundee's position as an eastern seaport. The John Zephaniah Bell, Burn-Murdoch, and Weinberg pictures were a reminder of Dundee's outward-looking past and were not the Dutch artist Jacob Maris and the North American painters John Kane and Albert Pinkham Ryder in the north-east of Scotland?

The nearest I came to the mystery at the heart of Dundee was when I discovered, or rediscovered, the work of George Dutch Davidson. During the process of cataloguing we had come across cardboard boxes containing works on paper which were a strange mixture of highly intricate, decorative draughtsmanship in exquisite detail, and brush drawings in body colour that were quite broad and displayed the wistful colours of the *fin de siècle*. These like all the works on paper in the collection were given new mounts and placed in solander boxes for safety. For one of these pieces which had received water damage it was already too late. The work was beautiful and I was enraptured not only by its quality, but also by its strange spirituality. It seemed that the art nouveau had found another original voice to add to those surrounding Mackintosh and his contemporaries in Glasgow; their slightly later Dundee equivalent.

The death at the absurdly early age of twenty-one of George Dutch Davidson (1879–1901) had called forth the Dundee Graphic Arts Association, and a *Memorial Volume* published by them. This work, of which 100 copies were printed, had fine collotype illustrations, with correspondence. It is one of the most beautiful books of that period. I began to work my way through the names that had been printed more than seventy years earlier. From Miss Helen Dutch, a cousin of the artist whose name I found in the Coupar directory, I was able to track down *On the Scheldt*, a beautiful canal view near Antwerp which I had desired with the passion of true love from the moment I saw its reproduction in the *Memorial Volume*, and I bought it for myself. Today this would be frowned upon. My reasoning to my chief was that as Dundee had not covered itself with glory in their care of the Davidson works in their possession, one would probably be just as safe with me.

There was more to come. Further down the list of subscribers was the name of the deceased artist's friend, the painter David Foggie. Foggie is not a very common name, and I discovered that his widow lived in Kirkcaldy in Fife. Mrs Foggie, whom I found as I found Miss Dutch by the simple expedient of going through the telephone directory, showed me a large portfolio with the words 'I think this will interest you.' The folder contained a further thirty-five works by Davidson, doubling the known *oeuvre*, and including some pieces of the highest quality, including the iconic *Self Portrait* of 1898 which is one of the most extraordinary documents in the history of the *fin-de-siècle*. It intuitively parallels the Freudian sexual psychology of Edvard Munch's *Im Menschenkopf* (1897) and Paul Klee's *Der Verliebte* (1923) – and would look perfectly at home in their company. At the same time it seems to situate the young artist's self-portrait within an aerial map of the Tay Estuary where he lived. Three watercolours which Davidson completed at this juncture are abstract in the theosophical sense of referring to cosmic space. These too were part of the Foggie group. Together with the *Self Portrait*, they made a much stronger case for Davidson as an original contributor to the iconography of the art nouveau in Scotland, who had gone far beyond the confines of the symbolist illustration of his period.

There was another stroke of luck. Researching the Dutch Davidson connections in St Andrews University Library, I realized that the library owned an 'association' copy of the *Memorial Volume*, and that its owner had sent a copy to the poet William Butler Yeats. To our joy there was an unpublished letter from Yeats offering thanks for the book, but also waxing lyrical about George Dutch Davidson's work:

> 'The book is beautiful with a kind of ritual energy – as of things that have by very energy of feeling passed out of life, as though precious stones were made by the desire of flowers for a too great perfection – all such art delights one as if it were part of a religious service speaking to the whole soul, the passions not less than the moral nature uniting it to an unchanging order. Of course one can see influences, but that is an original nature using all, a nature more delicate and sensitive but less cold and logical than Beardsley's – whom I knew. How strange that these lyrical and decorative natures should so often be short-lived – Beardsley, Shelley and lesser men whom one has known, though the world has not.'

Margaret Foggie's collection was bought for Dundee City Art Collections, and in 1973 we were able to mount an exhibition showing the entire output, virtually, of the city's most extraordinary artist, who had died so tragically young. The exhibition was titled 'The Hills of Dream Revisited', after one of George Dutch Davidson's illustrations to a poem of the same name by Fiona MacLeod (the pen name used by William Sharp), high priestess of the Celtic Revival movement:

> And a strange song have I heard there
> By a shadowy stream
> And the singing of a snow-white bird
> By the Hills of Dream.

The imagery of this quatrain – song, stream, bird, hills, dream – distils the other-wordliness of the *fin-de-siècle*. It recurs not only in George Dutch Davidson's work, but also in that of Jessie Marion King, and in their contemporary the poet Hugo von Hofmannsthal, whose libretto for *Die Frau Ohne Schatten* parallels it so closely it that one wonders whether he had read 'Fiona Macleod'. I can say that the music for the opera and some of the illustrations of Jessie Marion King evoke each other so strikingly in my mind as to create a vivid experience of synaesthesis, one sense invoking another, the music 'heard' in the art, the art 'seen' in the music. In Davidson the progression of style from material to dematerialization is complete. He is that rarest of artists, one who, however briefly, achieved an abstract style which was not connected to an applied discipline, a craft.

Another important work, *The Silent Pool*, was also tracked down for the exhibition, in a house next door to the Fine Art department of the University of St Andrews. I enjoyed teasing colleagues in the department about the treasure that had lain for years under their very noses.

In the meantime there were five large galleries to fill with revolving exhibitions in Dundee, one of them containing a makeshift picture store, and the main gallery doubling as a recital hall, complete with stage. These problems were gradually solved with the installation of a basement store with sliding racks and the restoration of the five galleries to their original role as picture galleries. This involved the demolition of the stage, but before this I remember the visit of the Amadeus String Quartet, who used my office as their dressing room for the evening. I politely suggested that they might enjoy our current exhibition 'Printmaking in Dundee' as a background to their recital. 'We will trrrry not to let it distrrrrrract us', said one of them, Norbert Brainin or Peter Schidlof. I was too disconcerted (pardon the expression) to respond. Or to paraphrase Tom Honeyman, I must have said *something* but I forget what.

Except for the Diploma Galleries of the Royal Scottish Academy, Dundee's Victoria Galleries are the grandest I've ever worked in. Certainly the grandest night was when we held a champagne reception to mark the publication of the *Dundee Catalogue* in the newly refurbished galleries, devoid of stage, picture storage, partitions, and a collection of musical instruments. 'The Hills of Dream Revisited' showed our new acquisition of works by George Dutch Davidson. My successor as keeper, Clara Young, filled the galleries up again and introduced mezzanines as modern paintings measuring 24 x 30 inches tend to look lost in the generous spaces of a Victorian gallery. Although I prefer the clarity of the previous arrangement, I acknowledge that her Royal Academy-style hang of Dundee's rich collection of Victorian pictures was beautiful.

It was satisfying, several years after I had left the Museum, to assist the acquisition by Dundee of the large *Loteria Nacional: Buying the Tickets* by one of the greatest of the London Scots, John Phillip. This splendid picture had belonged to Lord Wraxall whose ancestor bought it from the artist and its presence further enriches the Victorian displays at Dundee. This is buying par excellence to fit an existing collection.

Mr Boyd, my boss, was a product of Glasgow School of Art who had published a catalogue of Frank Brangwyn's drawings. He was happy to leave the Art Section to its own devices while he pursued his many other interests in Scottish silver, local archaeology and Dundee's history. His directorship saw the expansion of the Museum, which acquired keepers in Archaeology, Natural History, Textiles and Social History and Education. It was only after I had become his Depute and attended the monthly meetings of Dundee Corporation (the City Council) that I understood his effectiveness in wresting cooperation (and money) from our political masters. A mild-mannered and delightfully absent-minded man, Mr Boyd would wear down opposition in committees with long, closely argued speeches which would have the elected body surrender in desperation as the only means of inducing him to sit down. His passion was matched by his ambition for outlying branches of the department: the Mills Observatory, Dudhope Castle, Camperdown House, Broughty Castle, and the Barrack Street Museum – he championed them all tirelessly.

My ever-supportive chief allowed me to take January 1976 off to work on my book on Scottish painting. I had the bare bones ready – the work for exhibitions presented in the past – but what was needed was a push in other areas. I was touched by his support and pride in the project from start to finish. But soon I would be depute – and for six months I was acting director – and the paperwork and meetings began inexorably to mount. I felt I was learning more and more about less and less.

Mr Boyd and I went to Forfar to visit Mr Mann, the jovial secretary to the Camperdown Trustees (13/1/75), owners of the great painting by John Singleton Copley, *The Victory of Admiral Viscount Duncan at Camperdown*. It was on a long loan to the City of Dundee and hung, neglected and in poor condition, in Camperdown House. The painting was lined and restored by Diane Malloch, so that it could once again be displayed. The restoration involved lining the enormous original canvas with a reinforcing canvas which was pressed to it by the hot wax method then popular among restorers. For this a special hot table had to be erected: it was nerve-wracking, but the restorer worked with great care and the *The Victory of Admiral Viscount Duncan at Camperdown,* one of the great works of American painting in Britain, could again be seen in all its glory. I regret to say that for a time Dundee kept it in the spiral stairwell in the Albert Institute which is not often used by visitors. After some years, it now hangs on loan in the National Gallery of Scotland.

Alexander (Sandy) Dunbar, who as the UK director of the Gulbenkian Foundation in Lisbon had bought a lovely Donald Bain, banteringly said to me at this point that I had become the world expert on Donald Bain and Orchardson. But there was method in my madness: I was piecing together my history of Scottish painting which would be, in Hamish Miles's words, 'convincing to the onlooker new to the subject'. I was aiming at the onlooker who knew modern painting. The late Brian Sewell, the art critic ('Scottish painting – does it exist?'), was the kind of spectator I had in mind.

Relating Orchardson's studies to the finished works (or rather, to the exhibition-size works) was close to the world of the *catalogue raisonné*. Artists' techniques have not changed all that much over the centuries, unless one is looking at the works of Damien Hirst and all the many other followers of Marcel Duchamp and Dada. Of course their dependence on drawing applies mainly to figure painting. Because drawings were to some extent disposable parts of the creative process, and because the artists concerned were in the process of inventing and reinventing the whole Western tradition of figure painting, the old master ones have become enormously glamorous. Some years ago I was in the Henry Huntington Memorial Library in New York to identify a drawing there as made by Dante Gabriel Rossetti for Dundee's *Dante's Dream on the Day of the Death of Beatrice* which is probably the most important Pre-Raphaelite painting in Scotland. *Bingo*, as we say in the trade. Similarly, a drawing by Michelangelo was recognized by Sotheby's at Castle Howard. Slowly but surely the apprentice years become the years of expertise.

Not to be confused with the painter Orchardson, the wealthy foundry owner and philanthropist James Guthrie Orchar left his collection of some 400 works (paintings and prints) to the residents of Broughty Ferry. The James Guthrie Orchar Collection was kept for many years in Beach House in Broughty Ferry (the house was purchased as a temporary home for the collection in 1919), but eventually in 1987 it was transferred to the City of Dundee and the Albert Institute.

About 1970 my parents bought the Steele Road railway cottages directly opposite the smithy where my grandfather served his apprenticeship many years before; the next house a mile away down the Jedburgh road had belonged to a kinswoman, and Mains Farm in the opposite direction was another distant ancestor's house in the 1740s. As a family, we were *connected*. I later discovered that neighbours at Redheugh nearby were descendants of James Boswell, the biographer of Dr Johnson, and of William Wilkins, the architect of the National Gallery in London.

Again, take the house in Broughty Ferry my family moved into in 1972. It was sold to us by William and Norah Montgomerie; he was a poet and she a writer of children's books; they knew the painter J.D. Fergusson and his wife the dancer Margaret Morris, who came to visit them. Twenty years later, William Montgomerie wrote the monograph in which was a painting by Donald Bain which we had recently been given by the artist and duly introduced to the house. Do houses choose their owners?

In Dundee meanwhile there followed a series of studies of Scottish artists of the past. We must have been one of the Scottish Arts Council's main clients in those halcyon days when the council still regularly supported historical as opposed to contemporary exhibitions. The choice of subjects and the research were determined by areas I wanted to explore in my history of Scottish painting. When my book on this subject was published in 1976, much of the research had initially been carried out for exhibitions, which have the merit of uncovering unknown, forgotten or lost works. This gives the art historian working as a keeper or as a dealer a huge advantage over academic colleagues. Hitherto unknown works of art are rare indeed in the professorial contributions to the literature on Scottish art.

The book project was advancing rather slowly until I began a correspondence with Stanley Cursiter late in 1973. I never actually met him, because when I spoke to him on the telephone (from Tom Honeyman's house in Glasgow) he was about 86 and in the process of vacating his house at 14 Ainslie Place in Edinburgh to retire to his house in Stromness on his native Orkney. But I wrote to him several letters to which he replied, fortunately, as his replies are now in the National Library of Scotland. They contained a bombshell.

Perhaps it seems strange to say that the seven paintings of 1913 by Stanley Cursiter were the most important discovery I made, because he was a very well-known figure in Scottish art circles, not obviously in need of rehabilitation or lacking recognition. For decades he had been thought of as a landscapist of Orkney, a portraitist of Scottish notables, and a former director of the National Galleries of Scotland, who had published a well-regarded book on Scottish art and studies of Sir Henry Raeburn and Peploe. His earliest work was forgotten, partly because it had been produced immediately before the Great War before, as he wrote to me, he 'departed for the Somme'. In a creative burst that saw him move in quick succession from exquisite watercolour illustrations and lithographs of Norse legends, through a series of oil studies of the lovely Poppy Lowe (including one in which she is nude except for a wrist watch), the young Cursiter arrived at Futurism. By this I mean *futurismo*, the dynamic style derived from Cubism by Gino Severini and a circle of his Italian friends in Paris. Cursiter was well aware of their work and borrowed, for an Edinburgh exhibition, a Futurist masterpiece, the celebrated *Le Boulevard* of 1913 by Severini. This painting must have come straight from the easel.

When he wrote to me his series of letters of 1973 (now in the National Library) about exhibitions of modern painting in Edinburgh, he pointed out that not only had he appreciated the Futurists, he had also briefly painted in their style. In a letter to me of 18 November 1973 he wrote: 'For your amusement I enclose three photographs of pictures painted in 1913 – these were I suppose influenced by the "Post-Impressionists Exhibition".' Of these, one view of *Princes Street* was plainly unfinished although interesting in its treatment of the architecture which was Antonio Sant'Elia-like: could Cursiter ever have seen the young architect's work? Another, *Rain on Princes Street*, was a relatively severe work in black and white, with a pattern of black umbrellas and glimpsed faces of pedestrians beside the bronze lamp standards of Edinburgh's New Club re-formed to resemble Futurist sculpture by Umberto Boccioni. The third painting with its long title *The Sensation of Crossing the Street – the West End, Edinburgh* was by far the most complex as well as the most accomplished work. It was almost a Futurist tract, reflecting the subjective impression felt by the modern girl in the foreground of the hubbub of motorized vehicles amid a kaleidoscope of Edinburgh vignettes. It showed the right-angled junction of Princes Street with Lothian Road, Edinburgh. The vehicles included two omnibuses, a street car and a hackney carriage, in addition to the two dozen identifiable human figures which included a self-portrait, a policeman, and in the centre of all the mêlée, the delectable features of Poppy Lowe whose 'sensation' is depicted. This teeming composition was resolved in terms of myriad coloured triangles, very much in the manner of the Severini masterpiece *Le Boulevard* which Cursiter knew at first hand.

This was the missing piece of the jigsaw puzzle. The Scottish Colourists had worked in Paris and admired Picasso and Matisse, but where was the evidence of real engagement by any Scottish artist in the European avant-garde to which so much lip service was paid? Stanley Cursiter's two finished 1913 paintings, together with two delicious small works in the Scottish Modern Arts Association's Collection and a further two which belonged to the artist's daughter (*The Regatta*, unfinished, splendid, and reminiscent of J.D. Fergusson at his best, and *The Ribbon Counter*, wonderfully decorative and very futurist) provided such evidence, or as much of it as one was ever going to get.

With the artist's blessing I wrote to the Tate Gallery and to the Scottish National Gallery of Modern Art offering them *The Sensation of Crossing the Street*, the only picture of this group sent by the artist to an exhibition in London, at the Whitechapel Art Gallery. We thought that, as custodians of national collections, the Tate should have first claim on the most important picture. In the meantime, *Rain on Princes Street* was acquired for Dundee Art Gallery. *The Sensation of Crossing the Street*, however, was declined by both the Tate and the National Gallery in Edinburgh and I felt free to write to Dr Cursiter expressing my own interest in the picture. I explained how important I believed it to be, that I had a modest 'teaching' collection of Scottish art, and suggested that I would pay the same price that Dundee had for *Rain on Princes Street*; but I had no money. Dr Cursiter sent a telegram with a message to pay when we could, but in the meantime we were to have the picture which duly arrived the following day in a special crate at Turnhouse (Edinburgh airport). We were delighted by its lovely condition: it was 'bluer' in daylight than it appeared in the photograph, and the painting had a lovely, pristine surface. I sent Stanley Cursiter a telegram to Orkney expressing our delight and gratitude. A week later he died. Our cheque was sent to his executors.

When my *Scottish Painting* appeared in 1976, Steve Adamson at Studio Vista reproduced *The Sensation of Crossing the Street* on the front cover. The picture was requested for the 'Futurismo e Futuristi' exhibition which inaugurated the magnificently restored Palazzo Grassi on the Grand Canal in Venice in 1986. In Venice with the picture itself in April 1986, I saw my book in pride of place in a bookshop window in the Calle Campo Marzo XXII. The futurist cover had clearly intrigued the bookseller – a Scottish painting in an obviously Italian style.

We made several visits to Venice that year. The painting was hand-carried, which meant that it occupied its own seat in the aircraft, and we were then taken over the lagoon by *motoscafi* from Marco Polo to the front entrance of the Palazzo on the Canal Grande. We left it occupying a small room in the custody of an armed guard. *The Sensation* clearly caused a sensation, because it was requested for later versions of the exhibition in Barcelona, Paris (at the Centre Pompidou, where I met its curator, Jean Dethier) and finally in Tokyo, at the new Museum of Modern Art in Kiba. By this time the exhibition was less about Futurism and had a strong architectural and urban bias expressed in its new title 'La Ville: Visions Urbaines'.

The painting has also been in demand as a book cover. I turned down an application to use it for a German translation of a Doris Lessing novella, which was translated as *Die Terroristin* (The Female Terrorist). This just wasn't what the picture was all about. On the other hand, it was the perfect foil to Virginia Woolf's stream-of-consciousness novel *Mrs Dalloway*, and can be seen on the cover of a Penguin edition of that very suitable masterpiece.

Subsequently I sold *The Ribbon Counter* on behalf of Stanley Cursiter's daughter Margaret Hunter to an important Scottish private collection. One satisfaction of that sale was that we successfully deployed an unorthodox but we thought valid argument with the Inland Revenue to the effect that in the case of such an anomalous work within the artist's *oeuvre*, its value at that time should be the basis of calculation for capital gains tax, not its 1982 value plus interest. In 1997 I finally parted with *The Sensation of Crossing the Street* to a collector who had earlier declined three Peploes I offered him from the Harrison Collection. Much later the same collector bought one of the most expensive and controversial Scottish paintings of all time at Sotheby's, the *Singing Butler* by Jack Vettriano, famously copied from a painting manual.

Joining Cursiter's *Rain on Princes Street*, another important modernist Scottish painting acquired for Dundee (in 1975) was William McCance's austere *Mediterranean Hill Town* (identified by Patrick Elliott as Bogliasco in north Italy), dated 1923. McCance was influenced, like Cursiter ten years before, by Cubism, but in his case it was by the London version of Cubism proposed by Wyndham Lewis and the Vorticist circle. I first saw a work by McCance when their recently acquired *Conflict* (also dated 1923) went on display at Kelvingrove Art Gallery. I was enormously impressed by this evident masterpiece, so original and powerful, with strong colours, muscular drawing and bold handling. But who was William McCance, a Scottish artist who looked more like an American artist, say Marsden Hartley or Stanton Macdonald-Wright? Alasdair Auld, director at Kelvingrove, who had bought the picture for the gallery there, introduced me to the artist's widow, Margaret McCance. From this meeting resulted a touring exhibition which I assembled in 1975, mostly from her collection.

For a long time I owned *The Boat Yard* by William McCance, another very strong Vorticist work from McCance's London period; again, though, the Scottish National Gallery of Modern Art and other museums made no move to acquire this piece, a key work by a very rare Scottish artist which was sold privately. Only after a decade of seeing it every day did I find the source of its composition in a lithograph of 1919 by Christopher R.W. Nevinson, which was part of the Cursiter family collection I acquired in Tasmania in 1986. Perhaps this was mere serendipity rather than research, but I did travel halfway round the world and back again for that footnote to *The Boat Yard*. It proved McCance's link to London Cubism, or more correctly, Vorticism.

Arthur Melville's early work was well represented in the Wyhowski Collection, which came from James Cox, a mill owner famous still in Dundee for the eponymous factory chimney (Cox's Stack) that displayed his prosperity and power. Unfortunately I didn't make this find until after the Melville exhibition and after I had left Dundee. Later still we had two of the little oil panels that date from Melville's painting trip through Spain in 1892, as well as his large painting of *The Contrabandista* of the same year. Between one of the Melville panels *The Green Valley* and Fergusson's slightly later *Avenue de L'Observatoire* there is a strong resemblance which shows how close the Glasgow School and the Colourists were, compositionally and in the use of colour, when the Scottish Colourists were still young painters.

During the ten years I spent in Dundee I met and married Gillie, became the father of Andrew and Marion, moved from a top-floor flat in Baxter Park Terrace to a beachside terraced house (with cupola) in Broughty Ferry where we were visited one day by Peter Blake not long after he had become famous for designing the *Sergeant Pepper* album cover. I became an honorary lecturer in the French department of Dundee University, and was promoted twice. But I was terribly restless and confessed to my father that I had begun to feel ashamed of being a public servant, having to thole the inefficiency, waste and incompetence endemic in the public sector.

I wrote to the Hon Patrick Lindsay, Lord Crawford's son, and at the time a senior director of Christie's. That I am not still in Dundee is probably due to him, because after a year's waiting I was interviewed by two directors of Christie's, David Bathurst and Michael Clayton, and became a member of the famous auction house. There was a lovely *Courier* photo of Gillie with a very young Andrew, Marion and me.

I was about to test the truth behind the Wilkie dogma that 'to know the taste of the public is to the artist the most valuable of all knowledge.' To which one could add Mr Whitton's credo that 'there is no bad reason for liking a painting.'

6   The Third Man

When I joined Christie's as an agent working to the Wemyss Place office in Edinburgh, I had only two colleagues in Scotland, Sir Ilay Campbell and Michael Clayton. Ilay had three large houses in different parts of Scotland, but his Christie's business was conducted from the remote estate office at Cumlodden near the shore of Loch Fyne, Argyll. He was well known in Scottish society, had begun as a surveyor for Knight Frank & Rutley and adored working for Christie's. It was a constant education.

Michael Clayton, an expert in silver and gold who had vast general knowledge, ran the Edinburgh office, with its basement dining room and low purchase price. 'That must be the annual rent' said a London visitor, not realizing that London was still a lot more expensive than Edinburgh. Michael was a kind-hearted but difficult colleague who did not suffer fools gladly. As I was tentatively 'examining' a piece of silver as if it were a painting he could stand it no longer and shouted 'Pick it up'. This was a new world of people who breathed on silver to check for restorations, who crawled underneath furniture, who never used hotels if they could help it but always thought up someone interesting who might provide bed, dinner and a tour of the family heirlooms.

There was general merriment at a house sale on one occasion when, believing he was bidding for a fishing rod, Michael accidentally bought himself an ironing table. He said it would go to a good home. It was he who mentioned Christie's 'study leave' which took me to Venice for a week in the winter while Christie's and Edmiston's was being made ready in Glasgow. Michael also found that one could then travel one's family for almost nothing using tokens from Kellogg's cornflakes packets, advice that proved very useful when everyone had to be brought to London by train.

Through Christie's I began to see pictures which had previously been the stuff of legend; a Modigliani in Edinburgh; examples of Matisse and Van Gogh belonging to the Middleton family in Aberdeen; Fantin-Latour, Alfred Sisley, and Gauguin in a Glasgow collection; a Tintoretto, a Titian, an Annibale Carracci, a Giorgio de Chirico that was in Venice and was sold, through me, by John Lumley in London. Lumley's great knowledge of modern painters was accompanied by an extraordinary level of organization, and when I toured Canada looking for Scottish pictures in 1980, he generously let me have a copy of his Canada diary which was exclusively about collections; where they were, who owned them, and (not least) what arrangements owners had made for their future.

In terms of tradecraft one learned fast or else at Christie's. Every day was different. There was the major who gave me a bollocking for being late (satnav was unheard-of), and another who interrupted me in mid-flow with 'Stop talking!' There was Lady Maclean who said 'You can try, but it's a pepper mill' to my 'May I open the Beaujolais?' I was flummoxed when asked what I thought a certain wooden pole was, but I could identify it as a set of library steps (the rungs were inside the pole) when I saw another one weeks later. It was a new world of furniture – sofa tables, knole settees, longcase and bracket clocks, mystères, bonheurs du jour, porcelain caberets, gateleg or trestle tables, court cupboards, wine coolers, knife boxes, elbow chairs, Windsor chairs and so on ad infinitum. I collected for exhibition a Thomas Chippendale card table at Dumfries House, and before my arduous drive to London (which could not include a comfort break as my cargo was too valuable), I was given luncheon, served by a butler, by the Dowager Marchioness of Bute. At the time the kindly old dowager lived by herself in that secluded Robert Adam masterpiece.

I was able to give free rein to an interest in castles, often of the inhabited variety, with interiors I had hardly seen. There are still more than 1,500 castles in Scotland. Noble ruins like Bothwell, Craignethan, Tantallon, Dirleton and Kilchurn can be seen at any time; you can visit Dunnottar, Neidpath, Castle Campbell, St Andrews, Linlithgow (Palace) and on Deeside such beauties as Craigievar and Crathes (with paintings by George Jamesone and Archibald Skirving) and many, many others. A few of the ones I stayed in were Dunvegan, Floors, Towie Barclay and Kinkell. The National Trust of

Scotland and Historic Scotland have several finely restored castles. However, it seems that sometimes their curators are preoccupied with the chintz interiors, while I am much more interested in the buildings themselves. Many castles are still in private hands, and some like Dunderave or Harthill are occupied, perhaps because for one thing their stonework is in better condition than houses a tenth of their age.

In a Victorian castle on a remote Scottish island the dining room seemed more adapted for indoor cricket than conventional entertaining. But there was a good Scottish picture by William Crawford. I have only ever seen this one example of his work. There was also a large collection of pornography – contemporary, I noticed. Another castle boasted a painting by Johan Zoffany, yet another a huge collection of Victorian glass skeets, as well as the finest private cellar Michael Broadbent, Master of Wine and head of the Wine department, could remember seeing in thirty years. An original illustrated edition of one of John Gould's bird books was somewhere on the shelves, a bibliophile's prize indeed.

Late in 1978, Michael Clayton called me in for a confidential word in the basement dining room. Would I go to start the pictures department in Glasgow? I would also become a director of Christie's new auction rooms there. I agreed. To prepare me for this I went to Christie's King Street head office in St James's in London for six months during which time I stayed in one of the firm's flats in Ryder Street 'above the shop'. Christie's still had Fischer Fine Art opposite, and on Duke Street the St George's bookshop and an Italian café. While I was there Anne Simpson of *The Glasgow Herald* wrote an article about my job at Christie's under the byline 'The Third Man', referring to my status as number three in Scotland and hinting at the protocols and codes inseparable from an auction house.

Everyone in Christie's began with a spell at the Front Counter: it is an effective way of finding out who does what and where in that warren of offices, specialist libraries, warehouses filled with 'kit' or newly emptied after a sale, secretaries, porters, minions, and grandees all clustered round the Great Rooms. Experts could be summoned down to the Front Counter, as when I called Peter Arbuthnot from Ethnographical Art (I think it still may have been called Tribal Art) to see an elderly couple from New Zealand who had brought in a Maori carving. 'These are very rare in New Zealand' quoth the old lady. 'I am afraid madam they're very common in London' quoth he.

'Morning, I'm Bill Hardie,' said I, to Kathy Pritchard, the lady who ran the Front Counter of Christie's. 'Good morning William and take your hands out of your pockets,' she replied. This may not have been the first time I had committed this crime but it was certainly the last. First names were obligatory as they were throughout the art milieu, unless one was auctioneer that day, in which case it was 'Sir'. The dealers were 'the trade' but this was less pure snobbery than it sounds, as it merely distinguished between private and trade clients. Inside Christie's we didn't regard ourselves as 'trade', nor come to think of it did we ever shake hands with each other or wish each other good luck. Keeping our hands in our pockets in the presence of clients was taboo, as was 'Merry' as opposed to 'Happy' Christmas, 'your Grace' as opposed to 'Duke'. But the ultimate informality at someone's house was the removal of one's shoes, obligatory when standing on furniture to peer at a picture with the help of a torch. Visitors to Jeffrey Archer's London penthouse, having been asked to take their shoes off out of consideration for his carpets, would have been surprised to find the Munch painting *The Scream* among the novelist's collection – but it is only a good copy of the original.

Objects would be taken upstairs to the department concerned where people were busy cataloguing, researching, or reading *Alice in Wonderland*. 'Nothing to do with Korean,' snapped Sir John Figgess, our Korean ceramics expert, when I volunteered the owner's view of the origin of a pot. Rachel Russell's reaction to an 'Elizabethan chalice' was 'It's not a chalice and does she mean Elizabeth II?' Our experts tended not to mince their words. A client wanted advice on a Persian miniature and I rang Sophie Cavendish in Islamic works of art. She asked me who I was, and on being told said in crystalline Mitford tones: 'I didn't think you sounded like one of those upper-class boys at the Front Counter.' She was living in a 'little squat in Berkeley Square' and would be 'in the country' over the weekend. 'At Chatsworth?' 'Ya'. Sometimes the Front Counter was like being on the set of *Upstairs Downstairs*.

I toured the departments, spending a day or two with each one and trying not to get in the way. The more technical subjects like Modern Sporting Guns or Jewellery have their own workshops for testing gun barrels to make sure that they are in proof, or to check the weight and colour of gemstones as well as detect fakes. There was a power cut just before Christmas one dark afternoon when a jewellery sale was on view. All went black for a few seconds, but immediately generators boomed into life and light was restored. No doubt a certain number of zirconite 'diamond' switches were hastily replaced in pockets. Or so we joked; but the need for the generators was suddenly very clear.

Christie's was nothing if not theatrical. One of the delights of living in Ryder Street was its proximity to innumerable theatres. In Tom Stoppard's *Every Good Boy Deserves Favour* (mnemonic for EGBDF, the five lines of the stave), a musician who is a political dissident is being held in a Russian psychiatric cell, which he claims to share with an entire symphony orchestra. He is obviously mad. Then, in a stunning *coup de théâtre*, the lights go up to reveal onstage the full London Symphony Orchestra, hitherto invisible, with André Prévin at the rostrum. The play was on during my time in London.

In Christie's, all financial details, estimates, valuations and reserves are encoded via a simple system. It wasn't the done thing to quote numbers out loud, only letters, and this was *de rigueur* for paperwork. Cataloguing sessions take place in the basement warehouses in St James's where the goods are stored, lotted up, estimated and described for the sale catalogue. The cataloguing sessions differed according to the personality of the expert in charge. I noted that James Spencer (who afterwards became director of the Imperial Collection of Porcelain in Taiwan) would often be prompted by his very experienced secretary while he was mulling over a catalogue entry.

James Spencer would begin:
'A Kang Xi circular dish...'
She (typing away): '...with lobed rim...'
James: '...painted with dragons...'
She: '...chasing the flaming pearls.'
James: '10-inch diameter ...'
She: '...with the six character marks.'
and so on until the cataloguing was done.

Sir Hugh Roberts (Surveyor of the Queen's Works of Art) would eulogize the furniture he was describing, 'What wonderful carving'. Charles Cator, a master of the cataloguer's art, would pile description upon description in the demanding area of French furniture, with each detail of structure, function and exotic materials all falling into place in the correct order, that is, beginning at the top and ending, ten lines further down the page, with what the piece stands on. Charles once startled Michael on a visit to the Edinburgh office, while admiring a carved giltwood mirror, by asking 'But why have you hung it upside down?'

Pictures are subdivided at Christie's into several categories: Old Master, Nineteenth-Century, Modern British, Impressionist, Contemporary, English Watercolours and so forth. Because the picture warehouse floor undulates due to uneven foundations, a cataloguing session is called a 'hill', giving us 'to hill'. Pictures are hilled, not catalogued. Gregory Martin would treat a hill of Old Masters like a consultant on his rounds surrounded by medical students. 'Well, what is it?' Silence. 'Come ON!' 'French seventeenth century.' 'Le Nain? WHICH Le Nain?' Or, 'What's the subject?' 'Mother with a child and an elderly man.' 'Perhaps an Expulsion of Hagar?' In John Lumley's hills of Impressionist or Modern British sales with Francis Farmar and Carolyn Cumming I felt more secure on the familiar ground of the European twentieth century. My taste and that of Christie's were sometimes at loggerheads; Adrian Frazer at Christie's South Kensington was not impressed by my Liberty dining chairs from Murroes Castle because although beautifully made they were too modern.

Not everyone was happy that I'd left Dundee Museum for Christie's; Professor Sir Ivor Batchelor for instance was underwhelmed and did not want to see us when I was showing off Dundee collections to a Christie's visitor. My guest Francis Farmar was denied an opportunity to see Wilkie and Pre-Raphaelite drawings that are now in the British Museum.

By way of training I sat in the rostrum at South Kensington on a couple of evenings after hours with Bill Brooks and another director, the ebullient Christopher Elwes, firing bids at me. Brooks and Elwes were each clutching 'like a daisy in a coo's mooth' a well-nourished after-hours drink, and the session was good-humoured and peppered with practical suggestion: from the obvious ('Get a move on, they won't wait all day') to the technical ('Write with your right hand, hold the hammer in your left' – professionals abhor the amateur auctioneer's brandishing the hammer, which he probably refers to as a gavel, in the right hand) to the abstruse ('Never take bids from more than one bidder in the Room until you've passed the reserve *and* the highest bid in the Auctioneer's Book'). Other advice ranged from the commonsensical ('Move your head more, you have to see everybody') to auction good manners ('When you have a bidder in the Room, don't go on to another bidder until the first one has stopped bidding.' 'You have a reserve of £500 and a commission of £450, what must you do?' 'You have a reserve of £6,500, and commission bids of £4,200, £5,300, and £7,500, off you go').

Another lesson at Christie's concerned the numerology of odd and even numbers. The sequence 0-2-4-6-8-10 because it has five steps – an odd number – has the disconcerting property of putting an auctioneer on the wrong footing. Whereas the sequence 0-2-5-8-10 has four steps – an even number – and does not break down as the auctioneer sails serenely past the Scylla and Charybdis of reserve and proxy bids.

A reserve is the lowest figure at which a lot can be sold and a proxy bid is the highest the auctioneer is authorized to bid for a lot by an absent client. This is absolutely essential to the practice of auctioneering and if one neglects to practise it one can be facing some seriously upset clients. After my first auction at Christie's South Kensington, the Hon Patrick Lindsay, one of the grandees of the firm, asked me how I had got on. 'I missed a reserve by one bid,' I said ruefully. There was a pause. 'Don't do it again,' he said.

A quick-witted auctioneer will foresee any danger and put in a bid off-the-wall which brings the bidding 'right' again, but this is inelegant, can be spotted by the connoisseurs, and though not punishable by death, is regarded as clumsy and the sign of an incompetent or slack auctioneer. As an auctioneer I always felt like an ice skater preparing for a triple salko whenever multi-coloured ink commands in the Book indicated that a lot was coming up carrying bid instructions, none of them usually designed with the auctioneer's convenience in mind. In the good old days the auctioneer would have fun thinking up 'bought in' names before an auction – Dickens, Joyce, Orwell, Black, White, Grey, etc. Nowadays all bidders are given numbers which is certainly more efficient if more prosaic. I learned enough to be in 'General Practice' as a valuer; and I met half of the London art world, and more than half of that part of it I needed to know.

My first excursion as an auctioneer in a Christie's sale was at Christie's South Kensington in Old Brompton Road. I was to sell the first fifty lots of a sale of watercolours. This was considered one of the easy categories of sale, unlike Dolls and

Textiles, an auctioneering nightmare which only the toughest and most experienced auctioneer in the house, Bill Brooks, was man enough to handle. (So difficult were the dolly ladies: there had even been a fight at one of the Doll sales.)

Back again in Glasgow as the new director of a shiny new company I had the humiliation, because that's what it was, of taking the Lane Sale where things like old fridges were sold to the trade. But this period of selling ten-shilling lots was short-lived. Christie's wanted it as little as I did. Soon my quarterly Fine and Important sales were as valuable as they were supposed to be. I was able to concentrate on Scottish painting and who knew what I might find? But I did feel envious of John Lumley when he was auctioneer for the first Glasgow sale of the Wemyss Honeyman Collection in 1979. This was being sold on behalf of the executors, which meant that everything had to be sold without reserve. All John had to do was contain his excitement as the records tumbled. Why, a Peploe made £15,500!

Tiny offices are a Christie's tradition, and mine in Bath Street was shared with an assistant and a secretary. But the view of the narrow Sauchiehall Lane was exceptional, because I overlooked the south elevation of Mackintosh's Willow Tea Rooms at 215/217 Sauchiehall Street. The building and interiors of the Willow Tea Rooms were designed and built in 1903 for Catherine Cranston, who ran several tearooms in the city. These were the only tea rooms where Mackintosh had a completely free hand to design as he pleased. At that time this famous five-storey elevation in Sauchiehall Street was a sophisticated remodelling of Mackintosh's original building and designs which included a long window for the Room de Luxe inspired by the mullioned opening in the courtyard of Linlithgow Palace. In the lane to the south, Mackintosh seems to have given a Le Corbusier chimney to a plain country cottage. Given its proximity to the iconic Glasgow School of Art this aspect of the south elevation of the Willow Tea Rooms (at 215/217 Sauchiehall Street) is worth seeing. (In 'Timelessness' on page 158 I indicate the modernity of the chairs the architect designed for the Sauchiehall Street Willow Tea Rooms.)

Youthful enthusiasm, or perhaps I should say youthful inexperience, did not go very far in Glasgow. One day I was looking at items in a sale of porcelain when I came across a very nice French art nouveau vase, beautifully modelled and painted as a mademoiselle. It was high on a cabinet and as I reached it down I realized in a split second that it had a cover as well. Split is the *mot juste*: the cover flew over my shoulder and broke into a million pieces on the floor. What was worse, my first thought – immediately rejected – was to put the vase back and say nothing. Joe Mullen was completely all right about it although it must have been annoying to have a novice behaving like the proverbial bull in his china shop. The senior partner Charles Douglas, to my Mustardseed-ish 'I look forward to working with you Mr Douglas,' replied 'I am sure we will have a most courteous relationship.' Weeks later he accidentally spilled coffee, so that I found myself sitting in a pool of it, unburnt but wet; and I was wearing a fetching new suit. It looked briefly as if Charles would have to pay a cleaning bill. Fortunately this was not necessary as the coffee was black and dried invisibly. He was nicer after that. When asked slightly patronizingly by Christie's impressive Group Accountant who had come to vet us, 'What is your system of credit control Mr Douglas?' Charles replied 'It's very simple Mr Price. We don't give credit.'

At Christie's people in the rostrum were simply expected to behave themselves, not to indulge in jokes (at least not often) and not to fudge like amateurs. The auctioneer was looking after his own reputation as well as the firm's. Once after a picture sale in Glasgow, Michael Clayton told me that Lord Bute thought I as auctioneer had 'run him up' to the maximum of a bid he had left 'in the Book'. I had done no such thing and there had been an underbidder all the way. When Lord Bute was in Christie's again, I sought him out and mentioned what Michael had told me. I didn't attempt to vindicate myself, and simply said, 'I'd be pretty stupid to try to run you up.' He offered his hand without a word, we shook on it and that was the end of the matter. Some years later I was touched when he asked me to join a committee convened to discuss arrangements for Glasgow's year as European City of Culture.

It was typical of Christie's that one was left to sort out these corners of the moral maze for oneself. For example, Roy Thomas, who was Christie's and Edmiston's Head of Furniture, had an interesting lot, a chandelier at the Montgreenan House Sale, estimated £4/6,000, reserve £4,000 (in red), bid in the Book £28,000 (in green). Twenty-eight thousand pounds! But the chandelier was sold for £4,500. It obviously would be unethical to 'use up' one hundred per cent of a commission bid. This is what one does in a willing seller-willing buyer valuation, which is influenced by the buyer's view. But it might be reasonable to suggest that such a high figure was a more accurate reflection of the value of the item, and it was clearly a price that someone was prepared to pay. The auctioneer is after all the agent for the seller, not the buyer. I admired Roy Thomas for resisting the temptation to improve his sale figures, but I thought that perhaps the vendor had been hard done by, and discussed the matter with him. His belief was that the confidentiality of the written bid was absolute. I thought that perhaps the principle is closer to the point where one is being fair to both buyer *and seller*. The auctioneer at any point up to the last minute could recognize that he had seriously undervalued an item. We agreed to differ.

The news of John Lennon's assassination (1980) was given to me by Jackie Lacey, Christie's PR person in Scotland, during the Montgreenan House Sale. Michael commented, ever wayward, that 'it was no loss'. However, I was shocked at the loss of my father and the end of The Beatles in the same year. I remember feeling depressed; the world seemed a darker place that year.

There was always the possibility – the probability even – of surprise at House Sales, where the owners of the house were often resentful of the necessary presence of people (gangers, porters and specialists) who would be stamping all over their carpets or who would be estimating low a piece of lacquer which had cost an astronomical sum at Mallett Antiques in London. I found a Rembrandt etching in a chapbook at Fowberry Castle compiled by Joseph Crawhall Senior, an early Peploe at Solsgirth House, a J.D. Innes painting at Floors Castle and German pictures at Inzievar House. My missing corrected copy of 'Orchardson' turned up in the MacTaggart library when we sold Sir William MacTaggart's pictures and drawings in his house and studio at Drummond Place in Edinburgh. This House Sale was the most fun to do. It is the only experience I have had of being applauded by the room when the sale was over. For, as Paul Whitfield, Christie's managing director at the time, once said, 'When was the last time anyone said "well done" at Christie's?'

By way of contrast, at Blairquhan Castle, Jamie Hunter Blair (to whose father, Sir James, I sold the most important picture in his collection of Colourists, *Nude – Reflections* by Francis Cadell) was the ultimate host, tirelessly egging-on, aiding and abetting his guests who when they were not shooting, were playing golf, spillikins, croquet or innumerable other games. Or going for a walk, which might take all afternoon. Or a run in the car, finishing with a visit to the opera. I have no idea how much business he brought to Christie's but that was not the point. Everybody felt better with Jamie around. 'Come for lunch!' he would boom. And if something got broken, he would offer to pay for it, forgetting we were insured for that kind of thing.

I was well aware that a turnover of perhaps four thousand pictures a year represented a high level of exposure: there are quite a lot of things that can and therefore will go wrong. The worst case was a small wooden panel with a painting of a church interior in the style of the seventeenth-century Dutch artist Pieter Saenredam. This picture belonged to an old friend, Harry Woolford, a former chief restorer at the National Galleries of Scotland. The paint layer was very thin. Harry had done what he could to give it a surface clean, and it was entered in one of my auctions, where it made something like £600, within the estimate we had agreed. We thought no more of it until six months later I was told that the *Daily Record* had printed an article about it because it had just made £50,000 at a sale. This explained the embarrassment my presence seemed to be causing the porters that morning. I telephoned Harry. Above all I did not want him reading about this debacle before I could speak to him. He heard me out and without hesitating for a moment said, 'Don't worry, they've made a mistake.' Used to examining old master paintings at close quarters, he knew that this work wasn't 'right', and was able to assure me that the 'traces of signature' described in the auctioneer's catalogue had not been there when he had cleaned the picture. I was lucky that Woolford had been its owner and that the episode only made the tabloid *Daily Record*. I found myself having to tell people the story.

Subsequently all my attempts to find out what had happened were stonewalled, but I gathered later that a provincial European museum, having bought the work on the basis of an optimistic catalogue entry, afterwards returned the picture asking for their money back. The matter gnawed at my vitals and I tried to persuade the powers that be to intervene but I was told 'don't be too fussed'. And that was the end of the matter.

Certainly none of us tended to crow over rivals' mishaps: we all made mistakes and as sure as little green apples it was our turn next time. But it might have been better had there been more dialogue, because shortly afterwards there was a rash of forgeries which plagued the Scottish houses until a restorer was convicted and jailed for them. Because I had had my fingers burned I was highly sceptical of any work which had no convincing provenance, but some forgeries did find their way past several of my colleagues. In Glasgow the veteran dealer Ian MacNicol once told me that he had been shown a forged label allegedly from Ian MacNicol Fine Art which had been used to give credibility to a fake Fantin-Latour – in Argentina!

You had to be on your toes in Christie's. One morning a sale was within a hair's breadth of being cancelled because all the important pictures were sequestrated before the sale; at the last minute it was agreed that a newly created bank account could receive the sale proceeds. And one day the London dealer David Mason jumped the Harlamoff bidding up by £50,000 just to speed things along making the auctioneer – me – look pretty foolish in the process. There was, too, David Bathurst's dilemma in New York about 'buying in'. I suppose that if something is 'bought-in' it is 'sold' in some sense. But the New York court thought otherwise. A formal reserve is one thing and lays clear obligations on the auctioneer. But if there is no formal reserve and the auctioneer has discretion from the owner to protect the lot, is it wrong to give the impression that a lot has been sold when it hasn't? Bathurst was also up against the cartel question, which also looked like anti-British rather than anti-trust, when the London houses were galloping away with the American auction market.

Even the bad times were good though, and there were more good times than bad at Christie's. It was exhilarating to drive to Skye to see a portrait by Johan Zoffany or to Corehouse to see a Jusepe de Ribera, to see in a new light a manganese-painted Ming ewer (worth £650,000) which had fortunately never been drilled for electricity, or the famous study titled *Ide Collar* by Paul Outerbridge Jr which became the world's most valuable photograph, to find a *Merzbild* by Kurt Schwitters in the process of lotting up for a general sale of pictures. I remember how effectively the brush-mark codename – forerunner of the stock number stencilled to the stretcher of every picture – was matched by Christie's Muniments Room to the same picture in Glasgow a hundred years earlier.

There was something very comfortable about being in Christie's. And they were kind enough to send me on a tour of Canada to which I owed renewed links with Magda Salvesen and the late Tom Howarth, the art dealer Blair Lang on Bloor Street, the Gardiners whose porcelain museum was opposite Tom Howarth's apartment on the same street in Toronto, and the Thomson family. Nor should I omit to mention that apart from having a white handbag signed by Picasso, and paintings of her life in the frozen north, Kathleen Daly Pepper owned the big studio easel of Lawren Harris, one of the Group of Seven.

But that's probably enough about auctions. Like an actor allergic to theatres, I don't enjoy the excitement of the saleroom. I took it amiss that certain colleagues simply declared themselves unsuited to the task of wielding the hammer. Michael Clayton through from Edinburgh would naughtily put obscure requests on entry papers which we didn't have time for, just to test whether the new auctioneers were up to the job. The truth was that the only thing worse than taking the auction was not taking it. It was the final stage of the process of finding, cataloguing and selling a picture for the owner.

We will gloss over the telephone diplomacy which brought me a final cheque, the elderly Volvo estate which was now my property, and my last day at Christie's when I cleared out my desk after six years. As an old Christie's hand famously said 'When you join Christie's it's like getting into a warm bath, then the water gets cold and it's time to get out.'

7 Nineteen Eighty-Four

Sir Hugh Fraser, who had recently ceased to be chairman of Harrods, agreed to help fund me. Hugh was enthusiastic, indiscreetly so sometimes. One day we were in an elevator full of people and he was talking about 'when you've left Christie's' before it was a *fait accompli*. He punctiliously attended our two-man monthly meetings, telephoning if he was going to be five minutes late. He was brilliant at remembering names, the result of long years of training at House of Fraser with its huge staff whom he would address by name. In a social context, Hugh had another skill: he could remember anyone's favourite drink, although he was quite abstemious himself. 'Don't tell me – it's a whisky sour.' Playing the carefree toff who would cheerfully make a fool of himself – one week he would be photographed giving a giraffe to Edinburgh Zoo, the next he would be jogging, cigarette in mouth, round the pitch of his latest interest, Dumbarton Football Club – Hugh's private generosity, and that of his family, to medical and other charities was immense.

The agreed working capital was taking a very long time to materialize and only did so on the eve of our AGM nearly a year later. Hugh brought it in cash, in a suitcase. By this time I had managed without help for a year, and when Hugh asked for all his money back after a few months I concluded that I would be better off on my own. Hugh allowed me to buy back his shareholding, with interest, and we had an amicable parting of the ways. Since then I have had no financial partner except the bank, but if Hugh hadn't said 'yes' when it mattered I would never have had the courage to start my own business. Fiona Robertson joined me as secretary during the year and stayed for seventeen more years. The gallery could not have survived without her calm competence as gallery administrator whether acting as sales clerk for our auctions, hanging a new show, or holding the fort in my absence.

Shortly after I had left Christie's in March 1984 Miss Mildred Keith died in her magical house at the end of the world in Thurso. The auction at Christie's of the Keith Collection, which I had nurtured so carefully, took place within months. I was left without a role in its sale. It was equal in quality if not quite in quantity to the Wemyss Honeyman Collection, and records were broken for prices by several Scottish artists. Again, as an executory sale, there were no reserves and my successor as head of Scottish pictures had a dream debut. The argument that this should encourage me as it showed the strength of the market did not greatly console me, but it was consolation of a sort to receive a letter from the director of the National Galleries of Scotland, Hugh Scrutton, thanking me on behalf of the Trustees for the successful outcome of the sale. This had enabled them to invest a sum of about £250,000 in a bequest named in honour of Miss Keith's brother, the collector David Barrogill Keith. All I could do was buy a painting, not a very expensive one, at the sale – a *View of St Tropez* by Maclauchlan Milne.

It was bought from me by David Donald who was assembling a notable collection of Scottish art for Fleming's Bank in the City of London, and was the first of several pictures acquired from me by Fleming's over the years, including a lovely white Peploe of roses and a watercolour by Charles Rennie Mackintosh of flowers painted while he was staying at Dunglass Castle. Works by John Bellany, Millie Frood, E.A. Walton and James Morrison were to follow.

The late Mrs Murray Usher's Thomas Hardy first editions were another early glimmer of hope. I noticed that apart from the things Mrs Usher wanted me to look at, she had some nice books and took them to South Kensington. As a result of their success we were able to buy the Carstramon Reynolds (see page 120).

Later, more technically, it was possible to sell a valuable work for an owner at a figure which (he had had it for a long time, and the rules were different then) cut out the need for him to pay the dreaded Capital Gains Tax. Yet another collector wanted me to sell

Peploes with the promise that he would buy from me something by J.D. Fergusson; but he was a Lloyds Name and had been caught, with his syndicate, in a severe downdraught – from which we came away empty-handed.

The late Duke of Buccleuch wished me good luck, and the late Lord Thomson said that although this would be a busy time, after a year it would seem normal and I would wonder why I hadn't made the move earlier. Writing St Kentigern's centenary history kept me sane, or at least from worrying too much. Lydia and Ernie Lannie were very positive: being rich helps ('never look down') and so does being Italian ('there's only vodka and Irn-Bru'). But my mind still shies away from thinking about that period. A friend's wife actually joked to me 'I hear you're walking the streets' in a cheerful tone which only rubbed salt in the wound because it somehow suggested that this was a common fate which I could all too easily share. Why, a pair of black shoes that I bought then still has associations of anxiety. Our daughter had a long and worrying convalescence from a delayed operation on her appendix.

There is a photograph of Gillie in my new office at 10/14 West Nile Street, seated at a desk on which rests the Mackintosh clock for which we had arranged a sale when the family asked for it back. She looks very young and elegant, but too serious. Not for the first or last time I had doubts about the selfishness of pursuing my private ambitions.

Rock bottom was struck weeks into my new venture. At Christie's the board avoided membership of each other's clubs because clubs don't like members to talk shop: I was Western Club, Joe Mullen was RAC, Michael Clayton was New Club and Charlie Douglas was Art Club. (This is probably why Charles Rennie Mackintosh was never joined up to the Art Club by his partner-in-practice John Keppie.) But now that I was no longer with Christie's I could join the Art Club, and did so. In celebration I asked the critic Emilio Coia to lunch. All went well until he suddenly asked me jokingly if I'd left Christie's because I'd had my fingers in the till. I was speechless and furious. So – I resigned over a bad joke. I had probably irritated him by asking for a portrait (Coia had drawn my father). Later, we were on speaking terms again which was not a bad thing: he wrote us several good reviews in *The Scotsman*.

Like many other painters or estates, Alberto Morrocco had a gallery with exclusive rights to his work. We had never had anything by him, unfortunately, with the sole exception of an early piece. Alberto Morrocco had actually made the pot in this picture, as he explained in a letter to me. I see now that I was over sensitive in the Art Club and chez Mas Sekine. Being 'on your own' does these things to people.

The early months of the existence of the business were supported by a handful of loyal clients: Mike Thomson, who was downsizing from one beautiful house in The Mearns to another, was disposing of spectacular Colourists; Grant Honeyman and Margaret Wilson sent me important items from the collection of their father, Tom Honeyman. For Grant I sold the portrait of *Mrs Honeyman* by Wyndham Lewis. I had known Mrs Honeyman, a lady of reserve rather than severity, but whose portrait is regal in the manner of the same artist's portraits of *Edith Sitwell* or *Praxitella*.

> Praxitella, aloof, assents.
> Her creator, a genius naturally,
> Gave her the precise attributes
> Of an arctic, acid green

Also for Grant Honeyman I sold a lovely Ivon Hitchens to the Maclaurin Art Gallery in Ayr. There were several new collectors like Gordon Tourlamain and Michael Everist who had recently sold their companies and had the wherewithal to make major acquisitions. One of the satisfactions of a dealer is to be given something marvellous by a true collector, and then to find new enthusiasts willing to trust their own and his judgment sufficiently to spend an outrageous amount of money acquiring it. Everist began with a lovely William Bonnar and a romantic early Japanese E.A. Hornel, but he was able to tell me later that he had bought a London flat for a daughter from the proceeds of the sale of two Colourist pictures he had bought from me before the prices went sky-high!

Louise Walmesley, whose very fine early Hornel I was privileged to sell for her to the Hornel Trust in Kirkcudbright, once told me that the Glasgow dealer Ian MacNicol had made her fortune. I ought to add that all my four brothers did the decent thing and have walls festooned with my pictures, as do many friends too numerous to mention but not too numerous to forget.

After a year I was in profit, praise be! And the firm has survived ever since.

Auction houses in those days sold principally to the trade, whereas a gallery's customers are private collectors and museum buyers. Several collectors stayed loyal, and as any business needs a buyer and a seller, I was fortunate that as one collector in the east was disposing of his Colourists, another in the west was forming a collection of Scottish pictures. It was a pleasure to share the excitement of the hunt with a real enthusiast – in contrast to buyers at an auction, who are trying to conceal any excitement they may feel as best they can. A major Glasgow collection which included works by Gauguin, Sisley, and Fantin-Latour was entrusted to me for sale, although there was some worry that they would go instead to Agnew's, whose representative was beside me on the plane to Glasgow. They were stored in our newly-acquired strongroom in Washington Street prior to their being sent to auction. I discussed the details with John Lumley at White's, when I also arranged that Christie's should sell an important work by Giorgio de Chirico consigned by Gabriella Cardazza, whom I had met in Venice through an introduction by Richard Demarco.

During one of my visits to Christie's office in Wemyss Place in Edinburgh I had popped round the corner to visit Graham Munro in Heriot Row. The artist was now well into his eighties, but he knew of me and my book on Scottish painting. This helped to break the ice on my first visit which was the beginning of an affectionate collaboration between us two unequals: he in his 80s, settled in his imposing New Town mansion, I some forty years younger and after my departure from Christie's 'beating the drum' commercially.

Ever young in spirit, Graham Munro was full of enthusiasm for Steven Campbell's exhibition at the Fruitmarket Gallery: an artist half-a-century younger. I went to see it and still recollect it as the most exciting and innovative display of new work I have ever seen by any contemporary artist. It was that unfashionable thing, an exhibition of figure painting, but set in the context of a vast, complex, containing Nature. It reminded me of the late Titian painting inspired by the *Metamorphoses* of Ovid, a comparison that still does not appear to me to be disproportionate. Everything was on a grand, profuse scale like Nature itself, showing man's place in the unpredictability and complexity of the natural world. The old certainties of 'significant form' were about to receive a severe battering from this prodigiously imaginative young artist. I still regard this exhibition as the most impressive debut show I have seen.

What I could see of Graham Munro's oil paintings, hung in the front rooms of the Munros' town house in Heriot Row, suggested the work of a traveller-painter, like Maclauchlan Milne or Graham's friend 'Spanish' Macdonald. He then suggested I look at the Moroccan pastel studies he had made on a scholarship visit in 1926, which were stored in a huge drawings cabinet upstairs. These were altogether livelier and more spontaneous than his oils, with a real feeling for the pastel medium. I was delighted by their freshness, vigour and precocious technical prowess. There were two hundred sheets carefully preserved in tissue paper, having lain there for nearly sixty years. Richard Demarco offered me an exhibition space at Edinburgh College of Art, which he had booked in its entirety for the 1984 Edinburgh Festival. Thus our first exhibition was born in late summer 1984 – 'Moroccan Studies in Pastel by Alexander Graham Munro RSW'. People queued to buy them, and Fiona's typewriter nearly went on fire writing invoices. Graham and Ruth Munro were interviewed by Val Atkinson for Scottish Television and there was a piece in *The Observer* colour supplement. When the show was over, the work was still being bought by collectors, and I will long remember Graham, whose health was failing, reacting to my telling him in hospital that we had sold over 130 of his pictures by sitting up in bed to exclaim, 'No! Really?' We had given him the most successful exhibition of his long career.

Graham Munro's pastel studies evoked the light and colour of the wadis and foothills of the Atlas Mountains. There was also a large quantity of architectural studies in pencil of desert forts in remote parts of the country. Ruth Munro offered to give me these. I declined, but it would have been better if I had accepted, because the drawings were distributed piecemeal in auctions, diluting their value as a record of a bygone time in the desert communities.

I said later to Ruth Munro, 'It'll be difficult to follow that' to which she replied in her deep contralto 'You will have many more fine exhibitions.'

Our sequel in the same venue for the 1985 Festival also came from the Munro Collection: paintings by the New Zealand artist and close friend of the Munros for many years, Francis McCracken. Although we did not know it then, McCracken is regarded as one of the two main New Zealand artists, the other being Frances Hodgkins. Both are avidly collected 'down under'. On the eve of the opening of the show we had a telephone call from the dealer Ian Johnson in New Zealand offering to buy all the paintings in the exhibition. We explained that we had organized a private view to which we had invited a large number of people who would expect us to be able to sell them pictures. A compromise was reached: we would allow the exhibition to run for an hour, after which we would sell to him whatever works were not sold by then. Thus it came about that we had a second sell-out show. We could relax – for a while.

Visiting Eastern Australia and New Zealand led me to Lance Crawford in Melbourne and Ian Johnson in Auckland, who between them bought the remainder of the large collection of works by McCracken which had been entrusted to us by Ruth Munro, including the entire *oeuvre* on paper. I met Lance Crawford in Paris over a memorable weekend to divide the spoils. Ian Johnson came to the aid of the party in spectacular fashion by buying an entire exhibition of Francis McCracken oils from us.

Art Fairs from being a unique annual event became a norm. Although we should have been more at home in London than in Los Angeles or New York, we had a wonderful time in both places and even sold expensive paintings by German Expressionists and by Charles Rennie Mackintosh in New York. And LA was unique. We went back to Edinburgh every Festival until the Andrew Grant Gallery was no longer an option. In January, another fallow period in Glasgow, it was up, up and away to the Fair in Islington's old, restored Agricultural Hall on Upper Street.

The Edinburgh Festival, where we showed Stanley Cursiter, and Jon Schueler with Daniel Lang, seemed to bring us luck. We only abandoned it when we took over the West Regent Street premises in Glasgow, which cost so much to restore that we thought we'd better not wander from home. We later returned to the Art Fair scene with the Charles Heap Collection of early drawings by David Hockney, mostly done during his Bradford years, at the Royal College of Art at Kensington Gore. They had formed part of his portfolio for entry into the RCA in London – which was where the Fair was held. Not surprisingly, they sold very well there, and at least two of them went to members of the RCA staff. Glasgow Art Fair seemed less buzzy but perhaps I was biased: a neighbour sold the Andy Warhol print of Mickey Mouse for £4,000 while our more glamorous but much more expensive version at ten times the price went unclaimed despite being encrusted with diamante – a forerunner of the way Damien Hirst was to use precious materials. The Art Fairs accounted for a dozen of the 100 shows we presented; and it was a pleasant change from Glasgow.

Bill Samuel offered me a newly decorated space in the large red sandstone former bonded warehouse of the J & B Blend in Washington Street, which he had developed and was about to sell. The proposed new gallery would occupy part of the first floor of the Edwardian directors' suite. I accepted eagerly: we were sorely pressed for space, the two large rooms offered were attractive and light, and there was a strongroom along the corridor which would be ours. It was close to the river and it was easy to imagine shipments of the Black and White blended whisky, and of Heidsieck champagne and Gonzalez Byass sherries arriving to be warehoused in the building's heyday. Washington Street was one of the old commercial streets of Glasgow. Near us were two flour mills and a Victorian brick rice mill, now restored as an hotel. We ran the Washington Gallery, as we called it, with some success from this unlikely place for five years. It was good exercise running up and down the stairs with pictures, and our clients seemed happy to attend our private views until the street became more popular and parking became difficult. One day Eunice Kennedy Shriver (John F. Kennedy's sister) came in to see us, accompanied by her husband Sargent Shriver and an out-of-his-depth councillor who referred to 'Tosh', meaning Mackintosh. We had arrived! Later Bill Gates' mother-in-law Mimi and friends from Seattle Art Museum helped me to celebrate a birthday surrounded by pictures in our last gallery in Blythswood Square.

Forty bright brand-new oils by Marysia Donaldson, her new work, was the subject of our first exhibition in the Washington Gallery. It was the first of many contemporary shows. But I was inexperienced enough not to remonstrate over her prices, which were manifestly too high: as a result only a few pictures were sold. It was a social, but not a commercial success, and she repaid us some years later by forbidding her husband David to exhibit with us. Other exhibitions held there included James Robertson who gave us our next show (we showed him twice).

Clare Henry wrote in the *Herald* of the artist's 'avant-garde panache, his courageous throwaway calligraphic gestures', while Emilio Coia described Robertson as 'a truly first-rate artist'. There were good reviews, but not many sales. Another artist whose work we liked well enough to show twice (and, like James Robertson, to take to the Art Fair in Islington) was David Cook. Cook had made and then painted a chair made of beachcomber's debris – which made sense as he had spent time living on the beach – and his work was innocent, childlike and full of colour.

Washington Gallery was soon furnished with Mackintosh's easel, and a clock (destined to spend some time in Kentuck Knob, a residence designed by the American architect Frank Lloyd Wright near the village of Chalk Hill, in Pennsylvania), and another item from Glasgow School of Art, the day bed dating to 1910.

A collection of a quite different character, belonging to the late Andrew Wilson, made its way to our strongroom. The Wilson Collection comprised works of superb quality by nineteenth-century British and Continental artists including J.W. Carmichael and Sir David Wilkie, as well as by the French artist Léon L'Hermitte. Mr Wilson asked us to sell these privately. Dorothy McEwen took two or three works by Morel and Harlamoff to Toronto for us, and successfully sold the Morel. The large L'Hermitte paintings went to a Beverly Hills client, and the Carmichael to the founder of Aggreko Generators – a keen yachtsman who appreciated *Sailing Vessels in a Calm*, a typical work by the artist.

The Wilkie painting *The Pedlar* was painted with this master's usual exquisite touch on a wooden panel, and was borrowed for the Wilkie exhibition that was being arranged by Lindsay Errington for the Paul Mellon Center for British Art at Yale. The painting had been considered a lost work, known only as an engraving, until I drew it to Lindsay's attention. It was acquired from me for Mr Paul Mellon's own collection, which, with that of the Mellon Foundation itself, is the greatest collection of British art in North America. A year or two later, we sold to the Paul Mellon Centre for Studies in British Art in London a classic Glasgow School picture, *Blowing Dandelions* by George Henry. This beautiful and important work had come to us from a Glasgow lady, the late Muriel Lawson, who also sent us paintings by Walter Sickert and Russell Flint.

I was resolved to show, as well as the established names from the past, new artists whose work was exciting and which I found stimulating and relevant. To be more precise, it was my ambition to show the principal protagonists of the new figure painting in Glasgow: Peter Howson, Adrian Wiszniewski and Steven Campbell. The slightly younger Stephen Conroy was already out of reach because his work was commanding high prices and his gallery, Marlborough Fine Art Gallery, understandably reserved his not very copious output for their one-man shows of his work. Campbell was more prolific and Marlborough later loaned us his pictures twice. Since seeing the Fruitmarket exhibition in 1984 I had wanted to collaborate with Steven, when one day he came into the Washington Street Gallery with Adrian Wiszniewski.

John Byrne's *The Yellow Cigarette*, a self-portrait, went to Manchester Art Gallery, bought by Julian Spalding while he was director there. After checking with the artist first, we were able to reassure the City fathers, who wondered what kind of cigarette this was. Perhaps an image of nicotine use will soon have all the period charm of a picture of someone taking snuff. Many of John Byrne's self-portraits, even the most abstract ones, show him enjoying a good puff. And there was that notable series of douts (cigarette ends) painted in acrylics on tiny panels with all the control and painterliness of a Chardin, which we acquired from Billy Connolly along with another group of tiny watercolours of *Boots* (welly, cowboy, dominatrix and rustic) testifying to another minor Byrne fixation, footwear. For *The Marriage of Figaro* costumes (Scottish Opera 1986) he went to immense lengths to design shoes for the characters, demonstrated by several sheets of beautiful pencil studies of eighteenth-century shoes (see page 89).

Through Michael and Ann Thomson I met Dominique Moreau Granger who was staying on the Phesdo Estate, where Ann had a large aviary containing rare and exotic birds. Dominique is a Parisian and paints tightly controlled small oils of grand houses and their gardens or estate cottages: his little panel portraying Inveraray Castle as the gondola of a hot air balloon flying over Loch Fyne was bought from the exhibition by the Duke of Argyll, who probably had never before imagined his house being in the ascendant in quite this literal way. Jamie Hunter Blair commissioned a fanciful 'portrait' of Blairquhan with a fireworks display in the sky, and the very charming, very French little paintings, with their clipped gardens and ornamental birds, delighted Glasgow buyers. At the second show Dominique was very grumpy and threatened to call off the show half an hour before the *vernissage*. I had no idea what he was grumbling about, but I think it had something to do with our commission. I may have indicated that I intended to make him liable for my losses if the show did not go on. It did go on. Evelyne de Mascarel, Dominique's Paris dealer, smoothed any ruffled feathers and we made many sales.

Peter Howson's exhibition of 1986 was opened by Stanley Baxter. Before rushing to the King's Theatre for that evening's performance of *Mother Goose* (with himself in the title role) he told a long story illustrating the difference between irritation and aggravation. Irritation is caused when the same wrong telephone number is dialled a second time. 'Away an' bile yer heid' might be a predictable response – enough to provoke a certain type of Glaswegian to reach for the phone a third time and deliberately dial the same wrong number. *That* is aggravation. Told in the master comic's inimitable style – he later explained that he wanted to see how it would work on an audience – it had our large party in gales of laughter.

This was Peter's biggest show yet in Glasgow, and as there was a mixture of small as well as large pictures, and as a certain human warmth still pervaded his increasingly bleak view of the human condition, there were many sales. Peter was a delight to work with, not because he is particularly easy or businesslike (I think he would agree that he is neither) but because he has a ready sense of humour and a professional commitment to his work. It was fascinating to watch him finding titles for pictures. I became impatient when one title was taking particularly long to come to Peter: a painting of a man in a kind of harness. *Man in Harness* I suggested. Finally, the right idea came to the painter: *Man Walker* (by analogy with a baby's harness or 'baby walker'). I think it was for Peter's second show that we acquired a dozen or more paintings, some very large, from Gabrielle Harrison in London. We were able this time to offer a survey of the artist's development to date.

In Margaret and Murray Hunter's Edinburgh house were several very beautiful and important pictures. My immediate concern was with the fabulous *The Ribbon Counter* by Margaret's father Stanley Cursiter, as initially I wanted to photograph it for the second edition of my book on Scottish painting (of which it decorated the front cover). On one visit Margaret mentioned her cousin's family in Tasmania, who had a collection of paintings by Stanley Cursiter. I corresponded with the family and learned that although there were no surprise masterpieces among them, the collection comprised a choice group, mostly of Orkney landscapes. Realizing that the Cursiter centenary year was approaching, I resolved if possible to acquire the paintings for an Edinburgh Festival celebration of the event. The Pier Arts Centre in the artist's native Orkney was thinking along the same lines. But I needed to have some pictures to sell to pay for expenses and a bit over.

I flew to Tasmania, via Vancouver and the Mel Scotts, then via Fiji to Sydney and Melbourne where I held picture 'clinics' in my hotels. In Melbourne Lance Crawford, responding to my ad in the newspaper, introduced himself and he and Diane gave me dinner – the beginning of a great business partnership ended only by his untimely death. In Sydney as I was about to buy a ticket for Hobart, I heard the name 'Launceston' announced, which was where I was to visit Margaret Hunter's cousin. As the flight girl said, 'We're going to Launceston today.'

I was met at Launceston Airport by the family's solicitor Philip Gunton, and driven straight over to the house where I met the lady and her daughter. But we had to have lunch first. This was hospitable, but it also seemed to take an eternity and I wondered whether the conversation would ever turn to the matter I had travelled so far to discuss. Finally the subject was broached by Mr Gunton, who had evil tidings: Sotheby's had just been to the house and had prepared an appraisal. I suddenly felt a long way from home, where Sotheby's were always popping up out of the undergrowth, but *here* in Tasmania … With a continuo by Mr Gunton who was clutching his crib with Sotheby's figures and would react with a non-committal 'Hmm, interesting' to each of my figures, I completed the valuation. It was a relief when my total turned out virtually the same as Sotheby's, the only difference being one of emphasis: they had placed more value on the landscapes than on the portraits, which I had placed higher. The daughter was less disposed to sell the pictures than her mother, but finally an agreement was reached: I would buy the entire collection. We shook hands and Keith Tremayne collected me in his old yellow Mercedes for the drive back to Hobart. We arrived about midnight. But there was a message for me from the solicitor Mr Gunton. I telephoned him. The deal was off. I felt even further from home and had a night of Boswellian self-recrimination.

In the morning, with the courage of desperation, I telephoned again. I pointed out that auctions can take months to assemble, the proceeds take another month to be paid, and there is no guarantee that everything – or anything – will sell. I would stand by my offer, but only until my departure that day. Because the paintings were required for one event, the centenary exhibition, I wanted them now or not at all, and I wanted all of them, not just some of them. He replied within minutes. The deal was on again. After making arrangements for the shipment of twenty paintings to Glasgow, I returned via San Francisco, where I spent a weekend by the hotel pool or in it, enjoying the weightlessness of the carefree.

The 'Stanley Cursiter Centenary Exhibition' at the Edinburgh Festival was a great success with the public and with the reviewers. I was 'Glasgow's most serious and widely travelled dealer' according to Clare Henry, who was impressed with the fact that I had been to the USA, Canada, Australia, New Zealand, Germany and France in the space of a year in search of material for exhibitions. All the paintings acquired in Tasmania were sold. Ray Entwistle at Adam & Co told me it was the best Scottish exhibition he had ever seen. *The Evening Hour* (which had come from London) was perceptively snapped up by Timothy Clifford for the National Gallery of Scotland. The values of the paintings have trebled or quadrupled since then. There were also a Eugène Boudin watercolour and a lithograph by Christopher R.W. Nevinson; it was the latter that had some influence on William McCance. The show went on to our Washington Gallery in Glasgow and then to the Pier Arts Centre in Stromness, Orkney, with whom we published a well-illustrated catalogue with an essay by me on Cursiter's Futurist paintings of 1913.

Margaret Hunter also had a little painting which I thought magical, said to be by Jean-Édouard Vuillard. I was sure it was 'right'. In Scotland even then it was possible to see fine examples of Vuillard's work, especially in Glasgow, and I had also had the privilege of access to the Traill Collection in Edinburgh. (Isobel Traill was the daughter of Sir John Richmond, founder of the eponymous Chair of Fine Art at Glasgow University.) The picture was a typically subtle demonstration by Vuillard of a bold juxtaposition of blue and orange, which are complementaries. It had an inscription written on the reverse by Stanley Cursiter stating that it had belonged to Charles Hodge Mackie, who had given it to him. Cursiter had placed a question mark beside Vuillard's name.

There was another painting in the house which had also come from Mackie, a watercolour of a *Breton Peasant Woman* by Paul Sérusier. This had some alleged association with Gauguin although it clearly was not by him. This took me close to *The Evergreen* link with the important Mackie–Sérusier connection. I was reminded of the wonderful little *By the Bonnie Banks O' Fordie* by Mackie, which looked as if it might have been painted at Pont-Aven, bought by Andrew McLaren Young many years before for the Hunterian Art Gallery but varnished so that the card ground is no longer lightly coloured as it ought to be. The difference is that the Scottish painting is literary (it is an illustration of the ballad 'There was three maidens pu'd a flower'), whereas the French picture is a true intimiste work.

Excited to have the opportunity to acquire a work so potentially important, I bought the Vuillard. I wrote to Antoine Salomon in Paris, who was writing the big *Catalogue Raisonné* of Vuillard. He took an age to reply. His letter when it arrived was short but not simple: *Deux ouvrières dans l'atelier de couture* (Two Seamstresses in the Dress Shop) was his title for the picture. This surprised me because I thought, and still think, that the picture is a *Maternité* with both mother and father present and the baby as well. So little was I expecting the word 'couture', however, that I thought at first that Salomon was suggesting Thomas Couture, a nineteenth-century academic painter, as the artist. I was relieved to read further: '*Vous tournez le fer dans la plaie*' (you're turning the knife in the wound). Salomon had known of the existence of this picture and had wanted to track it down for his own collection. I owned the Vuillard for several years before it was bought by the National Gallery in Edinburgh.

The opinion of the Vuillard expert was authentication enough, but further corroboration arrived at about the same time from an unexpected source. The artist Charles Mackie's descendant in Peckham in south-east London wrote to me regarding an early painting he had by Hornel, and mentioning a diary written by Anne Mackie. I went to London immediately. The Hornel was a beautiful little Kirkcudbright work of the late 1880s probably bought by Charles Mackie at about the time he acquired the Vuillard. Thanks to the diary of Anne Mackie, we discovered when that was, because she faithfully recorded the visit paid by the Mackies as young newly-weds to Vuillard's studio in Paris in 1893. Here is an excerpt:

'The other studios [*she has just mentioned the opulence of Gauguin's apartment*] we visited were more workaday and poverty stricken. I remember Mons. Vuillard's little garret stacked with pictures as his buyers came but rarely and his kind command to take the picture we liked best. And we were so afraid of being greedy that we chose the smallest picture we could find but that picture is still a joy ...'

Anne Mackie's diary, which we sold to the National Library of Scotland, is perhaps the most significant document to shed light on the links between Scottish and French painting. At that crucial period when the *Les Nabis*, especially Paul Sérusier, but also as we learn from the diary, Vuillard and Gauguin, Maurice Denis and Paul Ranson, through meeting the Mackies, can be attached, however fleetingly, to Scotland. Here indeed were riches. Elsewhere, I mentioned the suggestion made in a letter written by Peploe's wife that the Glasgow dealer Alexander Reid 'knew Gauguin', and Dr Frances Fowle has referred to a mention by Gauguin of a Glasgow exhibition in which Reid is most likely to have been involved. I negotiated the sale of the diary to the National Library of Scotland. It offers charming insights into lighthearted days when the young people were united by belief in the unquestioned importance of what it was to be a painter.

Since we are talking about great painters, I heard Miron Grindea mention on the *motoscafi* to Venice that he had been drawn by Picasso, and by the time we had reached our destination I had arranged to see this portrait in London. This resulted in my being in Carola Grindea's friend's gallery in New York and our Glasgow show of the painter Arnold Daghani, whose work I viewed in his house which was crammed with pictures from top to bottom.

I made a video of Margaret Mellis's huge collection of the abstractions of her late husband Francis Davison in Southwold. She found objects on the beach here which were incorporated into sculpture – and went for a swim in the cold North Sea every day, which was why although in her 80s she looked thirty years younger. But a visit to Monte Carlo was less successful and I never saw Edith Petitjean's paintings by Marc Chagall because the maid turned me away at the door with the slightly off-putting remark, '*Madame est malade et ne peut pas vous voir.*' I had travelled along the Riviera coast in the Blue Train feeling rather pleased with myself. Some years later, after the old lady had died, the maid was imprisoned for stealing her money.

We showed the John Byrne costume designs which John Cox had commissioned for Scottish Opera's *The Marriage of Figaro*. I bought them in the darkened Theatre Royal from John during rehearsals. Our agreement had to be abruptly reached, as we were told to keep quiet by John Cox who was directing the performances of his cast. These drawings went far beyond what was necessary as far as the wardrobe mistress was concerned. Not a few of them had been through the photocopier while the costumes were being made but they were undamaged. They were executed with John's habitual incisive, exquisite touch as a draughtsman, often with touches of colour added in gouache. In fact, they were works of art in their own right. We found a white-gold finish (it looks like silver but doesn't tarnish) for the V-sectioned frames we had made for them, and they were eagerly bought by our clients. Kirsty Wark bought one.

Just before the opera opened in the Theatre Royal John Cox mentioned that the bicentenary of the 1786 first-ever performance of Mozart's *The Marriage of Figaro* would fall during its Glasgow run, and wondered if I might have any ideas as to how this momentous anniversary could be celebrated. I suggested that the Josef Lange *Portrait of Constanze Mozart* might be borrowed from Glasgow University for the evening of the exact bicentenary. John was enthusiastic, so I spoke to Sir Alwyn Williams, principal of the university at that time, who agreed to help. Thus this treasure from the university's collection of Mozartiana appeared in the Theatre Royal Charter Room for one night only, exactly two hundred years after the original first night. It was returned the following morning to the university and the obscurity of the Reserve Collection of the Hunterian Art Gallery. It is hard to believe that this treasure has hardly ever been displayed in their main gallery.

I only knew of the existence of this precious Glasgow relic of Mozart because I had visited Grant and Monica Honeyman in Brantford, Ontario to value their pictures, in particular the Wyndham Lewis *Portrait of Mrs T.J. Honeyman*. Grant lent me his rare copy of *New Mozartiana in Glasgow University* as bedtime reading. I stayed up nearly all night reading it through. It tells an incredible story. The *Portrait of Constanze Mozart*, and some fragments of musical MSS in Mozart's hand, belonged to the composer's son Franz Xavier Wolfgang Mozart, who had given them to his friend the Bohemian musician Hugo Zavertal, whose son, Vladislav Zavertal, found employment in Glasgow in 1874, where he became a popular conductor and teacher. Vladislav Zavertal brought the Mozart items with him, including the portrait of his grandmother, Mozart's wife Constanze, painted by Josef Lange, who was her brother-in-law. I believe Zavertal lived in Helensburgh. On his death the items were bequeathed to Glasgow University. The following morning I took the train back to Toronto Central from Brantford and as I stepped onto the platform I realized that the strains of 'La ci darem la mano' from Mozart's *Don Giovanni* were being played on the station's loudspeakers. I walked on air, the usual effect the master's music has on me.

The acquisition of Vuillard's *Deux ouvrières dans l'atelier de couture* by the National Gallery of Scotland was supported by the National Art Collections Fund (NACF). In its Annual Report the NACF chairman at the time, Sir Nicholas Goodison, who also served as chairman of the London Stock Exchange, singled the painting out as the outstanding purchase that year. I saw him at the Art Fair in Islington, and as he was passing our stand, decided to speak to him on the subject. I referred to the extraordinary series of events which had helped authenticate the work, expecting an enthusiastic reply. But the best he could manage was a sour 'I expect you got a pretty good turn out of it.' Not for the first time since I joined 'the trade', I was reminded of the parable of the publican and the Pharisee. But it was through the Vuillard that we were able to pay for the refurbishment of West Regent Street, where we made a smart gallery notwithstanding a dodgy tradesman who tried, while installing plumbing and central heating, to dampen our spirits and cool our ardour.

8   *Annus Mirabilis*

At the beginning of 1990 I spent weeks in the Borders revising *Scottish Painting* for Cassell. We were anxious to have the second edition of the book appear in the autumn 1990 lists of new books as this was to be Glasgow's year as 'European City of Culture'. I was able to incorporate new material and the book was to be illustrated anew. Proofs were read in May on the island of Formentera – a fortnight when I could enjoy abroad, working. For the new edition, however, there was no picture researcher. There was a lot of work to do, but we succeeded, and the book was published on time, approximately twice its original length although with only 150 illustrations. At this point Fiona took a short sabbatical and we closed the doors on Washington Street, retaining the big walk-in safe for the valuable Wilson pictures.

Richard Russell, architect of the much praised Dundee Repertory Theatre but best known for his brilliant concept for the Falkirk Wheel boat lift joining the Forth and Clyde Canal to the Union Canal, was the designer for the gallery space we had now found in the heart of Glasgow's business district at 141 West Regent Street. He was a personal friend whose radical remodelling of his own house in Broughty Ferry had astonished Dr David Brown of the Tate Gallery when he stayed with us. (David amazed the Russells even more, by talking dog language to their Irish setter: not for nothing had he spent years specializing in animal husbandry as a vet in Kenya.) Richard simplified the interior spaces and introduced more light (it was a semi-basement) and subtle details of finish and fittings which transformed the place. Our perfectionism received a temporary obstacle in the form of an over-hasty automobile but fortunately our railing could be repaired.

We were delighted with it and so was our landlord. It was all very expensive, but we were in a hurry and, thanks to the sales of the Cursiter and the Vuillard, we could afford it. One tended not to argue with our landlord, who would arrive in an enormous black Mercedes wearing sunglasses. One day he was complaining about an armed robbery at one of his licensed premises. I commiserated with him, but sympathy was wasted for as he said 'None of our staff was hurt and anyway we'll find the people who did it and teach them a lesson.' One knew where one stood with George. I liked him (I hasten to add), perhaps because one day he said to me, 'You're witty!'

We opened the new gallery with a museum-type show: 'James Morrison: the Glasgow Paintings'. One of the 'Seven Painters in Dundee' from twenty years earlier, Morrison is a very accomplished artist, trained at Glasgow School of Art, who had followed Joan Eardley in taking a studio at Catterline. He had produced a series of paintings of architectural views of Glasgow's sublimely smog-blackened Victorian terraces in the 1950s and 60s. When we were discussing the show, I suggested that as Glasgow now stood revealed, through a massive stone-cleaning programme, as a light honey-coloured city, he might like to paint another series. But no: his Glasgow would always be that characterful, magnificent black. David Walker, the safest pair of hands on any project relating to Scottish architecture, wrote historical and critical notes on the buildings for the catalogue, which included a reminiscence by Morrison and a notably gratuitous use of the f-word by *The Glasgow Herald*'s chief art critic Clare Henry who was never in danger of kowtowing to bourgeois expectations. It was all very Glasgow.

David Donaldson, the Queen's Painter and Limner in Scotland, opened the show and the gallery by commenting that we were the most intelligent art dealers in Scotland: I am not sure whether he considered this an oxymoron. Hundreds of people turned up. We had only one complaint: as the entire show was borrowed for the occasion, nothing was for sale. I resolved not to repeat the mistake. W. Gordon Smith gave us a kind review: 'Nothing that Glasgow does in its 1990 jamboree will celebrate itself more satisfactorily than the exhibition of James Morrison's 'The Glasgow Paintings' which, by happy chance, opens the fine new William Hardie Gallery in West Regent Street.'

The next show was just as academically ambitious, but this time quite a lot was for sale, and sold, mostly to museums. It celebrated another aspect of the Glasgow art scene: the New Glasgow Group, who had formed around J.D. Fergusson and Margaret Morris, returned from France in 1939. This was titled 'Independent Painting in Glasgow 1943–1956'. Louise Annand, one of the artists, helped us to secure loans and locate pictures from this stimulating period, including work by Jankel Adler and Josef Herman, as well as Fergusson himself, and a host of interesting satellites. 'Museum show' was no misnomer, as several important works went to museums. Perth Art Gallery bought a stunning Art Deco painting called *The Cocktail Hour* by John Laurie, in which gold leaf had been used for the elaborate coiffure of the haughty model; Dundee University bought a Klee-like painting by Hugh Adam Crawford, still remembered in the city as a principal of Duncan of Jordanstone College of Art; the Lillie Art Gallery at Milngavie bought a rare early 'cubist' painting by Flora Wood; Maryhill Library – Maryhill is the Montmartre of Glasgow, being on a hill in the north of the city – bought a work by their local hero, Donald Bain; Robert Fleming & Co (now the Fleming-Wyfold Foundation in London) acquired a marvellous neo-romantic landscape by Millie Frood, her masterpiece which my friend Patrick Bourne once obligingly described to me as 'one of the low points' of the collection. (I put this down to professional jealousy.)

Donald Bain's gritty, early *Renfrew Ferry* and Louise Annand's rayonnist *Heraldry* were bought by Murray Johnstone, and several pieces were bought for another corporate collection, that of Ernst & Young, including an abstract work by William Baillie of Hamilton. From the SNGMA we borrowed an outstanding Margaret Morris, *Les Toits Rouges*, which we had sold them earlier. One of the surprises of the show was a large abstract work by Morrison McChlery: a wonderfully confident, glowing canvas reminiscent of Serge Poliakoff. How had McChlery, well known in Glasgow as an auctioneer in his family's saleroom, kept his light hidden under a bushel for so long, and how on earth had he arrived at this very sophisticated style?

Another contribution to the European-ness of Glasgow's year as European City of Culture, or 'Year of Culture' as it was always called in Glasgow, was an exhibition of the work of the German Expressionists: 'From a Family Collection'. This again was a unique opportunity for people to see work which had never been publicly shown before, by a school not well represented or understood in Britain as a whole. What was extraordinary was the fact that the 'family collection' was a local, Glasgow family (whose anonymity we wished to preserve).

For the exhibition catalogue I translated the commentary by Hans Hess on his parents' visitors book (published as a slim volume *Dank in Farben* in 1959) taken from my own copy of the book which I had had since I went to Hamburg as a schoolboy that same year. *Dank in Farben* (thanks in colours) is special as it includes not only signatures and comments, but also original drawings, sometimes quiet elaborate, by such giants of German painting as Paul Klee, Wassily Kandinsky, Max Pechstein, Kurt Schwitters, and Lyonel Feininger.

The works in the exhibition were in fact borrowed from two branches of the same family, one in Glasgow, the other in Pittsburgh, Pennsylvania. There was also a watercolour by Emil Nolde, *Sonnenblumen und Mohn* (*Sunflowers and Poppies*), which, amazingly, also came from a collection in Bearsden, Glasgow and was for sale. Thus we were able to show major works by Lyonel Feininger (including a rare set of his photographs illustrating a children's tale *Die Stadt Hinter dem Strom*, photographed from little wooden models of houses, figures, yachts and locomotives made by the artist), Christian Rohlfs, Emil Nolde, and August Macke, as well as prints by Franz Marc, Emil Nolde, Wassily Kandinsky and Ernst Ludwig Kirchner. All in all, this was a creditable representation of one of the most important of all European schools, which had hardly been seen in the UK and to the best of my knowledge never in Scotland.

There were also two minor names associated with the Bauhaus, Alfred Ost and Ludwig Meidner, who were bought by the Hunterian Art Gallery and the Paul Kovesdy Gallery in New York. In order to place these artists in their context I drove to the cathedral city of Ulm and then to Weimar to discuss them with the curator of the Bauhaus Museum in Weimar, Herr Siebenbrodt. Near Weimar, I made a detour to the village of Gelmeroda, well known as the location of Feininger's great series of paintings of its church. Here I was greeted by the extraordinary sight of the church spire illuminated by shafts of sunlight penetrating the dark surrounding clouds, just as Feininger depicted the same scene in the *Gelmeroda* paintings.

With the American owners of the works in Pittsburgh I devised a means by which I could carry everything through customs by hand. A special lightweight case of portable size was made in Glasgow to accommodate the largest work, which was the majestic *Gelmeroda I* canvas by Feininger. This picture, like all the others, was taken out of its frame to save weight (new frames would be made in Glasgow), and all the

Arthur Melville,
The White Piano (1897)

Stanley Cursiter,
The Regatta (1913)

Emil Nolde,
Sonnenblumen und Mohn (Sunflowers and Poppies) (1930s)
Watercolour on Japan paper, 34 × 47 cm

Sir David Wilkie,
The Pedlar (1814)

Charles Rennie Mackintosh,
Chair with High-tapering-back
for the Hall (1901)

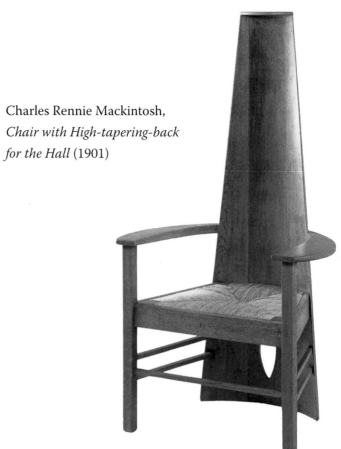

Christopher Dresser,
Linthorpe Pottery vase (left), Tea service (above)

Charles Mackie,
By the Bonnie Banks O' Fordie, (1892)

Lyonel Feininger,
Kathedrale, Titelholzschnitt zum Bauhaus-Manifest und Programm, 1919

Sir Joshua Reynolds,
Harriet Dutens of Craigforth (1772)

Attributed to Claude Lorrain,
A Procession with a View of Delphi (c.1645) *(top)*
The Marriage of Isaac and Rebecca (1648) *(bottom)*

Édouard Vuillard,
Deux ouvrières dans l'atelier de couture (Two seamstresses in the workroom) (1893)

Unknown artist,
*Gentleman seated in his study
with geological specimens*

John Laurie,
The Cocktail Hour (1936)

August Macke,
Auf dem Friedhof in Thun (At Thun Cemetery) (c.1913)

David Hockney,
William Hardie (1994) – reproduction of a video still
from *David Hockney New Drawings, 1993-94*

With Cyril Gerber and Paul Howard

With Tom Howarth

With David Hockney

With Jamie Bruce and his daughter, at Christie's first sale in Glasgow

Gallery front,
141 West Regent Street

A temporary obstacle

With Pat Lally, HRH The Princess Royal and Raymond Johnstone

With David Hockney

Steven Campbell

Peter Howson and Jill Gerber

Daniel Lang and Lady Orde

Blythswood Square

Gallery interior, West Regent Street

Taeko Seki

Arata Endo

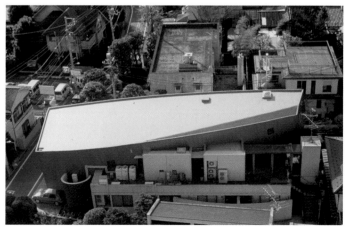

The 'piano' house
designed for the
conductor Watanabe
Shinichiro

other borrowed works were carefully packed inside the slim protective case, which was then fastened together with small screws. At each end of the journey, approaching security or customs, I was able – this was 1990 – to brandish a small screwdriver, to the visible relief of the officials, who saw from the paperwork that these pieces were only on loan and so had no VAT or permanent export implications. I have to confess that the scheme failed at the last hurdle, on the final flight from JFK back to Pittsburgh, because the airline insisted that the case be placed in the hold. I was allowed to witness it loaded but not unloaded, and it was an embarrassment to have to wait for it to be brought through by an official while I stood with the owner at the luggage carousel. He was remarkably stoical about it.

Subsequently several of the Glasgow pieces were sold from an exhibition I staged at the Morin-Miller Gallery on West 57th Street, New York City, including the precious little August Macke, which was bought by David Thomson, who also bought the Nolde watercolour. The Rohlfs went to Wolfgang Wittrock in Düsseldorf. Later we sold further items to Wittrock, including two important lithographs by Nolde, and to the charming Margret Heuser-Mantell, a specialist dealer also from Düsseldorf. Martin Hopkinson at the Hunterian in Glasgow purchased several prints by Ludwig Meidner. And that, it seemed, would be that. But we were in for two nasty shocks.

After the exhibition I had lengthy discussions with the owners of the Feininger, *Gelmeroda I*, by far the most important picture in the collection. They now wished to sell it. I went back to Pittsburg to stay with them and talk it over as I had done on previous visits. But the atmosphere had changed. I had revealed that I had a German buyer; and suddenly for this immigrant family, who had seen their whole community wiped out in Erfurt, the shutters came down. They no longer wished me to proceed. The picture was finally sold by the experienced New York Feininger specialist Achim Moeller. The odd thing was that I understood and even sympathized with the family: to me, the Jews represent an intellectual and cultural aristocracy whose modern history entitles them to deal as they wish in such cases.

I did have another image of Gelmeroda: Feininger's woodcut of the spire, which he titled *Kathedrale des Sozialismus* (the Cathedral of Socialism) which was used as the frontispiece to the 1912 *Der Blaue Reiter Almanach*, one of the key documents of Expressionism. This title's political overtones give a clue as well to the artist's intention in the painted series, where a 'red wedge opposes a white triangle' – these aren't just bits of geometry, they represent the mortal struggle of Bolshevism versus the White Russian faction. The Patrons of the National Galleries of Scotland bought the woodcut for the Print Room of the Scottish National Gallery of Modern Art. Ironically the SNGMA later bought another, lesser oil version of *Gelmeroda*, surely a missed opportunity since 'our' version was not only a greater work, but it also had a link to a Glasgow family. The two great social upheavals of the twentieth century were thus encapsulated in this tale of two versions of the composition: the Russian Revolution, with which I think Feininger identified from a comfortable distance, and the Holocaust, which had come only too close to the owners of *Gelmeroda I*.

Troubles come in pairs. The Nolde watercolour was returned to me by David Thomson after a short interval. Wolfgang Wittrock, his agent in Germany, had sent it to Dr Martin Urban at the Nolde-Stiftung at Seebüll in Schleswig-Holstein for authentication. Dr Urban condemned the work, and not just verbally or in writing. He had stamped the dread word 'Fälschung' (Fake) on the backboard (he had been dissuaded by Wittrock from stamping the back of the picture itself). This was a major reverse. David was a very important collector. Nothing like this had happened to us before. I returned his money, and racked my brains: where had we gone wrong? Our loss, potentially, was large financially and even larger morally. I went to London to speak to the specialists, especially Robert Levin, surrounded by his remarkable collection of pictures and Diego Giacometti furniture, and to New York to speak to the very experienced Serge Sabarsky. Both men had known the late dealer, Charles Locke, who had once owned our Nolde picture. But the trail was unpromising: Charles Locke, at the end of his career, had apparently had a brainstorm at an auction which had to be halted because he was outbidding the room on every lot. No one wanted to tell me where his widow, or his successors-in-business, or his executors were. His New York lawyers were unhelpful.

Months passed. Then I looked again, and read more closely the old Marlborough exhibition label, according to which the work had been included in their two-artist exhibition in 1960: 'Klee and Nolde'. I procured a copy of the exhibition catalogue, and our Nolde was indeed there, numbered as on the label. The catalogue's author was none other than Dr Martin Urban, who had just condemned the work. I wrote to him suggesting that perhaps with the passing of thirty years he had forgotten his original acceptance of our picture. He replied neither apologizing nor explaining and saying that he 'couldn't comment', but I felt free to send *Sunflowers* to auction where it was fully catalogued and sold well. Sometimes the solution to a problem lies close to the surface: on the label, even. Visiting the Nolde Institute at Seebüll more recently in its fine garden created by the artist and his wife, I found myself wondering whether the persecution Nolde had endured had rubbed off on his curator. As one of the artists included in the Nazis' 'Degenerate Art' exhibition, Nolde was forbidden to paint during the war years. He referred to the paintings of that period as his *'ungemälte Bilder'* (his unpainted paintings).

On this visit it also struck me that Nolde had adopted for the programme of his post-war series of paintings on the *Passion of Our Lord*, the same subject as the great altar screen by the woodcarver Meister Brueggemann in Schleswig Cathedral nearby. Nothing ever, or hardly ever, comes from nowhere. In this case I had been in Schleswig-Holstein, talking about Nolde as a schoolboy. Recently it struck me that the first portrait Reynolds painted of Dr Johnson owed its composition to a Hogarth which I had seen as a student, the *Portrait of Sarah Malcolm* shown in her room in Newgate Prison.

In autumn 1990, the opening of the new Glasgow Royal Concert Hall was imminent. The building, an off-the-shelf design from the era of the 1951 Festival of Britain by Sir Leslie Martin, was acceptable on the outside and acoustically miraculous inside the auditorium. It was hard to believe that it had proceeded so quickly from the hole in the ground which we visited months earlier to discuss a possible exhibition to mark the opening by the Princess Royal. Raymond Johnstone had already donated a Steinway grand piano to the Concert Hall, and now he was thinking of how to get some decent pictures into the place for the opening. Would we help? Most certainly. It was not a difficult brief, given that the project was close to Lord Provost Pat Lally's heart, and furthermore it was a congenial theme: the Glasgow School. Loans were quickly negotiated and a little catalogue was printed.

I was presented to HRH Princess Anne, Princess Royal, at the interval by the Lord Provost and Raymond Johnstone, who loyally offered the Princess a copy of my new book. She graciously leafed through it, the pages falling open at some of the more avant-garde illustrations. 'Hmm, some jolly funny things in here!' We all laughed. The moment was captured in a large front-page photograph of a radiantly smiling Princess in the *Herald* the following morning. I'm in the foreground; but my back is to the camera. Unfortunately, not even my mother recognized me.

The book received another memorable accolade. At a reception at the National Gallery in Edinburgh, Billy Connolly was standing surrounded by acolytes, dressed in what I can only describe as a cowboy outfit, with thongs, rhinestones, boots and a bolo tie. Was he wearing spurs and a ten-gallon hat? Quite possibly. I thought I'd leave him in peace, but he spotted me and bellowed, 'Bill, ah luv yur book, it's greeeeat!' Now that's what I call a compliment: the time, the place, the sentiment and the volume were all as Billy might say, 'ticketty-boo'. Billy at that point was presenting his own television series on Scottish art.

The Concert Hall exhibition was the backdrop to the launch of the second edition of my book *Scottish Painting* of which the publisher was able to send us 200 advance copies. These were all sold at the signing session which took place after Timothy Clifford's speech, the flavour of which was accurately captured by Ruth Wishart writing in *The Scotsman*:

> '...This is the kind of gratuitous information which is not quite, shall we say, music to the average Glaswegian ear. And that latter organ was similarly underwhelmed to be gleefully informed by a now-ebullient orator that while Aberdeen, Dundee, Kirkcaldy, Stirling and even Preston had shown great 'generosity of spirit' in lending works to the exhibition, the National Gallery of Scotland, which had among its Glasgow Boys collection the most significant work of all in William York Macgregor's *Vegetable Stall*, had regrettably been unable to respond because its own enormously popular exhibition was still running.'

Clifford in fact went on well over time, leaving me a minute which I devoted to offering him the address of my tailor (we were identically clad in chalk stripe suits). By the time Murray Johnstone's guests reached the tables of food they had generously provided, much of it had already been eaten by members of the Berlin Philharmonic Orchestra who had taken a lunch break from rehearsal. *Our* lunch. The great orchestra was in Glasgow as part of an ambitious series called 'World Orchestras' organized by Cameron McNicol, who was director of the Concert Hall. To hear them play a Haydn symphony under Kurt Hahn was spellbinding: just as a full *piano* requires a powerful choir, so a simple piece of music acquires pellucid stillness played by a virtuoso orchestra. If our food helped, I am glad.

After the exhibition involving the masters of German Expressionism I was determined not to seem parochial: 1990 was the fiftieth anniversary of the death of Jean-Édouard Vuillard and this provided me with an opportunity to build a 'small tribute to a great Master'. Richard Calvocoressi agreed to let us borrow the little Vuillard painting the Scottish National Gallery of Modern Art had just acquired from us. This was the nucleus round which it was possible, with generous loans from Kelvingrove Art Gallery and the National Galleries of Scotland, to create a small show of his work and was as much as we could rise to by ourselves, especially in view of the expense of insurance for such a valuable artist. Christian Neffe of Neffe-Degandt, the London gallery specializing in the work of the *Les Nabis*, was able to consign to us a dozen drawings by Vuillard, and many of these were sold. Disappointingly, the Couchmans in Ireland, whose local dolmen and Vuillard painting I had admired equally, had gone through a family rethink and had decided to send their Vuillard landscape to auction, where it fetched a mediocre price. The SNGMA insisted that 'my' picture could only be lent on a guarantee of 24-hour surveillance in West Regent Street. Security meant a night watchman rather than a commissionaire, who would wear a smart uniform and leap out to open car doors, so the considerable expense of his hire brought us no very visible benefit. But it was the only show anywhere that year to celebrate the Vuillard anniversary – and I was able to enjoy, or pine over, the little *Deux ouvrières dans l'atelier de couture* for a little longer.

We sold other beautiful works by members of the French School, perhaps most notably a lithograph of an *Odalisque* by Matisse, which came from the Scottish widow of Matisse's friend the painter Paul Maze. And there was a real rarity, sold for Dame Naomi Mitchison the novelist: a *Nature Morte* by the naive painter André Bauchant, which I collected from Carradale House. Here Dame Naomi had entertained Francis Crick; Crick and James D. Watson's *The Double Helix* is dedicated to her. Dame Naomi was not very kind about the New Glasgow Group, for whom she had once written a starry-eyed introduction. Ann Gloag bought a little Renoir *Head of a Girl* from me instead of a glorious Monet landscape which I had from Wildenstein's, the kind of reverse which hurts a dealer's credibility. But soft! Ann Gloag, with her decorator's eye, knew where a picture was meant to be hung in a house, and she sees colours that hide themselves in a painting. We do not complain of her and anyway she goes her own way impervious to all well-meant advice.

I prefer to forget how we were let in for an exhibition of the work of 'Princess Diana's favourite painter' Robert Heindel, who had been painting Scottish Ballet in rehearsal. But despite all the ballyhoo it was the most spectacular press event we ever had. I would like to think that the connection with Scottish Ballet was what hooked us. Certainly the girls from the company worked endlessly for the cameras in the gallery with their lights and even microphones. The dancers were in tutus and ballet shoes and spent the day trying for the perfect shot. This appeared in colour on the *Herald*'s front page the following day.

The year of 1990 closed with an exhibition of the work of Emma Fordyce MacRae who exhibited in America in the 1930s as a painter of stylized interiors and flowers and whose decorative work was brought to our attention by Jennifer Kissell. This continued a connection with American art. I've shown Daniel Lang with his more abstract compatriot Jon Schueler, and Andrea Tana, who works in London, and painted portraits of our two children. I still have Leslie Hunter's portrait of the Wild West writer *Bret Harte*.

9 The Go-Between

By far the major part of the paintings shown in 1990 were borrowed works by established earlier artists. They included some big names from the past: German Expressionists, Vuillard, the Glasgow School. An art gallery is a hungry animal, I was discovering; 141 West Regent Street had 200 linear feet of hanging space. Exhibitions of pictures emanating from many sources were just too expensive, and entailed a lot of research, as well as time spent persuading lenders and sponsors to give their support. It was increasingly clear that we had to give serious thought to shows by contemporary artists. There were the New Glasgow Boys and Girls – Jenny Saville and Alison Watt had begun to make their names – as well as the *nomenclatura* like William Crosbie, David Donaldson, Alexander Goudie, Alberto Morrocco, William Gear, Alan Davie, John Houston, Elizabeth Blackadder and John Bellany. Most were tied to other galleries in one way or another and in several cases I had to accept that it would be impossible for me to get new work.

Critics were something we hadn't had to deal with until now. I quickly learned to quote them in the ads, and there was no equivalent anymore of Dundee's Caird Hall's huge banners advertising these shows. Once I was moved to complain to the *Herald* about late reviews. Clare Henry in particular seemed to think she was reviewing a concert, not an exhibition; no matter how good the review, it wasn't hugely helpful if it was late. Bill Hare's London reviews were especially precious. Richard Cork had already singled out the Cursiter from my book, which he reviewed. W. Gordon Smith was thoughtful and many good reviews came from his pen.

Despite spending nine months in Provence as an *assistant d'anglais* in the Lycée Mistral in Avignon I had never been to St-Paul-de-Vence, with its fabulous associations: the Matisse-decorated chapel; the Maeght Foundation's collection with its Catalan School paintings by Joan Miró, Picasso, Antoni Tàpies and William Baziotes; the Colombe d'Or itself, a world famous hotel with special links with Picasso and Matisse; and more recently to 007 in the person of Roger Moore, the second James Bond.

Donald Bain, who had lived in St-Paul-de-Vence in the late 1940s, alerted me to the presence in the village of works by Leslie Hunter long before I went to see for myself. A number of fine pictures by Leslie Hunter were all still in the possession of the Roux family some seventy years after they had been given by the artist over the years to Albert Roux, *patron* of the Colombe d'Or, as payment-in-kind for food and drink in the restaurant. My approach to his son Paul Roux met a friendly reception, and it was arranged that I would come to see the pictures and uplift the ones I wanted to borrow for an exhibition in my gallery in Glasgow. The pictures were not framed so I had a stout wooden crate made to their size – 20 inches x 24 inches. Thus equipped I presented myself at the Colombe d'Or. Here I was given lunch which I had alfresco beside the large Alexander Calder painted mobile which was the main item of poolside furniture. I was not allowed to pay.

The Leslie Hunter paintings form a unique group, of lovely quality, with memorable still-life compositions and scenes of St Paul, including a view of the large open-air stone laundry trough which is still in daily use. The paintings had not only never been seen in Glasgow, they had never left the Colombe d'Or. We were very privileged to be allowed to borrow them for a while. When the pictures arrived in Glasgow we put them into very simple white frames. Hunter had stipulated white frames somewhere in his letters to Tom Honeyman.

We sold several Hunter drawings from the Honeyman group as a means of defraying costs. Norman Macfarlane supportively lent us several Hunter works on paper with scenes of St Paul. The exhibition was rapturously received. And then – glory be and what a life – it was time to take them back. Naturally we made the Roux family a present of the new frames, which did look rather stark. We should probably have 'distressed' them a little. When Mademoiselle Roux saw the frames she did just slightly wrinkle up her nose, then she smiled and said '*On peut les patauger un peu*' (we can smudge them a little). They are near the works by Picasso, Georges Braque, Jacques Villon and other masters and I'm grateful for the generous spirit which allowed these pictures by one of the most attractive Scottish artists to be seen in Scotland.

Back again with the Hunter pictures in St Paul, I visited a wonderful old *hôtel avec poutres* (a townhouse with beams), where the owner had known Donald Bain and remembered him and his love of olives. There was a crayon drawing by Donald still in the house. Donald Bain made many pastel studies of St Paul, and a few oils, one of which I bought for Dundee Art Gallery when I was keeper there. Bain also made a lovely little linocut of the bell tower. But this wasn't a picnic for Bain. He had written to J.D. Fergusson:

'... I have now reached the most critical point of my survival as a painter ... Had I to return [to Glasgow], all my efforts would have been wasted. Paul Roux came to see my paintings and was greatly impressed so he asked the loan of one and has placed it in the dining room of the Colombe d'Or. As you know people from all over the world visit the Colombe d'Or, it's more value than a show in London, and he has placed it near one of Hunter's still lifes, my painting is the one *Bottle and Jug* reproduced in my own book. I get on very well with Roux, he has told me some tales about Hunter.' (27 June 1947 from St-Paul-de-Vence)

'I am most welcome at the Colombe d'Or. Roux seems to like me, he is pleased to see me there, also his wife is really a good woman. He introduces me to people. Vanel said to me Roux will like you because he likes Hunter, she was right. You [Fergusson] will be among the notables at Antibes. The D&D [sic] of Windsor are there so is Picasso ... Agnes McKay [the author of a book on Arthur Melville] made a suggestion that some sort of note be put in my book about Montgomerie's mention of the 45 and the John Knox business, as a good many people out of Scotland don't know anything about it...

'As I returned from my evening stroll I met three guests who are friendly to me, they asked me to come and have a drink. I did and there was Picasso one table from us [D.B. drew his portrait] ...

'After an interval I now continue. Permeke the younger has been. He was most impressed and said I must have a show in Paris.' (29 June 1947 from St-Paul-de-Vence)

In a letter of 8 August, back again in Glasgow, Bain shows how important to him then were the collectors Vincent Singleton, George Singleton, Gordon Inglis and Tom Honeyman. He mentions the Château des Enfants (owned by George Davidson who had the Kodak shops in Europe) and the name of Constant Permeke. One can see that Bain found in Permeke encouragement for his own earlier work. It is rather like Sir George Reid mentioning Daubigny, but the actual connection is more obvious in the case of Bain. I suspect – but cannot prove – that he was aware too of such heroes of the School of Paris as Eugène Baboulène, Massimo Campigli, and Gustave de Smet. Bain certainly knew the work of Matisse, who would have been starting the commission for the nearby chapel at Vence. Bain's black wash drawings of this period are an obvious tribute to Matisse.

Earlier, we had shown John Byrne's drawings for the TV drama series *Tutti Frutti*. Concurrently with the Hunter show, a little exhibition of Byrne's drawings for his television series *Your Cheatin' Heart* occupied the small gallery. John, with his customary attention to every detail no matter how minute, had drawn the protagonists of his drama in character and in costume. The drawings functioned both as storyboard and as illustrations for the book which accompanied the series, which was produced and brilliantly cast by John. The show gave career-defining roles to Emma Thompson, Richard Wilson and Robbie Coltrane and several other actors. Robbie Coltrane opened the show with a practised speech. Later, on a visit to his house outside Glasgow, I admired his collection of 1950s American automobiles which were in keeping with his kingsize frame.

John Bellany was, typically, a one-off show with all the overheads and therefore no repeat economies. John is a forceful character, an artist whose work I only began to appreciate by writing about it (always a good way to learn). Earlier, in 1970 when I was assembling the 'Seven Painters in Dundee' show for the Scottish Arts Council, Bellany in Edinburgh had seemed to me almost anti-modernist in comparison with these 'cool' artists of the northern city, and Alan Bold had written me a note rebuking me for this slighting view of his hero.

The Bellany exhibition was on when David Hockney visited the gallery with Henry Geldzahler, his friend and a former curator at the Metropolitan Museum in New York. Geldzahler was the subject of one of Hockney's best known and most brilliant portraits, *Looking at Pictures*, and was also the subject of a Warhol portrait screenprint, of which I saw an example in Geldzahler's Long Island house. Both Geldzahler and Hockney were struck by Bellany's powerful handling of paint, especially in watercolour. David Hockney also liked Donald Bain's early watercolours of views of industrial Glasgow, in a naive style. I acquired several of John Bellany's paintings for the gallery stock. Subsequently I found myself being taken to task by the owner of the Beaux Arts Gallery for asking higher prices than the Bellany paintings he was offering in the Art Fair at the Royal College of Art, but there was really no arguing with the fact that as the pictures were mine and as I wasn't selling them on commission, I was entitled to ask whatever price I thought fit.

All the work was recent and benefited from the new optimism surging through Bellany's work since his operation, when, emerging from the anaesthetic surrounded by flowers, he immediately called for his brushes and began work, at first on a small scale and in watercolour, later in larger and larger oils. I still have one large oil of a Venetian masque from this period which is full of *joie de vivre*, as well as a big flower composition, *Aberdeen Flowers*. W. Gordon Smith wrote: 'This elegant Glasgow salon is ablaze with new canvases and watercolours … energy, heightened colour, and cheerful aggression.' Clare Henry: 'a brilliant show'. Emilio Coia: 'John Bellany does not so much exhibit at the William Hardie Gallery as take possession of it, so authoritative and intense are his paintings.'

An autumn offering was paintings of 'France and Scotland' by Donald Bain, followed by a Christmas exhibition of 'New Paintings' by the gauzy, dreamy Brenda Lenaghan. Because it was Christmas, festive cheer was provided by Carl Pinder, Principal House Clown at the huge circus at Kelvin Hall. I liked his naive paintings with titles like *Frig off Freddie You're Fired*. Glasgow had a sort of folk life and its fairground art, I hopefully thought, might be echoed in the gallery, which I could see as being a little like that of Père Tanguy in Paris: unpretentious, inconspicuous, but filled with wonderful things. 'Hankies' was the title given by John Byrne to an exhibition of early year 1992, 'the latest joyful tweak of his prodigious talent' as the critic W. Gordon Smith wrote in *The Scotsman*. Since *Your Cheatin' Heart* twelve months earlier I had pestered John for another show, urging on him the notion (as I've always regarded him as the most sheerly talented artist I know) that *pace* the theatre, he should devote more time to painting. I expect that theatre people advise him to stop daubing and return to his true *métier* as a playwright.

John Byrne had recently mentioned watercolours painted by himself, and my expectations were high when he telephoned to say that he had an exhibition ready for me. So I was puzzled when three tea chests containing John's collection of silk handkerchiefs arrived at the gallery. 'Where's the show?' quoth I. 'In the boxes'. 'Are they watercolours?' 'No, hankies'. 'What's the show called?' 'Hankies'. John then spent three days mostly recumbent on the gallery floor collaging the hankies into miraculously meaningful, decorative and even beautiful compositions, which were pressed behind plexiglass in frames. Again, they were bought in large numbers by his eager fans, and although neither of us became millionaires as a result, it was enormous fun to do this gloriously cheeky show.

I realized later that the handkerchiefs hadn't as it were come from nowhere, apart from John's secret hanky drawer and his favourite junk shop. There had been an earlier group of oil paintings, ostensibly self-portraits, which had featured forms broken up – that is too strong an expression, better might be 'folded' or 'streamed' – into shapes resembling scarves, pashminas, shawls, throws, chadors: the right word eludes me.

My portrait by John Byrne dated 27 September 1991 is the closest I have come to being psychoanalysed. I think it makes me look greedy and sly, cupidity personified. I asked about the little framed portrait of him I am holding. I am in my smart chalk stripe, the artist is unkempt and unshaven, like a refugee from cardboard city, blowing out his cheeks with the cold – or in indignation – 'We've got a right fruit here'. 'OK John I get it: dealer frames the artist'. John acts the innocent and denies this with a laugh. I then suggest, 'Is it "caring art dealer holds up to view the struggles of the artist: look folks, this is what they go through?" ' 'Aye, maybe, quite an ingenious idea that'. (John is too polite to say nothing was further from his thoughts.)

The left hand is professionally aesthetic and limp-wristed, the right is like a conjuror's producing a picture instead of a trump card or a white rabbit. My face owes more to Dorian Gray than Rembrandt. The tie is pure invention, like something the Slab Boys might have made and then rejected. It looks very nice but oddly I wish John had actually painted one of my favourite ties. I also wished he had painted the Vuillard I still had instead of the mocking self-portrait. A newspaper photograph of the portrait taken from the side flattened out the distortions in perspective, and, Holbein-style, made it look photographic. When Stanley Baxter saw the portrait he said 'He's done a Modigliani of you'.

James Campbell Brady came in unannounced one day in 1992. He looked a little like Sonny Bono of Sonny and Cher, but less *soigné*. Within a few minutes of looking through his portfolio, I agreed to show his work – a thing that had never happened before and never happened again. It was all on paper, but special paper made by Arches of Paris. That someone who so clearly hadn't two pennies to rub together would buy the best possible paper for his work impressed me. But the work itself was remarkable: technically it was beautiful as watercolour ghosted onto the page, using all the difficult things that watercolour does, runs, smudges, stains; and superimposing an understated imagery full of mystery, naivety, suggestion, import. The subjects ranged from Klee-like fish or angels to effects of light and colour on water, usually off the Western Isles of Scotland. Many of the titles indicated his love of the mountains, islands and waters of the Highlands, and his interest in the history of the region. All art has a motive; Campbell Brady's motive was the portrayal of the spiritual element in the landscape of places such as Canna, Quiraing and Buchaille Etive Mòr.

Brady appeared at the private view and the dinner afterwards, where to my delight he and James Robertson – amateur and pro – hit it off well. On another occasion he was returning from the Hebrides where he had made a series of charcoal drawings of the islands. I bought several of these immediately; I still have almost all of them. We also showed his work at one of the Islington Art Fairs, where examples were bought by such luminaries as Lady Conran, the Scottish Arts Council, and Fleming's Bank. I felt particularly pleased at each purchase, feeling that the buyer too had seen what I saw in the work of this completely unknown painter. He had hitchhiked his way from Bristol to Glasgow. I asked him where he was staying for the night and when he replied that he hadn't arranged anything yet, I suggested that he could bunk down in the gallery overnight. We were able to offer him the Mackintosh day bed, and the gallery had a small kitchen. The 'honour' of an overnight stay in the gallery was never offered to anyone else. I admired his sincerity and devotion to his craft, that was all. A year or two later I was contacted by Bristol City Council. Campbell Brady had died in a fire in his caravan and there was no money for his funeral expenses. Letters from the gallery had been found among his effects. I was invited to inspect all the remaining studies and finished paintings, which I bought for the cost of the funeral. I still have most of the work, except for the ones given away as presents.

It is difficult to convey the subtleties of Campbell Brady's work in words. The Hebridean drawings, being monochrome, were somewhat austere, but there were several paintings in watercolour or gouache which evoked the beauty of unexpected effects of light on colours in the landscape. The island of Canna is seen in bold outline against a clear sky or virtually absorbed by a cloudy background. In one study, the gunmetal sea contains one of those mysterious pools of vivid aquamarine that occur in balmy summer conditions. It was not until a recent visit (my first) to Assynt in the north-west of the Highlands that I understood the artist's fascination with that ancient range of majestic peaks mirrored in the lochs, now apparent, now hidden in mist or rain.

Looking at the *Nativity Angels* I saw another use of time by a painter, the time we spend absorbing the import and application of paint, the time it takes to see what the painter has seen and conveyed, whether an inner impulse or a sudden insight into an effect of weather, mist, wind, sunshine on land or sea.

James Robertson's paintings come from a different tradition, but as landscapes share some of the same concerns. They are gloriously celebratory of material, the stuff of art, and effects of light. Our 'Summer Exhibition' of pictures by Liz Knox and Cara McKinnon Crawford was even more optimistic – as one has to be in a Scottish summer.

The Charles Pulsford retrospective was opened by the late Bill Brown, then Chairman of the Scottish Arts Council, who staunchly read through his very carefully prepared speech to a disappointingly small but appreciative audience. Examples of Pulsford's extraordinarily powerful lithographs, some of them reminiscent to my eye of the work of Arshile Gorky introducing an early awareness of New York abstraction, which Pulsford had to communicate to students at Edinburgh College of Art when W.G. Gillies was Head of Painting.

There was an excellent review by the faithful W. Gordon Smith, and several early prints went to the British Museum Print Room. Surrealism is seldom seen in Scottish painting as it was in an impressive early work by Charles Pulsford, but it is an influence on William Baillie of Hamilton and on Ally Thompson. We gave lithographs by Pulsford to the Maclaurin Art Gallery in Ayr and to Dundee University, together with a snowy landscape painting by David Cook.

Other artists whom we showed at an early stage include Ben Henriques, Francis Farmar and Tom Deakins, one bought by a romantic couple who chose a painting of a tree in blossom to celebrate their late-flowering romance.

The Glasgow Orchid Festival of 1993 saw us present an appropriate exhibition. Nell Hardie's watercolour studies of local wild flowers were painted at the Cottages in the years from 1970 to 1980, when my father died. The artist then hung up her brushes, or to be more accurate gave them to the postman. The flowers could almost all be found within a two-mile radius of Steele Road (most of them were a short walk from the front door) and when we had them identified by the botanist Keith Watson, we realized that she had painstakingly described around two hundred species of plants, including some wild orchids. We exhibited some of the watercolours in the Orchid Festival and published a little illustrated book of them, a copy of which went to the Linnaean Society library. The book's value as a survey is more apparent with the passing years – and the passing of many species from the over-mown verges which used to provide their habitat.

Pamela Rachet, who is the sister of the Scottish writer Neal Ascherson but was better known to me as my guide in Provence thirty years earlier, came for lunch one Sunday in the gallery. I had not seen her for decades, there were just the two of us and we were surrounded by more than a score of new paintings by David Hockney. The Hockney exhibition has the next chapter to itself. It was paid for by the Andrew Wilson Sale as well as attracting the Charles Heap Collection and sponsorship from Murray Johnstone.

I had long hoped to show the work of John Gardiner Crawford, a fisherman's son from Angus, whose beautifully crafted paintings with their restricted palette and exquisite drawing evoke the natural history of the primeval north-east coast of Scotland. John is in a class of his own as a contemporary landscape painter.

The difficulty for us was that he is such a successful artist that he has no need to look beyond his regular shows with his Canadian dealers, the Beckett Gallery in Hamilton, Ontario. Fortunately the idea of a Scottish exhibition of his work had long appealed to him, and his friendship with my former chief at Dundee Art Gallery, James D. Boyd, was a factor in his decision to let us show twenty-seven new works at West Regent Street. These were received enthusiastically in Glasgow and we had several new buyers, including Alan Clark, whose political *Diaries* were then in the news, Lord Palumbo, a former chairman of the Arts Council, and the actress Jenny Funnell of *As Time Goes By*.

Although Crawford never includes the human figure, his landscapes or paintings of the sea have human resonances even when he is painting seabirds or a Pictish stone standing in a snowy landscape. The animals and birds are there as themselves, but the work suggests the common ground between creatures, their shared life which equates to survival. The compositions have great simplicity: *Sea Storm* is a painting of a white gull against a forbidding gunmetal sea; *Morning White* is a neglected rowing boat, its clinker-built hull showing rust marks against the beautiful washed white of its paintwork. There is constantly a sense of the passage of time; of aeons, in the depictions of Pictish stones and the cup-and-ring rock carvings of early man. John Gardiner Crawford is one of a number of artists like Ian Fleming, Will Maclean, Fred Stiven and Robert Cargill, who have taken the north-eastern coast as their theme. This would make a fascinating survey for another time.

In June 1994, the gallery showed Adrian Wiszniewski. The artist seemed distracted as the exhibition deadline approached. He had recently gone public with the depressing and not very original idea that 'painting is dead'. I was disconcerted by the recent work in the studio at Lochwinnoch: a few oils of various sizes which seemed directionless or unresolved. But the die was cast. A bilingual catalogue was printed (at the suggestion of his new Belgian dealer Micheline Lesaffre, who contributed a piece in French). The illustrations were of people throwing up, shooting up, or tied up, and also, dreaming or languidly musing, one or two pretty, poetic youths. Fortunately I had the wit to ask Duncan Macmillan to write the catalogue essay, which did cast a shaft of light on the artist's intention, not least in the case of a painting titled *Shafted* where a shaft of light illuminates the bound victim who is therefore 'shafted' in two senses of the word.

For me the illumination came later. Adrian made clear his displeasure at the paucity of sales, pointing to the excellent reviews the show attracted, notably from Clare Henry. Her review took the form of a candid interview with the artist. Clare Henry commented that a viewer could be forgiven for thinking that there were several artists showing. Adrian Wiszniewski: 'Everyone fights the boredom of the studio.' 'In the late 1980s people stopped looking beyond the surface of the pictures.' 'You had to try something new.'

As a protest at the isolation which is the lot of the easel painter, and at the same time as a penetrating critique of the decline of taste into banality, these three sentences strike to the heart of a contemporary malaise which must be apparent to anyone interested in the continuing vitality of art. How else explain the contemporary polarization of art into sensation in its tabloid sense (the apt title of an exhibition of BritArt at the RA), on the one hand, and accessibility of the blandest sort (Jack Vettriano, and a host of endlessly exhibiting commercially driven, essentially amateur painters) on the other?

I had become rather defiantly proud of the show. For all its forbidding subject-matter, *Shafted* was a masterly thing. If any new crop of paintings by an artist produces only one great work, that surely justifies the experimentation surrounding it at the same period. In a larger market city the new work of such an outstanding figure would have attracted interest from the museum community, but this was Scotland and the museums ignored the show. I record here that our accountants, Clements and Taggarts, paid for the illustrated catalogue.

Even more cerebral was 'The Constructed Space', a show concentrating on work illustrating, or inspired by, the work of the Greenock poet W.S. Graham (1918–1986). Nicholas Usherwood later gave me a book of Graham's poems, but that apart, we had no response to this nice little highbrow exploration of a literary and artistic rivulet, apart from good reviews. It was interesting to realize that W.S. Graham had had such an influence on Donald Bain, who produced at least one oil painting, *The Crowd of Birds and Children*, inspired by the poet, as well as illustrations for *The Seven Journeys* and a remarkable book cover design (in oils), probably for the publisher William McLellan but never used.

In the small gallery we showed the etchings and some designs by the glass painter and stained-glass artist John Kenneth Clark, who had recently made his name in Glasgow with a cycle of stained glass windows for Queen's Park Synagogue (now closed but the windows were subsequently moved to Giffnock and Newlands Synagogue). Safeway were building a new supermarket in Glasgow and when they asked us to recommend a designer for a new glass mural they wished to commission, we at once suggested John Clark. His mural at the Anniesland Safeway, where it has been seen by thousands of visitors every week, is a shining example of corporate sponsorship of art for a public space.

Safeway financed the catalogue of the show of new work by John Boyd, another undoubted maestro and beautiful painter in a very Scottish mould: rich, painterly work which never strays far from the motif, whether still life or figure subjects, often people at work in the field or fishing community. John was a dreamer with a firm grasp of material, like one of his own fishermen carrying a miniature fishing boat that is too solid to be entirely a dream, and too fanciful to be entirely real. Martin Baillie contributed the catalogue essay. Safeway's board bought five of the works and gave us a splendid dinner.

In 1994, from November to December, we had Steven Campbell's exhibition, 'Outside Right At The Sunset Gate'. Campbell's one-man show at the Fruitmarket Gallery in Edinburgh ten years earlier had marked his debut in Scotland. Before then he had been in New York, where his dealer Barbara Toll's letterbox was stuffed full of flowers when Steven found she was not at home on a day of rave reviews of his show with her.

Two bundles of small paintings arrived tied up with string: our exhibition. Steven was very articulate about these pictures, and I suggested he should write a narrative which we would publish as the catalogue, which we did. This is what he wrote:

'A boy of 7 one day left home to play. Being a very young boy he imagined he was older, so in his mind as he left home he was a young man. On passing the seat, the phone, the bell jar and eventually the door, he left his home to meet his friends and play football. As it happened, to do so, he had to walk through the golf course to get to the football field and as he did, he imagined years of golfing ahead as a young man does, leaving childish things behind. He was the kind of boy who stubs his toe, bumps his head, falls from trees. The walk to the football field passes a beach where cold bathers lay, alarmed as he ran by, his feet thudding the sand. The Thoughts and Many Others came to him on his journey. He was 7 years old, what he did not know was that it was the 7th of the 7th at 7 o'clock. Approaching the golf course, he was at the height of his maturity, years fell on him. He knew the weather was going to be bad, but immaturity left him vulnerable.

'When the lightning flashed he ran to a tree which at that moment seemed to bubble and boil, the sap appearing as amber balloons from the trunk. His Memory before becoming a weather system was of … .

'A girl who loved milk. This love became a problem. The girl on the phone, his parents kept saying, there's a girl on the phone and in his mind she lived there, reclining nervously, alarmingly, waiting. He remembered *Kangaroo Girl*, for him more real than Malcolm Mclaren's "Buffalo Gals", (he judged everything by his limited travel experience, which was only Australia). So these girls had tiny beautiful babies which travelled home. The sunset gate was something he knew well but on that day he imagined it had been plotting in a sneaky Art Deco kind of way. A picket, wrought or Tudor gate, would probably have enabled the story to knit less well and so, reduced the opportunity for disaster … .

'Lifting from the ground, of heat and of loneliness. As he rose into the air, as an angel does, the moisture in his body became part of the air and began moving away from him, establishing his own identity which was, as art is, creative. It moved around his home establishing small gardens, until the air became warm.'

Steven Campbell's show, which was described by the painter John Johnstone as 'a whole entertainment', was one of those special cases where I felt the gallery was contributing more than the space and all the things that went with the word 'gallery', because the artist was doing something extraordinary.

Another exhibition was by Francis Farmar whom I had known during Christie's days when he was head of the Modern British Pictures department. He had left the firm subsequently to devote more time to painting and a show with my gallery in 1995 was a nice connection. It has been rewarding to watch his development. His work starts with an admiration for the English watercolourists like Paul Nash but his repertoire of locations ranges from Findhorn in the far north-east to his native West Country, London, Provence, and Manhattan.

In 1996, since old habits die hard, I decided to start an auction arm in the gallery. The timing was opportune. Christie's had closed its Decorative Arts department in Scotland. Paul Howard was the specialist about to join the ex-Christie's club, and he agreed to join William Hardie Limited to run decorative arts sales for our clients. Naturally a posse of his own clients came with him, and his auction sales quickly became a fixture of the Glasgow antiques scene. Howard is a very capable cataloguer and took to the rostrum like a duck to water. For six years he organized four sales a year which ran like clockwork. I organized two pictures sales a year, the most successful of which included the Andrew Wilson Collection. It grossed £1.6 million, and split Sotheby's and Christie's claims to have the most valuable paintings sale in Scotland that year.

But I was discovering at the same time the litany of 3,500 private view cards per show + wine + advertising + pictures delivered and removed was very expensive. By the time we had added an auction arm and added a bookkeeper, the overhead was £250,000 a year, or as our accountant put it more alarmingly, £5,000 per week.

Two major collections passed us by which we might reasonably have expected to handle as auctioneers. The first was Iris Fox's collection of ceramics. She had been a famous dealer in Edinburgh who had been a client of Paul Howard's. I knew her solicitors. Thus the job of valuing the Iris Fox Collection for estate duty came to us, by far the biggest assignment of its kind, which Paul endured freezing conditions in the huge dusty house to accomplish. However, the bulk of the Fox Collection went to Sotheby's to be sold.

The second was the Howarth Collection in Toronto. I always knew that Tom would sell his collection rather than donate it to a public collection, and had often reminded him that the same clock was ticking that had scotched the sale by Sotheby's of Alice Bain's Mackintosh items (they had to be withdrawn from their Monte Carlo sale), namely the heritage laws of Canada which insisted on items held on Canadian soil for fifty years being subject to strict limitations on their sale. Tom had given up on the idea of selling to a museum or museums, and felt particularly thwarted when Timothy Clifford of the National Gallery in Edinburgh cancelled a meeting arranged to discuss the question on the ground that he was committed to a shoot that week. Tom knew that we had made a success of the sale of the Wilson Collection, but he sent his collection to Christie's, where it sold for record-breaking prices, with the the comment that the sale was 'too big for you to handle.' None other than Richard Green had said after buying the Harlamoff painting that 'top things sell well no matter where they're sold.' I did believe that with special publicity, and by staffing-up for porters and security, we could have coped. Perhaps Tom Howarth was right, but it is always painful to see a large job slip away when one had been close to it for many years.

I even dreamt about it:

> '... in the offices of the NGS, an apartment is designated to me (in Californian-ryokan style, panelled, parquet floor, leafy views) where I am to wait for Mr Clifford. I am offered pyjamas: it could be a long wait. I am regarded as someone who's not quite *comme il faut* by the secretaries. Two minor characters: a little cowed cleaning lady who whispers to me 'It's not right what they've done to you' and a short blond young man sumptuously got up like a Knight of the Thistle influenced by Bonnie Prince Charlie (plenty of rococo jewellery with his kilt) who emerges from a conference in the director's suite. I become restless and ask for Tim. I am informed in hushed tones that he is now sleeping. I plan to suggest that the meeting eventually takes place in my rooms, which I think might be suitably impressive, until I remember that I'm only a visitor there, just one more transient supplicant at court ...'

Clearly the situation was beginning to get to me. It's not Kafka, or rather it's Edinburgh Kafka, with eighteenth-century flummery added to twenty-first-century bureaucracy. There is something in this dream too of Orchardson's *The Duke's Antechamber*. Nothing comes from nowhere!

The neglect of such an opportunity by Clifford is perhaps unsurprising as his own interest in the byways of Italian art would not naturally lead to an enthusiasm for Mackintosh. I listened with growing dismay to his after-dinner lecture at the British Embassy in Rome and the long list of minor Italian drawings acquired for the NGS under his directorship. What is more noteworthy is that his then chairman, Sir Angus Grossart, who as a connoisseur of the art nouveau might have been expected to lend support to the acquisition for Scotland of the world's most important private collection of Mackintosh, failed to intervene. It is all the more surprising since this was occurring at the time when Grossart and Clifford were proposing to a hostile home crowd in Edinburgh that the National Gallery of Scotland should open a new Gallery of Scottish Art and Design in Glasgow.

The Howarth Collection was finally dispersed at auction by Christie's in London in 1994. A year or two after this debacle I was in New York with the Patrons of the NGS and asked Eleanor and Donald Taffner to allow me to bring a group to see their celebrated collection of Mackintosh. Although they weren't at home, we were very hospitably given leave to look at everything, including the Arts and Crafts (Tudric and Cymric metalwork and Moorcroft pots) but at the end of the scale if compared in the same room with the Mackintosh pieces.

Tim Clifford did once say to me 'If your gallery was in Edinburgh we'd buy more from you.' It was sometimes hard going. Our part in the setting up of the Keith Bequest, acknowledged by Hugh Scrutton, seemed not to be sufficiently remembered to guarantee fair play in the world of Edinburgh.

Once I had the temerity to sell a group of Mackintosh drawings in which Timothy Clifford expressed an interest to the Hunterian Art Gallery, believing that a bird in the hand was worth two in the bush. Tim was furious, or pretended to be: but why did he think I would believe he was serious this time? Ignoring the Scottish paintings which we offered to the NGS (because I don't want to be accused of sour grapes), one of which was under consideration for fifteen years, the items we offered at various times included a painting by Anselm Kiefer, *Die Drei Nurnen*, the Very New Hockney paintings, and the Feininger *Gelmeroda I*. A fifteen-year drought during which we sold nothing to our own National Gallery of Scotland while we were one of the most active galleries in the country was dispiriting. But Clifford did introduce me to the splendours of the Colonna and Doria Pamphilj Collections.

Matters were slightly better in Glasgow, where the Kelvingrove Art Gallery and Museum bought the John Ednie/Jessie Marion King screen from us, and (despite a critical letter I had written to the *Herald* regarding the city's collecting policy) large works by Peter Howson and Steven Campbell. I appreciated Julian Spalding's approach to the Steven Campbell painting which he scrupulously bought through us having seen the picture in our gallery's version of the brilliant 'Chesterfield Dreams', an exhibition originated by the Pier Arts Centre but shown also at Marlborough Fine Art, Steven's agents. And we would have more than our fair share of Museum clients both within and outside Scotland over the years.

Regarding the apparent commercial folly of writing the highly critical letter just mentioned, I reflect that business life is all about competition, which produces competitiveness, breeding combativeness, not one of the most beguiling human characteristics. But it sometimes has worse causes. Robert Graves is right:

> Fearless approach and puffed feather
> In birds, famine bespeak.
> In man, belly filled full.

An anonymous portrait of a *Gentleman Seated in his Study with Geological Specimens*, identified as the Edinburgh pioneer geologist James Hutton, was sold to the Royal Scottish Museum (now part of the National Museum of Scotland) on behalf of Harry Woolford. The identification was made by the keeper of Geology Ian Rolfe. Geology is one of the newest of the Earth sciences, and Hutton was a pioneer in the dating of the Earth, providing, as William Smith was doing at the same time in England with his work on ammonites and his great Geological Map, a time frame against which Darwin's *Origin of Species* could seem credible.

When reading Constable's *Letters* recently I was struck by a passage in which Constable wryly acknowledges the strength of the empirical evidence against the Creationists, who were still arguing that the Earth was 6,000 years old, and for the antiquity of geological upheavals, in his observations concerning oyster shells which 'must have fallen from Adam's table'. We noticed a similar phenomenon at Lourdata on Kefalonia, where the cliff path rising a thousand feet above the beach reveals a stratum of oyster shells close to the top of the cliff.

This whole area of the Mediterranean is earthquake prone: one afternoon a whole beachload of sleeping holidaymakers sat up bolt upright as a tremor disturbed their slumbers, and a tsunami at Myrtos Beach, another time on Kefalonia, flooded the siesta.

The *Portrait of Harriet Dutens* by Sir Joshua Reynolds was sold to the Stirling Smith Art Gallery and Museum at Stirling. I knew the Stirling Smith collections well, having drafted a valuation of its collections for insurance. One of its unexpected features is a fine large group of paintings by the Italian artist Filippo Palizzi, a contemporary of the mid-nineteenth-century Macchiaioli. These had been assembled by the founder of the Stirling Smith, Thomas Smith, who had travelled extensively in Italy and was a friend of the artist. The Stirling Smith also contains an important *Portrait of Prince Charles Edward Stuart* and the *Portrait of the Composer Arcangelo Corelli* and other unexpected treasures like the John Faed memorial portrait on ivory of a child or the *View of Crail* by the father of the Glasgow School, William York Macgregor.

I first saw Reynold's *Portrait of Harriet Dutens* at Carstramon House, Mrs Murray Usher's house at Gatehouse-of-Fleet. It was spring when I went; the drive wound through a wood carpeted with bluebells, like a painting by Hornel. Mrs Murray Usher wanted me to look at surplus silver, but when I found a first edition set of Thomas Hardy's novels it was decided they should go instead to Christie's South Kensington, where they did well. I was allowed to buy the *Harriet Dutens* picture. But initial research was a little discouraging. At the Fitzwilliam Museum in Cambridge Nicholas Penny liked the picture but observed that there was no entry for it in the meticulous 'Pocket Book' in which Sir Joshua Reynolds recorded portrait sittings. But there was a gap of several years in the entries, and Miss Dutens had married the Laird James Callander (later Sir James Callendar Campbell) in the middle of the period of the lost entries. At this point Hugh Brigstocke took up the research for us. The Dutens family, mentioned in Boswell's *Life of Johnson* and elsewhere in the period literature, were a Huguenot family who had escaped to England at the time of the revocation of the Edict of Nantes. M. Dutens had established himself at Court as a goldsmith. Brigstocke was able to gain access to the Huguenot Library, where he found further references to the family's history. He also found an absorbing diary written by James Callander. Harriet Dutens became his third wife. Perhaps he was interested in her fortune, but his interest in her person was clearly recorded, more in the language of a gentleman than a rake.

Once its authenticity was established, Elspeth King, the director of the Stirling Smith Art Gallery and Museum, was able to apply successfully for the necessary grants-in-aid. It was not possible to prove absolutely that the picture had once hung nearby at Craigforth House near Stirling, Sir James Callendar Campbell's seat, but it is pleasant to think so. In a real sense the picture was coming home to Stirling. The picture is solemn, perhaps with a premonition of the delicate-looking bride's short married life which ended with her death in childbirth nine months after the wedding.

The Black Gunpowder Factory at Roslin was acquired from me by the Royal Armouries, which had recently moved from the Tower of London to Leeds. With the Carron Works at Falkirk supplying his massive carronades and Roslin his gunpowder, Admiral Lord Nelson was well served in these parts. I had bought the picture from one of our auction clients. Neither of us had the faintest idea what it was. The only thing that attracted me was its detail: why go to so much trouble if the subject didn't merit it? The picture was on a large board, coarsely painted in dark colours, but it was signed twice and also dated twice: 1858? The artist's name meant nothing. What was the purpose of this group of severely utilitarian buildings, with a railway line and a manager's house? In style it was a little reminiscent of the earlier topographical views of New Lanark by Thomas Winning, but more crudely painted. The matter was explained and the subject and place identified by John Hume, the industrial archaeology expert at the Royal Scottish Museum in Edinburgh. I attempted first to interest the Explosives Division of ICI in it as a document of the early history of their *materia medica*. Not only would they not touch it with a barge pole, they explained that black gunpowder was extremely dangerous and unstable, and more or less implied that anyone wanting a picture of the filthy stuff must be mad. I can see that a picture of a nitro-glycerine plant would be much more attractive.

Cavernous were the roars (of laughter) inspired by another sitter, the actor and comic Duncan Macrae, whose rendering of 'A Wee Cock Sparra' at television's Hogmanay party stopped the nation in its tracks. His portrait was painted by William Crosbie and sold for Janet Wilkie to the National Gallery of Scotland. Stanley Baxter remembered his first meeting with Macrae, who said he would be carrying a copy of *The Times* when the ferry arrived at Brodick Pier, but this was unnecessary as the cloak and broad-brimmed hat worn by the great man could be discerned as the vessel was still a cable or two offshore. Macrae, according to Baxter, never knew what made an audience laugh. He was punctilious as a producer, making chalk marks on the stage – which he would then proceed to ignore when it was time to perform.

Carlisle Museum purchased two abstract drawings from us by Alastair Morton. Morton was a member of the famous Mortons of Morton Sundour Fabrics Ltd who commissioned textile designs from Charles Voysey (English architect and furniture and textile designer) and also produced a notable architect, John Gibb Morton. Alastair Morton had a house designed at Brampton, near Carlisle, by the leading British exponent of Modernism in architecture, Sir Leslie Martin, and his collection included one of the very first paintings by Piet Mondrian in British hands. I acquired the two drawings in satisfaction of an unpaid bill (not something that afflicts the fine art trade much, because most transactions are with people who know each other personally). A well-known gallery had acquired a small piece of sculpture from me, and a week later said they couldn't pay for it as they had gone 'through the pain barrier' into receivership. This makes me look like Shylock, but the timing grated, and I indicated that I would sue in an Edinburgh court, on their doorstep. So I was offered payment in kind and chose the Morton drawings from the gallery's stock. Gentle Reader, would you rather I had been left with nothing?

10 My Camcorder's Been To Hollywood ...

John Cox, at that time artistic director with Scottish Opera in Glasgow, and Bob Clyde came in one Saturday morning to see my pictures in the late Douglas Fraser's antiques place in Glasgow's Bath Street. It was September 1984, before I had my own gallery space in Washington Street and I was feeling rather low. It was no easy matter, six months after the *esprit de corps* of Christie's, to get used to having to do everything oneself and keep an eye on cash flow at the same time.

Bob Clyde always cheered me up; he is an ebullient character and with his talents why would he not be? Film-maker, cook, pilot, pianist and a scratch player who is poetry in motion on the golf course, he is an accomplished fellow. John Cox is a Fellow of St Edmund Hall, Oxford and has a world reputation as a producer of opera. In 1975 at a young age he had invited David Hockney to design sets and costumes for his production of Stravinsky's *The Rake's Progress* at Glyndebourne. This was Hockney's first commission for the musical stage and its huge *succès d'estime* led to further collaborations with Cox.

That morning it was John Cox who made my day by buying a beautiful Matisse-like oil of a *Bedouin Girl* by Graham Munro, in a fine gold frame. We spoke about his current production of *Idomeneo* at the Theatre Royal. By coincidence he had just sent me a letter because I had written to the *Herald* dismissing the poor review

123

by the paper's music critic, saying that we had been by turns 'uplifted, thrilled and moved' by the production. We had gone with our two young children to a matinée performance and had taken a box. As *Idomeneo* is an opera which has some of Mozart's most powerful choruses, we were surrounded by the music like its first audience in the Cuvilliés Theatre in Munich.

At that time I went to virtually every opera at Theatre Royal. Sometime in 1992 John Cox was asked by Covent Garden to produce *Die Frau Ohne Schatten*, composed by Richard Strauss. He engaged David Hockney again to design the sets and costumes, and began to commute to Los Angeles for conferences with Hockney and with the late Peter Hemmings, the very English head of the Los Angeles Opera Company. Since Cox over the years had urged me to do a show with David Hockney, I half in jest said to him on the eve of one of these visits, 'Can I come too?' To my considerable surprise he agreed. So it was ultimately Richard Strauss and Mozart who were responsible for our exhibition of new paintings by David Hockney.

Because of its location, the Beverly Hills Hotel, where Hockney had actually painted the wave pattern on the floor of the pool, was ruled out. As the purpose of all my visits to LA was to stick as close as I dared to David Hockney until he agreed to do the show with us, Sunset Boulevard at La Cienaga was an ideal location, near the artist's house up in the Hollywood Hills. When nothing in particular was happening, the art museums were easily reached by car: the Getty at Malibu, the Norton Simon at Santa Monica, the LA County Museum of Art on Wilshire at Venice, and The Huntington Library and Art Collections (home of Gainsborough's *The Blue Boy*) in Pasadena. One day I drove up the Pacific Coast Highway to Bakersfield to see the 1,000 giant orange umbrellas planted by Christo across many acres of Magic Mountain. This huge installation had to be seen from a car.

On my first morning in California I found myself breakfasting on the terrace of the Mondrian Hotel on Sunset Boulevard with John Cox's brother, the sculptor Stephen Cox, who was also staying in the hotel, and whom I was meeting for the first time. We were joined at table by Liz Lopresti, who introduced herself as a psychologist who counselled the astronaut Buzz Aldrin. Even in Los Angeles it is a trifle unusual to meet someone who knows a man who has walked on the Moon. (I once saw the first man on the Moon, Neil Armstrong, emerging from St Giles Cathedral in Edinburgh surrounded by photographers.) Liz took us on a tour of LA. Stephen and I went for a swim in the ocean, with the jets from LAX thundering overhead every other minute.

The Mondrian Hotel was David's suggestion. It was modernist pastiche painted red, yellow and black in the style of the abstract painter Piet Mondrian and by the architect J.L. Sert. The hotel had 1930s decor, all chrome, black glass and mirrors, a stunning view over the city below to the ocean, and a very LA clientele: the elevator would either disgorge soberly suited Silicon Valley executives, or people in sneakers, shorts and t-shirts ready for the beach; one never knew which it was going to be.

But the swimming pool was tiny. The current Hockney swimming pool (which is not the one in the early paintings) beckoned from Hollywood Hills, and thither Stephen and I took a taxi with a Mexican driver who had no English and didn't have a clue where he was going, finally arriving at David Hockney's house late. John Cox, who had been at the Hockney compound for a week, did the introductions. David was affable but abstracted. He was focused on the opera design, and seemed to have little interest at that stage in my proposed exhibition. The visitors had a swim and lunch, after which David fell asleep.

Waiting by a pool fringed with palm trees for the phone to ring is an essential part of the Hollywood experience. Especially if one is trying to persuade a very famous artist to agree to an exhibition.

For subsequent visits I always went to the Chateau Marmont on the other side of Sunset Boulevard. It is perfect for this kind of ordeal, being set in a quiet well-tended garden with butterflies and humming birds flitting among tubs of orange trees. Contrary to popular belief, people work hard in LA and there was never anyone around during the day. The rooms are quite small, with balcony views of the gardens, the service is low-key, there is an underground garage for your sports car, and above all, the place reeks of Hollywood history. Marilyn Monroe and Ava Gardner slept there, John Belushi died there. David Hockney planned *The Rake's Progress* there. But the Chateau Marmont is marvellously domesticated, just like living in – one's own chateau.

The David Hockney Studio in the Hollywood Hills, by contrast, was like a veritable dyer's cave with coloured pigments everywhere in the form of canvases newly finished or in the process of being worked on. It also contained two very large stage models, one of them with a light board for reproducing the lights which were synchronized with the sound track of the Wolfgang Sawallisch recording of *Die Frau Ohne Schatten*. There would always be several people in the studio besides David who was responsible not only for the design of the sets, but also for their realization. The director Peter Hemmings, producer John Cox, costume designer Neil Faulkner, and David's assistants Gregory Evans, Richard Schmidt and Bing McGilvray would usually be around as well. Gregory has been painted by Hockney in several famous pictures, and there also exists an unusually fine drawing of John. On each of my several visits over eighteen months the opera took precedence over all else.

Back at the Marmont I would fret by the pool and despair of ever making progress. After months of to-and-froing to Los Angeles, when he had completed both the opera and a group of twenty or more new paintings on canvas, I forced myself to allude to the idea of a Glasgow exhibition one last time. 'I've already said I'd give you an exhibition,' he replied. How had I failed to notice? I got the show after it had been to André Emmerich in New York City. We'd done it: David Hockney had painted another exhibition, the catalogue was settled and I was going to have the exhibition.

At the Biltmore Hotel downtown, where I stayed in 1993 to be near the Los Angeles Art Fair, the pool was impressive but the decor was a mind-blowing Spanish Renaissance inspired by the Ospidale della Santa Cruz in Toledo. The Biltmore Hotel is magnificent in a different way; it is showy, glamorous, a setting for Academy Awards nights with the flash bulbs popping. The Art Fair was opened by David Hockney, who listened with the rest of us to a fulsome panegyric from the Mayor of LA about 'the greatest Californian artist, David Hockney' and when Hockney's turn came he stood up, announced 'And I like LA too', cut the tape and sat down again. It was one of the shortest speeches in history and was rapturously received. He visited our stand where we were exhibiting large works by John Bellany, Steven Campbell and Peter Howson that looked stunning, daring and colourful. We experienced the 'Wagner Drive' devised by Hockney which choreographs to the music of *Parsifal* the jagged Hollywood Hills seen from his car, a Lexus, chosen for its quietness, driven by David in a torrential downpour.

Raymond Johnstone having said that Murray Johnstone would sponsor an illustrated catalogue, it only needed a text explaining the origin and the meaning of these unfamiliar new works, preferably in the artist's own words. I persuaded him to allow me to interview him in his studio. The resulting video shows me interviewing David Hockney, recorded by two cameras operated by Bing McGilvray. There are three versions of it, or four, if one counts the original spools taken by the two cameras from slightly different angles. From these two original tapes, the Hockney Studio made a *New Video View* which included a music track and optical effects. The third, most elaborate version, had filmed sequences dropped in. David in a sky-blue pullover was seen lecturing on perspective, with beautiful drawings on a blackboard. It was more tightly edited and was called *A View for the Curious at Salt's Mill*. I like it less because, at the end the frame showing David and me sitting talking morphs into a photograph, which David then tears in two. Ouch!

The interview:

I begin by saying 'This won't be the definitive exercise David, that will come another time.' There is a pause, I'm not quite sure whether he's heard me, then he says 'Definitive, that will come on the Day of Judgment and meanwhile we have got another chance.'

David Hockney begins by describing the sequence of events that led to the creation of the new paintings, which are linked with the opera 'somewhat tenuously'. He quotes Gregory Evans's observation that Hockney has developed a pattern of producing new work immediately after finishing an opera design. 'He thinks these are the most interesting paintings I do.' D.H. had been totally absorbed in the opera, 'a very complicated marvellous piece of theatre that I was very, very thrilled to participate in. I had been thinking about it for many years really, the music I absolutely loved ... it's visual music, it's theatre music, it's meant to be seen ... we very, very deliberately tried in the design to find the music.'

Hockney then explains the levels of meaning he sees in *Die Frau Ohne Schatten*: 'It's about creativity, it's about human beings getting together and making children at one level of creativity, a very deep and important level for us. But it's also about all other kinds of creativity, even creating the opera itself ... one of its main themes seems to be a life force that was represented in the opera by a river, we represented it as a river ... the life force itself is beautiful.' Hockney recounts that the paintings made after *Turandot* at the Chicago Lyric Theatre were shown only in Chicago's Richard Gray

127

Gallery ... 'though some people keep up with my work, not many people see it now unless we make a book or a catalogue and even then not many people see it ... ' and the paintings were then taken back to the studio. Here they were hung while Hockney worked on the next opera project, *Die Frau Ohne Schatten*, and explained that these recent paintings 'had begun to use what I call textural perspective'.

D.H. charts the development of his own thought through a critique of Western linear perspective, with its vanishing point on a horizon that disappears from you. 'That is the one the photograph makes, that is the one that dominates the whole world, actually right now the whole world is seen that way.' He refers to his photocollages which taught him that one way that perspective could be altered was through the use of *collage*. 'I knew that you could alter it, you could use collage' – a sentence that sums up Hockney as the empiricist that all painters are, moving immediately from optics, perception, geometry to: *collage*.

Then the massive stage models taking up painting space in the studio were left to be taken down by his assistants as David retreated to his beach house at Malibu to paint. On one of my visits to the beach house I was shown the tiny studio measuring only about fifteen feet square which stands a little apart from the house, behind and above it on the road side, its front door reached by a miniature electric funicular which David invariably used (holding a dog or two) instead of the steps. Here were painted the *Very New Paintings*: 'I just felt very free first of all and unburdened having I knew finished a very, very big piece of theatre, what would be in staging it, an enormous piece of theatre.' What he emphasizes at this point about the house at Malibu is the presence of the living, moving edge of the water: 'I've no doubt that that goes into the paintings as well.' But as he paints in the studio with his back to the water, and as the new paintings suggest – rather than a close-up view of the water's edge at Malibu – a bigger, panoramic scale, I ask if the viewpoint in the paintings isn't in reality the view from his house up in the Hollywood Hills?

This dichotomy may not have occurred to him – that the beach house view contributes a sense of movement and the house in the hills a sense of scale – and D.H. puts the question to one side for a moment, saying that he 'realized they are more internal landscapes than external landscapes' into which he had put things to give scale or height or suggestions of other things. His friend the master printer Ken Tyler had called the paintings 'narrative abstractions', but 'I never meant to do them that way'. He then refers to their theme or themes, and gives the instance of the early works in the series which he 'kept referring to as a mother and child simply because the shapes and tenderness of the links could suggest it.'

W.H.: 'But of course that is part of the theme of *Die Frau Ohne Schatten*'.
D.H.: 'Nevertheless I did not set out to paint a mother and child. In fact the drawing was done actually very freely and then I would let things suggest themselves to me … there aren't two things like abstraction and representation, each must contain the other. There's only one. I think it's that that deeply interests me now.'

Hockney develops the discussion of perspective and the limitations of photography as a picture of our time. In the edited version of the video is inserted a clip from D.H.'s film about Chinese scrolls. He is standing at a blackboard having just executed freehand an immaculate drawing in white chalk demonstrating perspective. The vanishing point is at infinity. In this view of perspective, the static viewer can never reach the infinite. Then Hockney superimposes a diagram of *reverse* perspective. This shows the viewer in movement, implying the passage of time, and the infinite is everywhere, including the viewer himself. This 'makes better theological sense'. 'Movement', he adds, 'is life'.

What now follows is an exposition of visual imagery in contemporary society, and the effect this has on our perceptions of the world. Cubism (employing reverse perspective) was an attempt to suggest the element of time, but the invention of moving pictures at about the same time was far more influential. The image on the cinema screen though 'has lost a lot of its magic. Actually I live in Hollywood and I'm quite interested in that idea.' There is further discussion of the disembodied quality of two-dimensional geometry, and the effect on us of depictions of space, implying movement and hence time.

D.H.: 'Remember the paintings were made in a small room. I'm living on my own down there, I haven't forgotten the opera, but I am exploring all kinds of visual ideas and really playing spatial games.' We identify two concrete sources for the vocabulary of shapes in the *Very New Paintings*: little abstract collages that he had made from opera set models, and a tiny 'automatic' pencil drawing that formed the compositional basis of the *First VN Painting*. Here there is a moment of unintentional comedy, because as

129

I am saying 'you're moving away there already from the shapes created for the opera', David is literally moving away out of shot to the far end of the studio to find the little drawing, which is then shown to the cameras.

He reverts to the viewpoint question: 'Remember when I live at Malibu I also live with … mountains behind. Those mountains I of course painted and explored in various ways … I do a drive, a Wagner drive that's highly choreographed, the music matches the scenery, it was done after I'd [done] *Tristan and Isolde* … it's all playing its part, I mean some of the paintings do have suggestions of fairy stories. Again that's coming from the opera.' Friends had suggested that Hockney, who is hard of hearing, was trying to paint sound; he thought there might be something in that idea.

I launch forth on a hobby horse at this point. In many of the paintings there are little objects like stooks of hay that have shadows suggesting daylight coming from a specific direction. There are other similar bits of shorthand, like a linear grid which echoes the actual appearance of LA far below the Hollywood Hills, clear references to sky and shore lines, to the ocean, to a bridge, even to a stage curtain. My question: are these painted shadows symbolic as the 'shadow' is symbolic in *Die Frau Ohne Schatten*, where only mortals have shadows?

D.H.: 'Perhaps that's unintentional. The shadow in the opera represents … humanity, and remember technically it's difficult to avoid giving a shadow on the stage … I live in a place [LA] where there *are* shadows. In Bradford where I come from there's no shadows because there's no direct light … somehow the little shadows infer a kind of crisp light, therefore giving other colours and other shapes more literal and metaphorical meanings than you consciously do.' Later he volunteers the thought that 'The *Eighteenth VN Painting*, which has the artificial light of the stage, because of hints like dropping light on the top and the light coming down, the light's actually coming from all over like it does on the stage. But it does in a Cubist painting as well. There's no one light source.'

Raised on the idea of 'painterliness' which is close to the heart or pineal gland of any historian of Scottish art, I am intrigued by Hockney's very controlled, calculated marks, which are the opposite of spontaneous. He will use sgraffito (the wooden point of the brush handle), flicks with the knife, dots, deliberate curlicues. These slow the movement of the eye, so that the viewer lingers over time on individual passages of the painting. Rather than give each a title which would narrow its meaning, he numbered them in chronological order. There were originally 26 in the series: some are better than others, several to my eye are masterpieces like the *Seventeenth* and *Twentieth VN Paintings.* With closer apparent links to the opera, the *Seventeenth VN Painting* has suggestions of a river, a bridge, and above all a male and a female figure, which could be seen as 'the Emperor and the Empress of the Spirit World' in the opera. David responds 'Yes but I thought I would leave it to the viewer.' In the *Fifteenth VN Painting* there is the unmistakable indication of the White Bird and ubiquitous spermatozoid marks would appropriately illustrate 'The Song of the Unborn' from the opera.

The discussion touches on the lithographic prints which Hockney made at this point 'carrying on the ideas' developed in the paintings. These were printed at the Gemini presses in Santa Monica. On one visit there with David I briefly met Robert Rauschenberg, one of the New York School who put twentieth-century American art on the world map. He reminded me of photographs I had seen of the poet Robert Frost, with an avuncular appearance surprising for an *enfant terrible* whose work was perhaps the most uncompromisingly revolutionary within that group of Abstract Expressionists.

We conclude the videoed discussion with a comparison between Mozart and Strauss:

W.H.: 'There's such a strong parallel which Hofmannsthal [Hugo von Hofmannsthal librettist] and Strauss were very aware of between *Die Frau Ohne Schatten* and *The Magic Flute.'*

D.H.: 'Yes, especially in the last act and ... it's like *The Magic Flute* until the couples meet each other and then it deals with the future, and the future is the unborn, the future is also that life force that I interpreted making the golden river become the tree of life, sperm, a force that is bigger than us, greater than us and that we acknowledge, and actually that life force propels me as well, and propels me into this work.'

At the end I gave David a relieved pat on the back. He is a disciplined worker who is in the studio at an early hour every morning. Thanks to this demonstration of his mental power we would be able to offer to 'anyone in Glasgow who has not seen my work for a long time' a detailed introduction to the latest paintings of the most famous artist in the world. I knew we had done the right thing when John and Helen Bellany, on a rare quiet day in the my gallery, spent an hour watching the video from beginning to end. The catalogue was focused on explaining the paintings in the exhibition, but I later suggested, in a chapter called 'Novelties' in the Manchester University Press monograph on him, that ideas are trailed quite early on in Hockney's long evolution.

Viewing the video recently, two things struck me to which I hadn't paid much attention before. As Hockney points out, the 'life force' which is the main theme of the opera was represented on stage by a river, seen first at night in a valley. It floods at the end of Act II, and is variously depicted as the Golden River and the Tree of Life which at the end is transformed into sperm. I must have absorbed this motif unconsciously when I saw the opera at Covent Garden. (I took Moira Baxter as my guest and introduced her to David during the interval. An actress to her fingertips, she loved the colour and drama of that first night.) The second point was the discussion's focus on one-point perspective, a subject which Hockney has researched as deeply, probably, as anyone alive. Not only is his analysis remarkably penetrating, his critique of the limitations of Western perspective and photography – 'the way the world is seen now' – carries social implications which I had missed. He gives as an example of the power of the visual image the servant girl in Gustave Flaubert's story 'Un Coeur Simple' who has never left her village. She sees a picture of a monkey carrying off a girl and thinks that that is what happens in the outside world. Images can lie and perhaps nothing is as influential as imagery.

What did I do to pass the time in Los Angeles? Along with the Hockney entourage, I went to a big restaurant that had roller-skating waitresses. David and I went to a Korean restaurant, stopping on the way to buy some music or books at Book Soup in West Hollywood. In the Hollywood Hills there was a dinner with the film director Tony Richardson and a fat English actor; we had lunch at the Hockney house in Mulholland Drive several times, and also at the beach house. David was hospitable. There was a cook.

I also had dinner once with Jennifer Bute's LA daughter and also with the Hemmings, a haven of upper-class Englishness: we watched a huge 'domestic' going on opposite as we sat sipping our gins and tonic on the porch. What did I do the other nights? For the life of me I can't remember. I didn't know anyone else in LA. Maybe I just slept off the jetlag between sessions of reading about Hockney, notably for a lecture at Chestertown. I remember once going to Arata Isozaki's bleak Museum of Contemporary Art in downtown LA expecting the usual soulless drivel, to be confronted with a huge photograph of Giles Robertson, the Bellini expert. 'I know him!' gabbled I excitedly to the attendant. On another rainy day I went to the farmers' market.

Back in Glasgow, a striped mini-marquee was erected in the small courtyard behind the gallery, filling all the available outdoor space and lending a festive atmosphere to the four private views held on successive days, all of which David Hockney attended. He was the perfect guest, charming the many Glasgow art fans who had come to see him and his latest works. We put him up in One Devonshire Gardens, and one night had him to dinner at home. He is always excellent company, amusing and amused. On the last evening of his four-night stay, I gave a dinner in Devonshire Gardens for David and for our friends and supporters, Raymond Johnstone and Nick McAndrew of Murray Johnstone and their wives. Tim and Jane Clifford were there too, Tim asking with his usual tact why Murray Johnstone were spending all that money on Hardie's gallery rather than the National Gallery, and complaining about his insufficiently prominent place at the table. Without intending it, we had scooped both the National Gallery and Kelvingrove. Julian Spalding at Glasgow Museums had tried to put a Hockney exhibition together without success. I was delighted and touched when he sent me a letter of congratulation.

The gallery looked wonderful. We had a pair of standard hydrangeas in tubs at the gallery gate, which were a perfect shape and were in flower. In the forecourt on the stone flagstones stood three of Laura Antebi's wire sculptures – a stallion, a mare and a foal. They interacted with each other, and at night they sparkled, the floodlights turning the wire to silver. I heard a small boy going past the window with his mother say 'that shop looks nice.' I hope it made a lasting impression, perhaps on a future artist.

David did a portrait of me at Bridlington. From the Charles Heap Collection I had acquired an early drawing by David of his father Kenneth Hockney, which I said I would swap for the drawing of me, although the one of Kenneth was the better drawing. 'I've already agreed to that,' said he. Again I had failed to notice. And another time I was in the pool, and David said apropos nothing in particular, 'people think that Kasmin is my dealer, but I don't actually have a dealer'. I was too polite or something to take him up on this.

At the start it was rather unnerving to be the subject of such fierce scrutiny. Hockney 'fixed me with such a look as he would draw me' as Ophelia said of Hamlet. 'Don't move, don't speak, look at me' but I was also observing David and although it is rather unusual to be invited to stare straight back at another's face for over an hour, I gradually realized that there was nothing to feel self-conscious about since David in a sense was miles away, his whole attention concentrated on the task in hand for which I was only a pretext.

11 ... And Conholt Park

The following year, encouraged by the success of the Hockney video, I took the same Fujix camcorder to Conholt Park in Wiltshire to record a discussion between Richard Demarco and Caroline Tisdall about the collection of items given to her by Joseph Beuys. I had described the excellencies of the Toyota Municipal Museum of Art in the city of Toyota to Richard who mentioned to me that the Tisdall Collection was for sale, but only to an approved museum. I thought it could be of interest to Toyota. I knew the chief curator of the museum, Aoki-san: he had bought several important Mackintosh items from us. As a sculptor himself, he was deeply interested in the work of Beuys, and had already bought important Beuys items from Anthony d'Offay, with whom he had formed a close business relationship. Mr Aoki expressed interest in the possible acquisition of the entire collection.

Caroline made it clear that the suitability of the buyer was of maximum importance to her – she was determined not to sell to the Tate and did not want to use the obvious London dealer. Another condition of its sale was that it had to be kept together as a collection. After I had spoken in praise of the new Taniguchi-designed Municipal Museum in Toyota, she agreed to proceed. As far as Richard Demarco was concerned the timing of the exercise rested on his belief that Caroline and her partner Paul van Vlissingen would use part of the proceeds to help fund the Demarco Foundation in Edinburgh. From the outset there were misunderstandings between the three parties – four, if one included the Toyota Museum, and five if one included the tenacious Yamamoto-san of the Fuji Television Gallery, who advised the museum.

The idea was that the resulting video could be used to interest the Toyota Municipal Museum of Art in the collection, as well as providing an interpretation of its many-layered meaning. Caroline Tisdall, whom I had met in Edinburgh working as a reporter for *The Guardian* in 1972 at the opening in the RSA of my Orchardson exhibition but had not seen for many years, invited me to come to Conholt Park with Richard Demarco to record an interview and discuss the sale of her collection.

After lunch, prepared by Caroline, we trooped into the attic, six of us in all plus one of the Conholt deerhounds whose name was Wednesday. The curator of the collection and his assistant Kate unpacked and arranged the various 'bits and pieces' as Beuys himself called them, which were brought up to Richard and Caroline who were seated at the window for the sake of the light. This time I was the sole cameraman. Although there was a tripod, the camera was mostly hand-held because space was tight. The quality is much poorer than in the Hockney video. We were running on batteries, so I kept fading the shot to save power – only to have to fade in again as Richard or Caroline embarked on another sally. Despite these drawbacks, I was pleasantly surprised by the video when I viewed it recently. Prompted by Richard Demarco, Caroline Tisdall is incisive and clear in her explanations and the sound track makes up in content for what it lacks in technical quality. There is none, probably, more expert than they on Beuys, and the video also provides a good record of some of the outstanding pieces in the collection.

I had seen Joseph Beuys in person only once, at the Edinburgh Festival during the now legendary exhibition 'STRATEGY: GET ARTS' (the title is a palindrome, which is its main justification: *any* palindrome is impressive). Arranged by Richard Demarco, this featured the work of Beuys and his Düsseldorf Art School contemporaries at the Edinburgh College of Art. At the front entrance to the college the visitor was greeted with a procession of sledges with survival kit strapped to them. Beuys had devised a performance or 'action' for the Festival exhibition. I attended one of the three-hour performances with Magda Salvesen. As far as I could see, it consisted of Beuys, wearing his trademark hat and a waistcoat that was too small for him, from which was suspended a metal triangle, very slowly carrying small squares of fat up a ladder and down again on the other side of a screen or partition. That, as far as I could tell, was it; the sum and the substance both. After half an hour we left. I was only dimly aware of an element of Dada which seemed to inform Beuys's work – an iconoclastic use of ready-mades for instance. Richard Demarco lent me a small book illustrating Beuys's early watercolours which seemed to continue the legacy of Paul Klee.

Partly because I knew my understanding of Beuys to be strictly limited I took my Beuys studies seriously, flying to London and back from Tokyo for the sole purpose of hearing Caroline's lecture on Beuys at the Tate Gallery. (Mr Yamamoto told me he thought he himself 'should study Beuys more'.) But on my return to Japan, Mr Aoki, the chief curator at Toyota Municipal Museum, dropped a bombshell: Mr Yamamoto had advised him that he could obtain the collection for a substantially lower price than we were suggesting. I contacted Caroline who admitted she had simultaneously been negotiating with Mr Yamamoto at Fuji Television Gallery.

I had gone to see Mr Yamamoto on my very first visit to Japan. His old-world courtesy belied a fierce competitor who was one of the most successful dealers in Western art in Japan, especially Picasso and the Impressionists. For the creation of the Picasso Pavilion at the Hakone Open-Air Museum for his employer Mr Suzuki, of Fuji Television, he had visited Picasso in his studio on several occasions. It didn't occur to me in my naivety to make him a financial partner in the Beuys matter, although he himself told me of his ties with Anthony d'Offay, who had made himself the most important dealer in the huge Beuys market, not least in Japan. I was later to learn of the scarcely less close ties d'Offay enjoyed with the chief curator at the Toyota Museum, who had bought major items by Anselm Kiefer and Beuys for the museum. It was hard to avoid the impression that Mr Yamamoto, having realized that I was not about to offer him commission, had effectively thrown a spanner in the works.

But Caroline affirmed at an emergency meeting at her riverside house in Chiswick that she supported my approach to the sale and gave me a letter to Mr Yamamoto and Toyota Museum certifying that I was her sole agent. Mr Aoki consented to my price of £1 million plus, announcing at the same time that he felt his agent had 'lost his face'. All seemed to be well – until Caroline changed her mind again and announced that she did not want to sell the collection after all.

I then received a Christmas card from Caroline 'with love from Paul and Caroline' with a Yoko Ono-influenced message about 'you make the future' alongside a less charming one stating that she did not want me to do anything more about selling the

Beuys material. No reason was given. I didn't think this was what Christmas cards were for. If this was a thoughtless act it had exactly the same effect as a malicious one. It was now my turn to lose face with Toyota Museum, who cancelled at the last minute the journey from Toyota to London on which their curator of paintings was about to embark. So as with the Hockney exhibition we made no sale.

At one point during the video shoot in the attic at Conholt Park, Paul appeared with his deerhounds, making a joke about stopping the dogs eating the collection. I am not sure how sorry I would have been if that had happened. It would have been an example of thoughtlessness on the part of the dogs, I guess. That we got as far as we did was probably more of an achievement than we realized, but to fail so close to the finish was a great frustration. So the only creditable result of the saga is the video.

The interview:

The video begins with the Beuys Collection being unwrapped and taken out of various boxes in the attic. The first objects requested by Caroline are a grey felt hat by Lock of Piccadilly (with its hatbox) and a pair of well-worn leather boots. These had belonged to Beuys, and had been chosen by him, like everything else in the collection, as items which taken all together would represent all the themes of his *oeuvre* in miniature. Thus the hat and boots are not only personal mementos, they are emblems of the artist's work, mental and physical. In this they are like the palette motif employed by Kiefer which symbolizes the vulnerability of art and the artist. C.T. points out that they also symbolize the earth and heaven, and the energy flow between the two. But they also *protect* the artist in his work: the hat was a kind of helmet (Richard Demarco). In fact Beuys wore a hat constantly for the practical reason that its warmth protected an old shrapnel wound in his cranium. Felt is a compressed, not woven, material and is an effective insulator. C.T. remembers that Beuys would jokingly say that the hat was 'for the next time' and that 'the hat could do it all on its own'. It had become his trademark, like Dali's moustaches. The boots were the ones Beuys wore in his action titled *Coyote* performed in New York.

Then two less accessible but still familiar items are discussed: 'Irish Energies' from 'The Secret Block for a Secret Person in Ireland' exhibition, Irish peat briquettes with Irish butter sandwiched between them; and a small square of grey felt impregnated with butter upon which are laid two toenails from Beuys's own big toes. The peat is an obvious source of compressed energy – Beuys is 'constantly amazed and delighted by the way nature helps you to survive and helped him to survive' (R.D.). Again, the reference to survival is biographical. It is well known that Beuys crash-landed his aircraft and, dreadfully burned and wounded, was found by Magyar tribespeople who coated his burns with fat and wrapped him in insulating felt. These materials saved his life and occupy a central place in his work. The toenails are explained (C.T.) as an example of Beuys as shaman. The shaman gives away parts of himself as a means of conveying his strength to others. C.T. recollects that the artist would call such pieces his 'pocket money'.

There ensues talk about the materials chosen by Beuys – felt, fat, peat – which play with the conventions of sculpture. C.T. describes the work as containing the universals of all religions, including Buddhism and Shinto. R.D. refers to the idea of transubstantiation and C.T. agreeing warns that this is only a starting point as the work eludes attempts to appropriate it to any single religion.

Next is a group of three more items from 'The Secret Block for a Secret Person in Ireland' exhibition. C.T. says that to Beuys there were only *questions* and *secrets*. First is shown the manuscript of the catalogue in Beuys's hand of all the exhibited items. Then, a saucer with a squeezed-out tube of UHU glue which was used to mount the watercolours in the show, the first big exhibition of his work outside Germany. R.D. comments on the beauty of the saucer with the tube, and compares it to the 'Poor House Door' piece – now in Mönchengladbach's Museum Abteiberg – which similarly relies on a found object. Here there are echoes of the Boyle Family's discovery of the unexpected beauty of the most ordinary fragments of man-made streetscape chosen at random. Lastly, there is a two-piece work called 'Northern Irish Tongue', which juxtaposes a tongue-shaped fragment from a bombed building with a photographic negative of an image of Beuys with bullet holes through it. The negative is from his *Coyote* action, titled puzzlingly 'I like America and America likes me'. Beuys had refused to go to America for the duration of the Vietnam War. C.T.: 'Very few artists in our time have been able to make statements like this.'

Now a box of Irish milk filters, bearing Beuys's *Hauptstrom* (mainstream) stamp which features a Greek cross, elicits from C.T. a comparison with the Celtic carved crosses at Newgrange, then, prompted by R.D., an exposition of the cross as points of the compass, or again as a dynamic representation of the right angle, the 'biggest man-made holder of energy'. Filtration was a key idea in Beuys's thought, we are told.

'The Samurai Sword is a Blutwurst' is the title of another work, a piece of German sausage carved to resemble the broken-off top of a sword blade. Beuys was in awe of the steelmaking skills of the Shinto armourers. I wonder (silently as behoves a cameraman) if the presence of the idea of 'blood' in the title is in some way anti-war. C.T.: 'an extraordinarily powerful little object'.

Next we focus on another assemblage, the 'Secrets Box', a well-travelled little leather suitcase into which Beuys would put objects as they occurred to him: sulphur tablets (for making wine); two acorns (reminding us of his great '7,000 Oaks' project); a piece of Irish seaweed ('there would have been no famines if the Irish had used seaweed'); a wooden wedge representing *in parvo* a big 'multiple'; pieces of lead and white felt; a metal cigarette box (he loved cigarettes) enamelled with the rubric 'Flow gently sweet Afton'; a postcard of geological formations in Iceland, and two boxes of *pâté de lièvre* (hare pâté). This last is greeted with delight as both C.T. and R.D. recall that Beuys often said he was the hare, and hairs from Beuys's own head are also found, punningly. Talk on the interest of mythological beasts ensues, and the relationship of man the hunter to sacred beasts of mythology like the stag. Several of the individual things are singled out as being of extraordinary beauty. I am struck by the simplicity of the sentiment that underlies this venerable leather case and its contents, literally something found in an attic, and reminding me of the Victorians' love of personal mementos like a locket of hair, or perhaps like a bell jar full of pretty things preserved that were once alive.

Richard Demarco again seizes an opportunity to give a Christian, indeed Franciscan gloss to the interpretation, but this is again resisted by Caroline Tisdall as too constricting a view. This time she prefers to advert to Beuys's love of cooking and food: 'He was great fun. There's a whole life in there isn't there? You recognize that life don't you?' 'I certainly do,' he replies.

From the *Coyote* action comes 'Battery', a bundle of copies of *The Guardian*. Beuys said that if newspapers were all that was left of civilization, they would carry in concentrated form, like a battery, an enormous amount of information about the energies that drive human life. The string with which the newspapers are bound forms a cross, and there are smears of the coyote's droppings and hairs on the top copy: 'That's (coyote's) contribution' to the paper (R.D.).

C.T. holds up a cardboard box that had had butter (that most Beuysian stuff) placed in a corner, thus juxtaposing a material that alters its form according to its temperature (butter) with a 'crystalline' right angle. The butter has not only melted into the box, but has seeped through it, producing changes said by both speakers to be beautiful. 'Look at the lovely changes that happen' (C.T.). Viewers of Beuys are counselled (C.T.) 'they should just relax'. To her the work has a self-evident beauty.

Several double images follow two fruit 'like that great work "Show your wound"' (C.T.); 'reality twice' (R.D.). The most poignant of these, for reasons that Beuys could hardly have anticipated, is the 'Cosmas and Damian' piece, a reproduction of an early painting of the two saints who were inseparable and performed medical miracles on their travels. Across this is laid a sprig of *dicentra spectabilis*, the 'broken heart' flower. Caroline Tisdall explains that Beuys called the Twin Towers of the World Trade Center 'Cosmas and Damian'. His work of this title was created in 1974. C.T. recalls that Beuys liked to say that he and she were also Cosmas and Damian as they travelled together performing their miracles.

A paired (as opposed to a double) image is created by a piece juxtaposing a sliver of Beuys's shaving mirror, the silvered backing well rubbed, with a piece of rock crystal of hexagonal prismatic section. 'The remembered and the immemorial.' (C.T.)

C.T. says that the one item which could not leave her possession is the blank notebook given to her with the Joycean inscription: '*Und jetzt sind sechs weitere Kapitel fäellig*' (and now only six more chapters [of *Ulysses*] are needed). She mentions that Beuys read the entire works of Joyce while still at school in Kleve; he admired Joyce as an innovator in the use of language.

Another echo of the early life of the artist is a standard Wehrmacht bandage kit, from the Nazi era in the year immediately before the war,1938, duly dated and stamped with the *Hauptstrom*. 'All he has done is recognize it and make it part of his line of thought' (C.T.). The stamp, apart from the cross, also bears the *Krumstab* (the crooked stick) and the arrow indicating flow. This is paired with another item in a negative-positive relationship, 'Kaiser Natron', which is the brand name on a packet which used to contain lemon sherbet. The brand name sits uneasily with the figure of a nymph and the inscription '*mild und bekoemmlich*' (mild and easy to digest). The Kaiser and a gentle nymph. I ask: 'When he gave this to you, did he say you were the nymph?' C.T.: 'Yes.'

The two most important works come last. The first relates to the period of 'Tramstop', the name of the piece he contributed as Germany's representative in the Venice Biennale. A borehole was sunk through the floor of the German pavilion. The small 'Tramstop' piece in the Tisdall Collection consists of detritus brought up from the hole at the level of the water table which supports the lagoon above. Items found in the bore sample included very old pottery, a piece of old leaded glass, a mussel shell, and an animal bone. Beuys has 'linked' them all by superimposing a piece of tangled string on top of these objects.

At the end of his life, when he was already very ill, Beuys gave Caroline the 'Butter Pots': a pair of stags' skulls, the empty brain cavities filled with butter, the element which always conveys the idea of transformation in Beuys's iconology. This was his last gift to her. C.T. explains that butter conveys the idea of change and of warmth. She reads a passage from 'The Secret Block' exhibition catalogue:

> 'The stag appears in times of distress and danger. At the same time it is endowed with spiritual powers and insight. When the stag falls dead or wounded it is usually the result of shame or incomprehension. The mercurial nature of the stag is expressed in its antlers. The flow of blood through them represents a twelve-year cycle, the mobility of blood sap and hormones, yes, and death. Death is quite a complicated thing ... the purpose of Western thinking and the science that grew from it is to reach material but one only does that through death. If you take the brain as being the material basis of thought, as hard and blank as a mirror, it becomes clear that thinking can only be fulfilled through death – a new life for thinking.'

Thinking, Beuys seems to be saying, is the true life.

The Conholt Park video's technical failings are obvious, but they are like the rain which shrouded the view of Loch Lomond. Beuys – the perfect guest – wouldn't let Richard Demarco apologize for the Scottish weather, saying 'All weather is good weather' and enjoying the fact that the elements had conspired to deny him the conventional glories of the scene. So it is with the jerky, on-off video. Precious things are lost no doubt but much remains. Caroline Tisdall plays at least an equal role to Richard; often they complete each other's sentences. After ten years I found it unexpectedly moving, elegiac. I watched it in the wee small hours in a very cold room in Tokyo. Perhaps this austere setting had something to do with my reaction, but I shed a tear at the end, as can happen at the movies.

The merit of the video is that it brought together two individuals, Richard Demarco and Caroline Tisdall, who had supported, admired and understood Beuys, in the presence of an anthology-in-miniature of his life's work. And although Hockney and Beuys produced very different work, they sum up better than any others what were the main preoccupations of art towards the end of the twentieth century.

12   At The Edge Of The Wood

Although Charles Voysey, Charles Robert Ashbee, Baillie Scott and Edwin Lutyens were more popular then, today it is Charles Rennie Mackintosh (1868–1928) who is a household name. No architect is as well represented in the public collections of his native city. As befits his international standing we have sent pieces to North America, Japan and London. We were lucky enough to represent his few major commissions (Windyhill in Kilmacolm, The Hill House in Helensburgh, Glasgow School of Art, and Miss Cranston's Willow Tea Rooms in Glasgow's Sauchiehall Street) with works which show his gifts in the graphic media, in furniture and applied art, though not, of course, in architecture. (The Hunterian-led authoritative survey of the architecture of Charles Rennie Mackintosh now provides a richly illustrated online *catalogue raisonné* of all the known architectural projects by Mackintosh from 1888 to 1920.)

I was fortunate to see the three main private collections of his work when they were intact; those of George Smith in Glasgow (now in the Hunterian Art Gallery), of Tom Howarth, whom I visited regularly in his Mackintosh-filled apartment in Toronto (the furniture was sold to Japanese collectors, among others), and of Donald and Eleanor Taffner in New York (some furniture has gone to the Metropolitan Museum in New York).

What Mackintosh achieved spatially in furniture and architecture is beyond most pens to describe. In this chapter, I resort to a form of verse to attempt this most teasing analysis (pages 158–160).

The interpretation of Mackintosh's three key watercolours, *The Tree of Personal Effort,*
The Sun of Indifference, and *The Tree of Influence, The Tree of Importance, The Sun of*
Cowardice, and *The Harvest Moon,* is arrived at through the presence of two female
figures in *The Harvest Moon* and identifiable features – suns, buds, leaves, stems,
breast plate, fruit, a 'tiny female figure' – in the other two. This is what I wrote in my
book *Scottish Painting 1837 to the Present*:

> '*The Tree of Personal Effort* whose healthy roots are visible, thrives in the
> hostile climate of a freezing sky and arctic sun – *The Sun of Indifference*
> – wonderfully suggested by subtle washes of slate and emerald. Its leaves
> and blooms, though little, are healthy, well ordered and beautiful in
> colour ... But the "personal effort" and "indifference" of the title are
> anthropomorphic and can only refer to the artist and his public. The
> symbolism is clear: the artist will create and thrive, through his own efforts,
> in a climate of indifference. Whereas, in the companion watercolour, the
> baneful glare of *The Sun of Cowardice* produces in *The Tree of Influence,*
> *The Tree of Importance* (which is rootless) a crop of imposingly large fruit
> which, however, tend to break their own branches, together with sinister
> flowers as large as flags joined to a strange vegetable form shaped like a
> *cuirasse esthetique* or classical breastplate – a familiar prop of the antique
> class of contemporary art education and the "influence" referred to in
> the title. Here we have a portrait of the very soul of the artist in travail,
> personified by the tiny, shrinking female figure of the tree itself, whose
> artistic growth is stunted by a "cowardly" dependence on past influences
> and material reward.'

What I've amassed of Mackintosh hardly illustrates what I've written because his work
as a symbolist watercolourist is nearly all held by Glasgow School of Art, mostly in
The Magazine. A large perspective drawing for an architectural project completed in
1899, *Queen Margaret's Medical College* (our only contribution to the big centenary
exhibition), shows the new building with Edward Lear-like trees and sky, and two
studious maidens walking in the glebe. *Flowers at Bowling* went to the Fleming
Collection; the wild flowers were probably painted at Dunglass Castle. Eleanor Taffner
chose the cultivated *White Tulips* which accompanies *Yellow Tulips* in her collection:
the artist was consciously making a work in tones of white. More colourful and more

geometrical is *Flowers on a Black Background* (the BBC film on Mackintosh shows one of these designs of about 1916 with a strident jazz accompaniment); but the third watercolour Eleanor bought from us is the most mysterious. *At the Edge of the Wood* was given as a wedding present to the daughter of Mackintosh's lifelong supporter, the head of Glasgow School of Art, Fra Newbery.

Some idea of the frequently complex references hidden behind the ever-elegant design of Mackintosh is provided by the metalwork with which he embellished Glasgow School of Art. The Scottish architect Hiroaki Kimura proved that metalwork details are influenced by Japanese *mon* (emblems). For the meaning of the motif we need to think in terms of the archer, and thence to the idea of the school as a structure *on the defensive* protecting art and at the same time *on the offensive* shooting its flower-like arrows of art out into the community. (Eric Aumonier's famous statue *Archer*, which dominates the main entrance façade of the Bauhaus-inspired East Finchley Tube Station, is the speed of the train as it hurtles into London.)

Mel Scott's clock by Mackintosh which had accompanied me back across the Atlantic (it had come from Vancouver and had originally travelled from Glasgow to Vancouver), despite Kenneth Chapelle's careful instructions, failed to start at Kentuck Knob in Pennsylvania. Peter Palumbo, Hayat and their son Peter gathered round while I tried with might and main to start it. Not a flicker. It was kindly suggested that design rivalry was to blame (Frank Lloyd Wright was the architect of the house). Fortunately Ken Chapelle had given me the address of a horologist based a mere two or three hundred miles away in Pennsylvania, who was summoned after my departure and got the clock to go. But the Palumbos let me take the white 'stretch' back to the airport the following morning while they walked the long beautiful drive with its wrythen hedge in the fine morning air. At Peter Palumbo's thoughtful suggestion, I made a detour to Fallingwater, Frank Lloyd Wright's famous masterpiece five miles distant. When I finally arrived in Pittsburgh in the very large white car with driver, my hosts commented 'We thought you'd been to a wedding.'

I had decided to try to work with the Toyota Municipal Museum of Art and the Hida-Takayama Museum of Art on the basis of a long discussion with Jenny White and Sakurai-san of the British Council in Tokyo on my first visit. Eventually both museums became clients. Other museums whom we contacted on our own initiative – and there is a long list, Gunma, Mito, Urawa, Kanazawa, Toyama, Hiroshima, Utsunomiya, Kochi, Naoshima Island, Ise, Setagaya, and Fukuoka to name but a few – were uniformly polite but what we were offering, which included works by Maurice Utrillo, Picasso and other French painters whose work had sold so well during the years of the 'bubble' economy, was too expensive or not what they wanted. It was enough, fortunately.

I visited the Toyota Municipal Museum of Art in 1995 while it was still being constructed, and was cordially received by Mr Aoki, chief curator, Mr Tomio Kitagawa, the curator of paintings, and Miss Shiho Takyo, the curator of decorative art, who was responsible for everything to do with Mackintosh, for whose work she had a deep regard, indeed a passion. Miss Takyo curated the inaugural exhibition of the museum, a small display of Mackintosh, the chief exhibits being two versions of the Argyle Steet Tea Rooms high-back chair designed by Mackintosh for Miss Cranston which had been acquired by Toyota from the Howarth sale.

The theme of passion can seldom have been better illustrated than when I sold to Toyota Museum one of the pair of hall chairs from Windyhill, the house originally designed by Mackintosh for his friend and faithful patron William Davidson. The chair was owned by the actress Gudrun Ure, who once played Desdemona opposite Orson Welles's Othello in London's West End. (In the bedchamber scene, Miss Ure was virtually strangled for real every night by the great actor.) Daughter of Alan Ure, who owned Windyhill, Gudrun Ure during her career as an actress was a contemporary of my aunt and uncle, Moira Robertson and Stanley Baxter, at Glasgow Citizens' Theatre Company. At the age of nine I had actually met her at the Citizens' Theatre backstage after a performance of *The Tintock Cup*. Her father, the self-appointed guardian of the secrets of Windyhill, admitted me as a visitor, having turned Tom Howarth away.

I initially believed that the case for the Windyhill hall chair was unassailable because of its impeccable provenance. It was one of two identical chairs that had descended from Alan Ure to his daughter, according to whom they had always been in Windyhill while the Ure family lived there. The fact that a *third* chair of this design existed (in the collection of the Hunterian Art Gallery) although Mackintosh's instruction to the cabinetmaker asks for *two*, could be explained by supposing that William Davidson, the original owner of Windyhill, had later asked for a third one to be made. Indeed, the original Annan photographs of the Windyhill interiors show two chairs in the hall, and a third in the dining room. However, as soon as Miss Takyo saw the colour photograph, she asked why the Ure chair we were offering wasn't dark-stained like the Davidson one in the Hunterian. The two chairs belonging to Miss Ure had a light, natural colour and had clearly never been dark-stained. Mackintosh's scheme for the hall of Windyhill included, with the two hall chairs, two different-sized tables which could be used as occasional tables or placed together to form a dining table, the hall chairs doubling as dining chairs.

As a governor of Glasgow School of Art I was very familiar with the two tables from Windyhill, because they had been given to the school by William Davidson and had come directly from the house. For years they stood in the so-called Mackintosh Room of Glasgow School of Art, where board meetings were always held. I conducted a long campaign to have these two very valuable tables moved to the safety of the Museum room in the School of Art partly because I had noticed that the green-stained oak had lost most of its colour on the table tops through decades of wiping. The green stain had the flimsiness of wash rather than the permanence of stain. We examined the Ure chairs again and sure enough, both bore traces of green, which was also visible in the photographs we had sent to Japan. Furthermore, Mackintosh's own watercolour drawings for the tables and the hall chairs were in green wash – an indication of how he wished them to be finished. Other pieces designed by him at this period around 1900 were also given a green wash.

To verify this, Miss Takyo took a flight from Nagoya to the Art Institute of Chicago, where Mackintosh's drawing for the chairs was on exhibition alongside the Hunterian chair, and she was convinced that all the evidence suggested that the true original colour of our chair was neither natural nor brown-stained, but green-washed oak, as indicated in the drawing. The hall chairs are armchairs and had a dual role: they could be stood against the wall or occupy opposite ends of either or both of the hall tables. In either case, a dark stain would have been incongruous as it would have clashed with the green-finished tables. A dark brown, on the other hand, was a more likely colour for dining-room furniture by Mackintosh at this time, and so would have been a suitable finish for the third chair photographed by Annan in the dining room of Windyhill. An Annan photograph suggests that the hall chairs are the same colour as the tables.

The effort involved in actually dealing in Mackintosh pieces can concentrate the mind wonderfully. The next stage was to ship the chair, in a special wooden case, to the Toyota Municipal Museum of Art on approval. As this cost something in the region of £10,000 including insurance, it was a somewhat stress-inducing experience, despite reassurances that the museum committee normally approved items selected for review on the museum's premises. Also, the museum gave permission to have a replica rush drop-in seat made for the chair, because the old one was very worn. To Japanese eyes old rush, like old tatami, would look unseemly. The rush used by Piers Kettlewell Cabinetmakers in Glasgow was slightly coarser than the original, which could not be matched from any source: a pity, since the rush was a subtle part of the design. The seat had expanded microscopically in transit and had to be coaxed into place when the chair was unpacked in the Toyota museum.

Some days after the delivery of the chair, the telephone rang in Tokyo. It was the museum, with the committee's verdict. The conversation in Japanese was interminably long and seemed very downbeat. Finally though, Miss Takyo raised her arm and made a fist. I made an expecting-the-worst thumbs-down sign to which she replied with: thumb up! Toyota had acquired a masterpiece; and we had sold what was then the most expensive twentieth-century chair on record. I wrote something about the complexity of this simple-seeming chair in my poem *The Rectitude of Chairs*.

The ever-exigent Toyota Museum asked us to repatriate to Britain a large fragment of a stencilled wall covering by Mackintosh because its import papers for Japan customs were not quite in order. We complied, made the necessary adjustment to the paperwork, and sent the item back to Japan for a second time, where its acquisition by the museum exactly defrayed our expenses. Here again we found ourselves involved in an unlooked-for discussion with the museum regarding the colouring of the stencils. This time we were indebted to Roger Billcliffe for an argument based on the characteristics of the orthochromatic film used by Annan to make the early black-and-white photographs, which were the only record of the interior of 14 Kingsborough Gardens (in which Mackintosh had created the stencilled wall). Miss Takyo told us that this item, like the mantel clock with its replacement hands, would become part of their Mackintosh Study Collection. The museum also purchased some books from us with covers designed by Mackintosh for Walter Blackie. But with the advent of a new committee, and particularly a mayor who was more interested in civic projects that had nothing to do with Western art, relations were abruptly broken off.

A large garden seat with a wave-pattern back from The Hill House, or rather from its garden, became part of the gallery furniture. It was extremely robust and heavy, but as far as we were concerned it was precious and was for papers, not people! We also had the beaten pewter washbowl from the famous White Bedroom in The Hill House. This bowl, another simple-seeming object, was in actuality part of an extraordinarily complete scheme of proportion and symbolism at The Hill House. It was added to the collections of the Art Institute of Chicago.

Timothy Neat's painstaking reconstruction of the links between the events of Mackintosh's life and his work, and the Eleanor Gregh study of The Hill House in terms of golden section proportion and her brilliant analysis of the great ironwork gates of the house, have immensely stimulated discussion on Mackintosh.

For twelve years I was a governor of Glasgow School of Art. The board work sometimes was more privilege than pleasure. It was no mean feat at meetings to stop the board using the Windyhill tables for the tea and coffee urns. But I was not successful in another long-running campaign, the merits of which seemed to me glaringly obvious but did not excite anyone else, namely the idea of reopening the original quarry which had supplied stone for the School of Art. This would have ensured matching stone for the inevitable restorations in the future and could have proved useful given the damage sustained to the original Mackintosh building during the tragic 2014 fire.

At the Scotland Street School (designed by Mackintosh, but closed in 1979 and now a museum) the exquisite carved stone decorations in a red sandstone are in a borderline state of preservation, and I hope the city fathers know where to go for the original stone for that building as well. However, the museum committee that I chaired was pure pleasure, with a multi-skilled team who propelled a successful bid for a Heritage Lottery Fund grant of £6.5m to help develop and promote the museum.

I went to the opening of Mackintosh's '78 Derngate' in Northampton with Peter Trowles, curator of Glasgow School of Art, and put some thoughts about the little house in lines called *The Wrythen Newel* (see page 159).

As a governor of Glasgow School of Art, my main contribution was to secure the Tetsuya Mukai Scholarship in exchange for an exhibition of Mackintosh works borrowed from the school by the Hida-Takayama Museum in Japan. I had vigorous support from the then director of the school, Dugald Cameron. When Mr Mukai came to Glasgow I was able to introduce him to Graeme Davies, the principal of Glasgow University at the time, and to the Lord Provost, in each case on the basis of an impromptu telephone call. I was delighted and so was Mr Mukai by the spontaneous welcome they gave our self-effacing Japanese VIP and benefactor. In recognition of his generosity in founding a scholarship at Glasgow School of Art, the school asked Mr Mukai to address its annual graduation day ceremony in 1998.

Murray Grigor was the owner of a dark-stained oak chair designed by Mackintosh for the Back Saloon of the Willow Tea Rooms in Sauchiehall Street. It went to the privately owned Hida-Takayama Museum built by Tetsuya Mukai in the foothills of the Japanese Alps at the end what is quite possibly the most romantic train journey in the world. Made in quantity, these Willow armchairs have a stocky, reliable appearance which earned ours the nickname of R2D2, after the doughty little robot in *Star Wars*. Its simplicity belies a subtle purity of rectilinear geometry; it seems less wilful, more a spirited play of abstract form, than the exactly contemporary chair by Frank Lloyd Wright. My poem *Timelessness* (see page 158) suggests this chair's – timelessness.

The same museum also purchased from us one of the sculptured plaster panels taken from the Willow Tea Rooms in 1978. It is the subject of one of the most perfect of all Mackintosh's drawings in which he has used an architect's steel ruler for the curves (Hunterian Art Gallery). I couriered the fragile and heavy panel, measuring over two metres square in its case, from Heathrow to Narita via Alaska, sitting behind the pilot of the JAL 747 freight plane. The conversation in the cockpit was a little surreal. 'How is the weather over Siberia today, Captain?' 'We're not going to Siberia, we're going to Alaska. What is so valuable that you need to travel with it?' 'A big wedding cake.' For takeoff and landing, the cockpit crew of three has one hand each on the joystick. The crate containing the panel was placed in its own container. The purpose of a courier is to make the handlers of a work of art more nervous, or rather more alert. I marvelled at the skill of the forklift driver who could lift the crate into the container with great delicacy, and wondered if he would have been quite so delicate if I hadn't been there. It was then roller-bedded onto a low transporter and hoisted by a scissors lift into the entrance to the 747 hold in the nose of the plane under the cockpit. Once inside, the crate was moved on rails and clamped in position for the flight.

I was the courier, but the courier had to have a minder in case he insisted on being flown somewhere else or otherwise made a nuisance of himself. There were only four of us, plus the minder, on the Boeing 747. It was night time, and three of us five were flying the aircraft. My minder was a young man from the airline who was going to fly straight home again to London after arriving at Narita. His mode of address to the two Japanese pilots, who were half his size but many times more qualified to be in the plane, was embarrassingly matey. The other member of the crew was the engineer. He was Italian and his job was to make sure the four engines were all turning at approximately the same rpm. He had so many controls to watch that his chair travelled on a track for him to read the array of dials. He explained that the JAL custom is to assign each individual aircraft to the same four maintenance engineers, whose names are recorded in a plaque on the aircraft, in the same way that Aston Martin cars are signed by the team that built them. Anchorage was like a very large mock-up for *Ice Station Zebra*, the runway continuously cleared by teams of giant snowploughs under great arc lights. The return journey by passenger plane over Siberia was almost an anticlimax.

The panel was destined to be finally fixed in place in the reconstruction of the dining room for the House of an Art Lover made by Piers Kettlewell Cabinetmakers in Glasgow. The whole room was shipped to Japan in time for the opening of the new museum in brilliant sunshine, with bands playing the national anthems of the two countries, a piper, a ribbon-cutting ceremony, a sake barrel ceremony (opening with wooden mallets), toasts drunk in sake, and a kabuki performance afterwards. The hospitality was not merely lavish, it was done with taste and above all with great consideration for the foreign guests. In fact, it was princely. The Western curators, including me, were interviewed for national television by NHK. Mr Mukai wondered why I hadn't taken photographs of the journey.

The British embassy had been silent on the subject. In a rare case of blatant lobbying I described Tetsuya Mukai's remarkable generosity to Glasgow School of Art and mentioned to the British ambassador to the UN, at a New York party, that we could get no official British response, in what was after all the Year of Britain in Japan. Magically

H.M. Consul came from Osaka and made a speech in fluent Japanese at the opening. The ambassador in Tokyo, Sir Michael Wright, contributed a message to the catalogue. Perhaps I should lobby more often.

A second panel from the Willow Tea Rooms was sold to the Royal Scottish Museum where it joined two large panels (designed and painted by Alf Webster, Scottish stained glass artist and master-craftsman, for James Craig's Tea Room in Sauchiehall Street) which we had sold to them. The Webster panels had been straightforward; Hugh Cheape of the Royal Scottish Museum (latterly Head of the Scottish Material Culture Research Centre, National Museums Scotland) was enthusiastic about rescuing these fragments of Glasgow Tea Room history. The Willow Panel was a more complicated affair. We had X-ray photographs taken (through the courtesy of Glasgow Dental Hospital, who brought their heavy X-ray equipment into the gallery). The beautiful large-scale X-ray photographs gave a clear picture of the internal construction of the panels, and proved that they were 'right'. The Royal Scottish Museum wished to augment their funds with a grant from the National Art Collections Fund. But the NACF's assessor declined to recommend a grant, without seeing either the panel or the X-ray. The Royal Scottish Museum and I had been confident of the outcome of the grant application, and the museum now had to reschedule the purchase, which was delayed for nine months while the museum assembled the required £90,000 (which, like the Hida-Takayama panel, included a museum discount of 10%). The delay was unwelcome but we got there in the end.

The third and last panel from the Willow Tea Rooms was sold to David Thomson in 2007. The best preserved of the original panels, it had been used to make the mould from which the panels of the restored Willow Tea Rooms were produced. It had been strengthened behind for this reason but it remained the closest of the three panels to Mackintosh's original idea.

Other examples of Mackintosh included his tall rectangular flower holder, and that unlikely candidate for pioneer status in twentieth-century design, the hat stand, for the Willow Tea Rooms, which seem a distant ancestor of the Solow Building at 9 West 57th Street, Manhattan by Skidmore, Owings and Merrill. Even if this were to be repudiated as a source by the architects, it makes no difference to my view that the formal vocabulary underlying aspects of their work is undeniably present in Mackintosh on a small scale from an early stage. It would not be the first time a monumental design first saw the light of day as something little. The Philippe Starck design for the giant head of beer at the top of one of the two large buildings that make up the Asahi Breweries headquarters in Tokyo, began life as a design for a door handle.

The unworldly George Smith was kind enough to suggest another active Mackintosh collector to me. Stewart Grimshaw (partner of the late Simon Sainsbury, philanthropist and art collector, and Honorary President of the Glasgow School of Art) bought several items which had come from Gudrun Ure, including four white metal lamp shades which were a rare if not unique example of design potentially aimed at a volume market (they reappear in several of Mackintosh's interior designs) although no more than perhaps a dozen were ever made. The Hunterian Art Gallery, which houses one of the most interesting collections of Mackintosh, bought several of his working drawings for Glasgow School of Art. A rare coloured menu by Margaret Macdonald for Miss Cranston's White Cockade Tea Room (at the 1911 Scottish Exhibition of National History, Art and Industry held in Kelvingrove Park) was bought by Tom and Kara Conti.

The hold of Mackintosh on the public imagination has not abated since the Edinburgh Festival of 1968. This is true also of a few of the figures who were his contemporaries, like John Ednie. Ednie is best known as the architect of the Arts and Crafts house at 11 Whittinghame Drive, for many years lived in by the late Sir Henry (Harry) Jefferson Barnes, a former director of Glasgow School of Art. Ednie also designed furniture for Wylie & Lochhead. We sold his masterpiece, a three-part carved screen with silver embellishments which contained elaborate drawings on vellum by Jessie Marion King, to Kelvingrove Art Gallery in 1985. This, and a brass and enamelled alms dish designed by Elizabeth Mary Watt, were the first items of decorative or applied art we handled.

A rare item we sold was a small wooden figure carved by Peter Wylie Davidson in a Vorticist style, very unlike the 1900s manner which he seems to have retained during most of his career as head of design at Glasgow School of Art. Davidson was also the author of a *Treatise on Metalwork* in which he illustrated the famous 'Swallows' choker in silver, silver wire and seed pearls, believed to have been designed by Mackintosh. We had this lovely piece, and a silver brooch by Herbert MacNair, husband of Frances

MacNair. They belonged to the Rowats, Fra Newbery's wife's family. I was easily beguiled by such gewgaws!

An exhibition at the Cooper Hewitt Museum in New York and at the V&A in London provided a reassessment of the work of a Glasgow-born designer, Christopher Dresser (1834–1904), who was even more influential in his own day than Mackintosh was in his. I had admired his work since the Fine Art Society began to assemble exhibitions of it in New Bond Street, and I had seen examples of Dresser's work in the collection of Andrew McIntosh Patrick, who was acquiring ceramics as well as metalwork and had some capital pieces, including the celebrated 'diamond' silver teapot.

Because one of my colleagues in the antiques trade knew that I was interested in Dresser, I was able without stirring from my chair to assemble a nice little group of about twenty examples of Dresser's Linthorpe pottery. This was helped when Muriel Brew in Helensburgh left me a green-glazed ewer in her will, but apart from that one piece, my collection of Dresser was brought to me, item by item, in the gallery. As it was invariably reasonably priced and because I enjoyed a mode of collecting that was positively sybaritic, I invariably bought whatever was on offer. It was used to decorate the gallery.

Then, visiting Koriyama City Museum of Art, a two-hour journey on the *shinkansen* from Tokyo, I learned from Mr Sato, the curator, that he and the museum were involved in a large show of Dresser's work which would be seen in Oslo. Koriyama City Museum of Art has collected British art since its inception in 1993 (its designer is Takahiko Yanagisawa who also designed the Museum of Contemporary Art in Tokyo). I sent photographs of my collection, they liked it, and I sold it all to Koriyama.

A year or two later I was offered a magnificent parcel-gilt silver tea service, made by Hukin & Heath to Dresser's designs, with chased chrysanthemum ornamentation. It had a St Petersburg collector's mark which underscored the luxuriousness of the piece, although the collector proved impossible to identify. Again, Koriyama City Museum of Art was the buyer. The tea service caused a small stir – forgive the pun – as I took it through customs in Tokyo airport. The enshrinement of honourable tea and its appurtenances (teapot, milk jug, hot water jug, sugar basin) in silver-gilt vessels shaped like the rising sun and chased with the Imperial flower, resonated with the ever-polite Japanese officers. As the tea service was the most valuable of its kind in Japan, its value resounded too.

Dresser was a pioneer in the appreciation of Japanese art in Britain, and Japanese collectors immediately see the Japanese element in his work which gives it special relevance there. The Linthorpe ceramics have a timeless quality, apparently unconnected to Victoriana, and they looked quite at home in Japan.

Timelessness

The Willow Tea Rooms' mullioned window to the Room de Luxe
Is an echo of a window from another room de luxe
Four centuries before, sketched at Linlithgow Palace.

In Sauchiehall Lane behind The Willow,
The apparent cottage with the Corbusier chimney
Contained chairs, RB 1903.4, ancestors of R2D2.

Ancestor Worship

The Hill House has an ancestral home
Nearby, at Dunglass Castle.
There the architect drew wild flowers in the glebe
Beside the great obelisk erected to the creator of a Comet, Bell –
That same turnpike, that dovecote, that L-plan, an
Inglenook that might have been designed for talk
About the unbuilt Hill House.

Near the Talwin Morris headstone in Dumbarton
A low ziggurat of stone among the laurel and the angels
I found its twin, incised with a single name:
A fellow-member of a Rosicrucian cell?

The Wrythen Newel

At Derngate, a wrythen newel as counterpoint to geometry,
And a tiny Scotch Corner, link this new house to ancient burghs
And to gnarled nature.

Autograph

The fortress
School of Art, protected by artillery
And ordnance, is a domestic fortification
To the east like Maybole Castle;
To the south an E-plan curtain wall like Fyvie;
To the north, a front welcoming like Montacute,
With huge mullioned windows behind a line
Of iron bows and quivers full of tulips.

The west door's an enigma solved in stone.
Aloft,
Library and Architecture dream
Dreams above unassailable railings
Ranged like pikes.
The Library oriel windows
Are in inscribed relief on the south wall;
At the corner, on a giant scale,
Two tiny reductions in wall depth
Are led in long lines upwards
Over several storeys to reconciliation
With stepped recesses between the great windows,
In the single plane of the pediment.

You couldn't draw that.
He must have thought of it on the site.

Trapeze

The Windyhill Chair inverts the tapering trapeze
of Walton's Abingwood Chair likewise of oak
whose heart-shaped finger hold
is Arts and Crafts
of the period,
instead
tapering upwards
to a flat vesica-shaped cap
which leaves an after-image of itself,
below the seat, a void whose radius
equates in section to the chairback in plan.

Only by this curve
can the outleaning back
optically return to plumb
when seen, as hall chairs are,
always from the front quadrant.

The Chair deceives the eye
As to its own rectitude.

The truth is visible in the void.

13 Kimono

My earliest encounter with Japanese art was a little book of colour woodcuts by Hiroshige. I thought *ukiyo-e* was quintessentially Japanese (Japan is the first home of colour printing), without realizing that other phases of Japanese art are equally authentic and equally characteristic. *Ukiyo-e* is merely the aspect that is best known and most imitated in the West.

Other earlier manifestations reach an equally high aesthetic level: the courtly art of the gold-ground screen painters of Kyoto often illustrating Murasaki Shikibu's *Genji Monogatori*, which is a kind of Japanese *Decameron*; the landscapists of the Kano School whose ambition was to transmit the master's style unaltered to their successors; the realism of Tani Buncho and others who flourished under the aegis of the Shogun's chief minister in Edo (old Tokyo), Matsudaira Sadanobu. These were as characteristic as the statues of the Buddha and Kannon from the high antiquity of Japan.

During my time at Christie's, being in general practice, one had to respond to netsuke or inro carvings, or Imari ceramics, bronze tsuba (sword hand-guards: the swords themselves, which it is taboo to touch, were a deeply serious specialist subject), and other types of object usually collected adventitiously, like the Japanese jar in the David Wilkie painting *The Letter of Introduction* (NGS) or the tsuba from which Ernest Gimson made a chandelier.

161

Hiroshige's *Fifty-three Stations of the Tokaido* recorded the stopping-places along the arduous route in coloured woodblock compositions, many of them showing Fuji-san. I wonder if the artist was influenced by the poet Bashô Matsuo's sequence of haiku describing a much earlier journey, *The Narrow Road to the Deep North*. Bashô's poetry is all about nature, mostly landscape which often reverts to an inscape of his own mood.

Another famous *kaido* (road) linked Edo to the Tokugawa Shrine in Nikko to the north, the magnificent trees giving a sense of ceremony to a journey with a splendid destination. The old Tokaido toll road winds three hundred miles from the capital Edo to the south of the *Tenka* (the 'Heavenly Realm' of the Emperor). Here at Motohakone its passage is marked by the red *torii* shrine gate at the lakeside, where the remains of a stately avenue of *cryptomeria* (Japanese red-cedar) still stand. Near Hakone bus terminal there is a Shinto cemetery plot with very old stones, a further vestige of the once-famous road. After 1633 under the Tokugawa shogunate all the vassals of the Emperor would troop along this highway and through Hakone Toge mountain pass to pay their respects at court in Edo – and then troop home again to their distant estates.

Or was the journey itself its own destination? For the haiku poet Bashô (1644–1695), travelling the unfrequented Tohoku way north, the point of the journey was – the journey. And the last thing the Shogun wanted, unlike Colbert and Louis XIV at Versailles, was a pomp of provincial lords milling around in the capital at the end of their journey. Hosokawa Yashiki in Tokyo at journey's end is one of many examples of houses where the travellers' families were quarantined as hostages in Edo. The courtly travellers were unlikely to rebel against the energy-sapping biennial corvée of the Tokaido. They were not exactly willing tourists, but the Hiroshige prints suggest that at least in the later years of the Edo period the arduous journey had its pleasures as they trudged to escape Fuji-san's daily reminder of how far they still had to go. Bashô's cabin in Bunkyo Ward in North Tokyo can still be visited.

I first visited Japan in summer 1995. I had two motives: to see the country which had long exerted a fascination; and to find clients for our small but select group of works designed by Charles Rennie Mackintosh and Christopher Dresser. I had waited until I had a firm contact in Japan and some prospect of business. I wouldn't have dreamt of going as a tourist. Laid end to end my visits since then add up to not much less than two years' residence in Japan, much of that time spent on travel inside Japan.

Two postcards from my first visit: one is the famous image of the *shinkansen* speeding like an arrow past Fuji-san, a hi-tech experience of the Tokaido journey with the benefit of tunnels through the mountains; the other, showing the Keio Plaza Hotel bent like a bow or perhaps a cutlass blade against a blue sky, was on my mother's mantelpiece when I returned to the Cottages. (She died within a week of my return.)

Beautiful nature as a background to elegant technology (a white skyscraper framed by blue sky, a locomotive by Fuji-san), and using images from archery or fencing, seemed to sum up Japan. The postcard images seem to relate to *kyudo* (archery) or *kendo* (sword fencing). With all the expertise of a few days' experience I concluded on my first visit that the 'the strength of modern Japan comes from traditional Japan'. The samurai disciplines – swordplay, archery, tea ceremony – are as deep-rooted in the Japanese psyche as the image-bank of the *kanji* script is in the spoken language.

In Hakone's Ashinoko Museum of Fine Art a gold frame surrounds a dazzling view of Mount Fuji, white against a blue sky. But it encloses a window, not a painting, and I realize that I am looking at the real Mount Fuji, covered with February snow, twenty miles distant. If I move to the right, the view changes to a bare branch seen against Lake Ashinoko, to the left, and I will see the giant red *torii* arch of Hakone Shrine across the water. From this viewpoint Fuji-san is a serene vision of perfection, its symmetrical white cone rising above foothills beyond the bright lake. Later in the day the mountain has absorbed the colours of a paler sky and, nearly invisible, seems less substantial than a passing white cloud. A tiny sickle moon has appeared. Such views recur times without number in Japanese art.

On Lake Ashinoko the ferries are replicas of British and French Napoleonic men o' war and a Delta Queen paddle steamer. Up in the nearby hills, cheerful little cable cars connect from the funicular terminus to the lakeside. The easiest way to get down to Hakone from Tokyo is a train journey on the Odakyu Electric Railways Romancecar. Not to mention the local Tokyo train that takes you from your corner of Tokyo to Shinjuku Station on the Yamanote Line. Then onto the Hakone Tozan Railway (a switchback mountain railway with the steepest climb in Japan) to the funicular railcar and the summit of Mount Hakone. Let's see, that's a train to Shinjuku, the Romancecar train to Hakone, the mountain train to the funicular railcar then *two* separate cable car rides over the mountainside and down to the pier at Togendai, and finally the ferry to

Moto-Hakone Port. Oh, and then a bus to Hakone Station, the return to Shinjuku on the Romancecar train and the Yamanote Line train back to Mejiro (a residential district in the city of Tokyo where I was staying). About ten changes of vehicle not counting museum diversions. Or you could go by car.

This convoluted, man-made stravaige to a place offering one of the best views of Fuji-san was an aesthetic experience in itself, but, in Hakone, bus and taxi rides were still needed to visit the three art collections assembled by Suzuki Tsuneshi of Pola Cosmetics, helped by Martin Summers of Reid & Lefevre; the Picassos in their pavilion and the Henry Moores in the open air of the Hakone Open-Air Museum, gathered by Suzuki-san of Fuji Television aided by Susumu Yamamoto at Fuji Television Gallery; and the most beguiling of the three, the charming Ashinoko Museum of Fine Art with its anonymous founder, where foreign visitors are given a copy of the catalogue of their choice collection of French masters, and where the fine French restaurant has a verandah with the ultimate view of Fujiyama.

In Japan, nature is hindered rather than helped: or rather, nature is hindered as a way of helping nature. Nature is implicit rather than obvious. Even the celebrated development in Tokyo by Tadao Ando at Omotesando Hills (2005) is mostly underground out of respect for the zelkova trees of the boulevard outside. Tokyo has as beautiful a collection of place-names as could be wished: the Valley of the Nightingales (Uguisudani), Cherry Orchard Gate (Sakuradamon) and High Field Stable (Takadanobaba) and countless other names hark back to the old wood-built city of Edo and its natural features, long obliterated. Many family names come from landscape, not villages: Mori, Harada, Tanaka, Yamamoto, Yamanaka, Matsuda, Kawayama and so on. They all describe landscape in general, not a particular place.

The seasons are marked by flowers. The cherry (*sakura*), azalea (*tsutsuji*), iris (*ayame*), and wisteria (*fuji*) flower in successive seasons, and are celebrated with their own special festivals, as are the autumn colours (*koyou*). Mejiro Dori (Mejiro Avenue) is lined with pollarded gingko trees, as is the main avenue on the campus of Waseda University. In autumn gingko leaves keep their shape when they fall and lie like piles of gold doubloons on the ground. Where we have bank holidays, Japan will take a cherry-blossom holiday, or an 'admiring autumn colours' holiday. Food is seasonal as in other countries but the new season's bonito or the silvery new rice *shin mai* and the luscious peaches are celebrated or rather cautioned by Bashô. These are very Japanese and in Shinto all things Japanese are sacral; religion and religious art are entwined with the landscape of Japan.

Funerals (always cremation, at which the family and friends witness the placing of the departed and attend the collection of the ashes) are solemnized by Buddhism, while 'going to the shrine' (which is Shinto) is normal for newborn infants. Buddhism and Shinto (in Japanese kimono) and 'Church' (in western clothes, white for the bride and morning suit for the bridegroom) combine at *kekkon shiki* (weddings). The domestic incarnation of Buddhism is the *bodatsu*, or Buddhistic shrine, which occupies a corner of virtually every Japanese household. These are lacquered and gilded and ornamented and contain the paraphernalia of prayer, including a little bell to summon the gods. They are also expensive, as is everything to do with Buddhistic ritual. To a Western observer, it can seem reminiscent of the sale of indulgences and the like which sparked the Reformation. By contrast, Japanese households will also have a Shinto shrine, but you would never know it was there: just a toy arrow with bells on it, a charm or two, and that's your lot, all reminiscent of something unpretentious assembled by Joseph Beuys.

It was only after frequent visits that I began to look at the architecture. The fabric of society is interwoven with aesthetic awareness, and that is most obvious in the landscape and how a poet like Bashô and a courtier-painter like Sadanobu responded to it. Yet the building types are very distinct – and very Japanese: the wooden *yashiki* (country mansion); the fireproof *kura* (storehouse) of moulded cement, in a completely different style; the *shiro* (castle) which is a fortified structure built in the seventeenth century under royal licence; the *jinjya* (Shinto shrine) always announced by the red painted *torii* (gateway arch) and the usually more elaborate *o-tera* (Buddhist temple), accompanied if very important or venerable, by a many-tiered pagoda.

Castles in Japan, like castles in Scotland, are fortified strongholds licensed by the Crown to local barons (*daimyo*) during the sixteenth and seventeenth centuries. Differences of military technology between the two nations mean that the Japanese castle is a graceful wooden structure, but with foundations, barmkins, and outer walls often hewn from the bedrock, whereas the Scottish castle is entirely of stone. The cyclopean base of Hiroshima Castle survived the atomic blast almost unscathed although the upper storeys, today restored, were vaporized. Himeji Castle near Kobe is known as white heron castle (*shiro sagijo*) because of its beautiful lines; its contemporary Craigievar is equally, consciously, a beauty. Both Scottish and Japanese castles distill a perfection of national style. (Masahiko Tsugawa took a nineteenth-century 'castle', Milton Lockhart House, stone-by-stone from impending dereliction on the banks of the Clyde at Rosebank to Takayamamura in rural Gunma.)

Walking in the narrow streets to the north of Mejiro Dori, we came across an old farmhouse on its original, unadorned plot of land complete with its own *torii* (Shinto shrine gateway) painted the traditional red. Surrounded by a high hedge and wall and girt by tall trees (the sign of an old property), it is easy to miss, and will surely soon disappear. The old lady was happy to talk and show us round the garden. She explained that several of the surrounding modern houses had been built on her family's land. Many a Mercedes Benz or Jaguar and an occasional Ferrari or Bentley adorning the narrow porch of a new house announces the owner as a recent seller of land.

There is a tiny shrine nestling beside a humble house and yet another hidden away near Mejiro. I found it on the map, but even then it was hard to track down. These venerable little shrines are always a delightful surprise, often the only sites of any antiquity in a wilderness of drab modernism. I found one in Nerima, at the start of the Kawagoe-Kaido, which Taeko-san identified as Sengen Jinja and which Bashô passed on his way to Nikko and then on to 'the great North' in 1691.

The architecture of Mejiro includes two Protestant churches, one in a delicate twentieth-century gothic with stained glass, the other a brutalistic concrete affair. But it had its own wooden shingle late Victorian manse or rectory which looked for all the world as if it might have been uprooted from New Hampshire *circa* 1880. This unique building was demolished for the sake of its land.

I walk to the bus stop past several traditional shops, including specialist makers of *shouji* (painted paper screens) and *tatami* (tight-woven straw floor mats), a soba noodle shop, a *komeya* rice-seller, a bottle shop dignified by the old appellation of *sakeya*, which still bears its traditional *kanban* (carved wooden shop sign), always an indication that the business is an old-established one. Further along Mejiro Dori there is a 'Fencing Company' (sword-fencing), a dealer in Japanese antiquities with a Samurai suit of armour in the window, a kimono shop, and an *inkanya* who makes name-seals. The shop-fronts of the traditional Japanese métiers cultivate an old-world, traditional look, often with the old *kanban* signs in calligraphy. I have a name-seal with my name in *katakana*, but I am discouraged from using it: 'too Japanese'.

The *shinkansen* journey from Ikebukuro in north Tokyo to the terminus at Morioka was swift and quiet. On the way, a huge wooden water wheel slowly turning in a rice field; a house feigning earthquake damage in the very latest architectural style; a transition from the blue sweltering heat of Tokyo to grey mists in the north. One satellite mega-town, Omiya merged with Saitama, two bodies without a soul (except that Omiya has a large and venerable shrine and *kaido* which you can't see from the train); townships of tiny houses providing habitat to the world's shiniest automobile population; Sendai with its castle; neat paddy fields looking like the written *kanji* for rice-field (four joined squares). Coppices of bamboo give way to pines, needle-straight, then to the cedar forests on the hills, populated by monkeys and bears, each rail tunnel opening to successive stages of the journey north.

We are on time in Morioka and halt precisely in line with the markings on the platform. Less efficiently, I manage to leave the presents on the train – rice cakes from Tokyo. Replacements are bought in Morioka, no harm done: it will make a more interesting story. The bus journey to Hanawa takes another hour. It is nearly dark when the taxi finally drops us at the old wooden mansion house. The garden is overgrown and dripping. The outer screens are drawn and the house is dark; it smells of cedar and new straw tatami. Some of the inner screens have been re-papered. The house seems quite bug-free after months lying empty, the effect of the cedar wood. Ikeuchi-san, the part-time housekeeper, has left everything spruce and has even plied her needle. Beside the pile of duvets is her workbox. She has also left a night picnic and has not forgotten that I like the local Towada red wine.

In two days it will be the O'bon, the Festival of All Souls: there will be fireworks and a great procession of floats carrying musicians which will wind its way round the town until dawn. The florists are selling flowers for the souls of the dead. The supermarkets have miniature sweetmeats for the gravestones or *butsudan*. For the living, a klaxon sounds at 7 a.m. every morning and again at noon as it has done for fifty years, a reminder of the days when Hanawa was a company town housing miners, and workers in the sake brewery, preserved as the merchant's house, Sekizen, with its wonderful snow-roof.

The *yashiki* (country mansion), Sekisou, was built 100 years ago of wood, plaster and paper on one raised storey. The upper storey has flyaway ridge roofs. The house's delicate appearance belies a subtle adaptability to extremes of weather, from baking summer heat to winter snowdrifts which touch the summit of the roof. The carved shrine-like front entrance gives access to a lower hall and then to a corridor which runs round three sides of the most important reception room or *zashiki* (a room completely spread with *tatami*). The corridor provides adjustable insulation and has inner and outer sliding screens. Two low tables and three big bookcases with old books are the only furniture. At the far end of the room are the *tokonoma* (alcove) for the flower arrangement and the *kazaridana* (shelf) for the sculptured figure, which, as Frank Lloyd Wright saw, are always in the same position. Tradition is omnipresent. Like the girl singer of *minyo*, who misses nary a click or a shake in a performance of great soulfulness and purity. Respect for the past informs the present. The past is visible, if you look for it.

Rooms are measured in area by the number of *tatami* mats on the floor. At Sekisou *yashiki*, the *zashiki* is a 25-*tatami* room, 10 on one side and 15 on the other, divided by a screen. *Tatami* act as a kind of module of interior design. This is because of the 1:2 proportion, which allows *tatami* to fit together as the length is exactly twice the breadth. Therefore a 1:2 rectangle (the *tatami*) dominates the interior plan which is carried through to the elevation. Whereas the golden section or ratio is the dominant Western proportion especially in the form of the golden rectangle, in which the ratio of the longer side to the shorter is the golden ratio (5:8 proportion). The golden section is geometrically exact but arithmetically an approximation. As its name announces, it is a line so *cut* that its overall length to its greater length equals its greater length to its shorter length. It is an amazing idea and also an elusive one as its proportion is actually a prime number, that is, indivisible by any number apart from 1. It is not surprising that Japanese and Western architecture differ. They are based on different systems of proportion.

In Japanese architecture there hasn't been the classical–gothic conflict. The basic categories were unchanged until the advent of Modernism, beginning with the Art Deco of Teien House built for Prince Asaka and the Imperial Princess Nobutu (now the Tokyo Metropolitan Teien Art Museum). Wood was the material for all except the *shiro* (castle) which was stone and wood and the *kura* (storehouse) which was cement. When Mortimer Menpes wanted a Japanese look for his house in London, he plumped for the temple style, all gold and red lacquer. Frank Lloyd Wright was influenced by the *yashiki*, while in Japan there were buildings by Arata Endo, a young architect and Wright enthusiast who was hired as Wright's chief draughtsman on the Imperial Hotel project. During his stay in Japan Frank Lloyd Wright designed, among others, an Arts and Crafts school for girls – the masterly Jiyu Gakuen Girls' School in Ikebukuro – as well as the Imperial Hotel which was one of the glories of Tokyo. The new aesthetic produced several such designers and it was perhaps the last great age of craftsmanship. Wood, iron, stone, and plaster were still the main building materials, glass technology was relatively unchanged and the maimed rites of steel and concrete were yet to come.

Back again in Tokyo, Mejiro needs to be seen from the street because here it is the Italian social ritual of *passegiata* that matters. This Europhile quarter of Tokyo has old bookshops, a teashop for literati called 'Betjeman and Burton', a delicatessen with as good a collection of single malt Scotch whiskies as one could wish for, a French pâtissier, a ditto chocolatier, and French and Italian restaurants as well as various Japanese ones (catering for devotees of soba, sushi, teppanyaki, sukiyaki, teriyaki, yakitori) together with other Asian restaurants. Crown Princess Masako lived in her new married quarters nearby and there were accounts of sightings of her flanked by her bodyguards in the local 'Peacock' supermarket. Makiko Tanaka, then foreign minister in Mr Koizumi's cabinet, who was at a gallery party, also lived here, as did the family of the old Shogun of the Tokugawa Shogunate whose large house and larger *kaikan* (meeting hall) nestled among very old trees in the centre of the Tokugawa village comprising Western-size houses for high-flying foreign executives and diplomats.

Mejiro (its name comes from the 'white-eye' bird, like a greenfinch) is like a large village in the city. There are little public gardens and a small shrine near Mejiro Station, the prettiest railway station in Tokyo with painted glass windows and the advantage of being on the Yamanote Line, which is the equivalent of the Circle Line. From my apartment I can see an almost exclusively post-war mass of expensive detached houses, The Running Man of Takadanobaba. The few traditional wooden *yashiki* become rarer every year, but one or two examples are still here, venerable but not venerated. Their existence is under constant threat.

The skyscrapers of Shinjuku, one of the four downtown areas of Tokyo, are in the middle of my view from my apartment. (In all Tokyo, this is also the building where the architect Endo-san lived; the spectacular thing is that the grandson and his father before him lived here in this very apartment block in Mejiro in Tokyo). Shinjuku qualifies as one of the four *hankagai* (downtown areas) of Tokyo because of its skyscraper hotels, posh department stores, vast railway station, corporate headquarters, and other indicators of metropolitan status. Its name means 'new inn' from its position as one of the gates of old Edo. The distance of several miles makes the giant structures look almost dainty. From Mejiro, this view of Shinjuku is full of reminiscences of icons of European architecture apparently locked in a private conversation literally over the heads of the passers-by.

The newest addition to the cluster of very tall buildings is the DoCoMo building which has a familiar profile. It is a giant Big Ben twice the height of the original, complete with a finial occupying perhaps five storeys, and a single clock face facing this way via the busy South Entrance Plaza of Shinjuku Station. Big Ben's presence on the Tokyo skyline chimes well with the Tokyo Tower, a faithful copy of the Eiffel Tower (but thirteen metres taller) visible over to the left in Roppongi. Other icons of the European cityscape in Shinjuku include the huge Tokyo Metropolitan Government Building building by Kenzo Tange. Its twin towers are his homage to Notre Dame. It lacks 'Geneviève', Notre Dame's great bell, but Tange-san has provided the Cathedral of St Mary's nearby with a real carillon of bells.

Another skyscraper, the Yasuda Fire & Marine Insurance Building (it was to become the Sompo Japan Head Office Building) contained the celebrated Van Gogh painting of *Sunflowers* bought for £40 million, flanked in the 40th floor viewing room by a Cézanne and a Gauguin. Love or despise it, PoMo can be very European.

The economic bubble of the 90s coincided with exhibitions, very often in busy department stores, which brought collections or artists to a huge and avid public. Musically too there was and is always something happening in Tokyo, usually classical or romantic music. Western performers are prized, but there are extraordinary Japanese exponents like Minae Fujisaki the soprano, the organist Junko Wada, the conductor Ken-Ichiro Kobayashi, and many, many others. Perhaps the wholesale borrowing of Western ideas has its only equal in Renaissance Italy.

It was only after seeing this view for the first time that I understood that wit and charm can coexist with very large-scale architecture. Charles Jencks, who coined the term Post-Modernism, told me this kind of playful pastiche isn't Post-Modernism, it deserves a less serious title: PoMo. From the other side of the apartment can be seen the Toyota Building in Ikebukuro. This is pure PoMo. Shaped like a gigantic designer shopping bag, complete with handles, what could better symbolize the consumerist culture of Japan than a Toyota bag in which to carry away your shiny new car?

The Toyota Building offers further light-entertainment at night when a skein of neon provides an animated display, for example Santa and reindeer at Christmas, pure cartoon art, *manga*. And at night the DoCoMo clock six miles away can be read from here. But the Japanese building type that relies most on lights is the pachinko pinball parlour, which features riotous light displays on the façade and inside bright fluorescent white lighting and very loud techno-music accompanying the racket of cascading steel pinballs.

Nearby is the Sunshine Building. Its windows remind me of Mackintosh's Glasgow School of Art boardroom pilasters, carved like musical notation, in which no pattern is repeated. Mackintosh was producing designs – we have already looked at the humble flower-holder and the unglamorous hat stand – that might have had relevance to the skyscraper architecture of the later twentieth century. The Sunshine Building's tiled surface is articulated by plain rectangular windows with roller blinds. This way of articulating the façade with an ever-changing pattern of illuminated windows is now commonplace. As there are 400 of them on the main elevation, the pattern presented to the viewer is one of infinite permutations of rectangles, depending on which blinds are raised or lowered. The building's appearance changes from hour to hour. The Sunshine Building is not the highest in Tokyo but its rooftop views are still second-to-none because of its elevated site. A much higher new Tokyo Tower, the 610-metre Tokyo Sky Tree, is planned for Asakusa which will then be the latest winner in the absurd contest for the world's tallest building.

Overwhelmingly the architecture is modernist and as everywhere in Tokyo, straight lines have all but banished curves. There are several *enpitsu biru* (pencil buildings), tall and very narrow, hence their soubriquet, emphasized sometimes by a gold pencil-like column added to the façade. And there is a masterpiece of domestic PoMo, the 'piano' house designed for the conductor Shinichiro Watanabe and his concert pianist daughter-in-law Terada Akiko. This can only be appreciated from above. I asked why the building down there resembled a grand piano beached by a tidal wave, and received this matter-of-fact-explanation, as if it was obvious that musicians might wish to live in a piano-shaped house. At street level it blends unobtrusively with its neighbours, so that the passer-by has no inkling of the architectural pun.

In Shibuya I spotted a beautiful little name-seal shop got up like a precious Art Deco box made of green onyx. Architects tend to revert to enlivening surfaces with the ingenious snakeskin or fishscale patterns of coloured tiles. Surface is everything in Japan – *hon ne tate mae*, the inner or true meaning (*hon ne*, the book's content) and the surface or face (*tate mae*, the façade). The earth's skin itself is a thin veneer. In a high-rise building which exaggerates the effect of an earthquake tremor however slight, a tiny motion, like being on water, occasionally reminds one of this constant in Japanese life.

The Sword, the Mirror and the Jewel are the Three Sacred Treasures which are the Imperial Regalia of Japan. They stand for prowess, self-knowledge and wealth. The fifteenth-century sword blades I had been taken to see in the National Museum in Tokyo could have been made only yesterday. Swordplay is one of the samurai disciplines. When a 'fencing company' appears in Mejiro, you can be certain it has nothing to do with gardening and everything to do with swords. In the Butsudan I saw the national sumo championship. All visitors were given not one but two goody bags stuffed with onigiri and other calorie-rich delicacies; were they trying to turn us all into sumo wrestlers?

Nearby in Tokyo I had a family commission to see the Sword presented to the Yasukuni Shrine (the rough translation of Yasukuni is 'glorious motherland'). It and the Yasukuni Museum have the ugliest *torii* or announcing arch: brutal and without the subtle curves of all the others, it is sited beside the martial arts centres. Our reception was courteous but guarded. Fair enough, we had given no notice of the visit, hoping that the Sword would be on display as it had been six years before. The errand was on behalf of distant family; my brother's father-in-law's friendship with his comrade-in-arms Lord (formerly Mr Speaker) Weatherill, by whom the Sword, captured in Burma, had been returned to Japan. This had been a simple act of the military people on both sides. Personally I had convinced myself that Mr Koizumi has a perfect right to honour the memory of Japan's war dead. An hour's visit to the Shrine War Museum convinced me that he is wrong to do so *at the Yasukuni Shrine.*

The purpose of the second visit to Yasukuni was to see the Sword which had not been available for viewing on the first day. The young curator/priest who was dressed in the blue and white robes of the priests of the Shrine did not keep us waiting and we were ushered into a small meeting room and offered the normal courtesy of green tea. He then spread a white cloth on the table, and brought in the sword in its scabbard. It was heavy. I admired the scabbard, which was leather with a wooden lining for the blade. He then brought me a pair of white gloves with which to handle the sword. The first thing I noticed about it, after its weight, was the obvious strength and sharpness of the blade. The only military swords I had ever handled were the regimental or navy standard issue swords of the nineteenth century. This sword was in a different class. The unsheathing of the naked blade was like looking at a loaded gun. There was no apparent signature. He answered all my questions politely and fully. I was anxious to show respect without a hint of disapproval – all soldiers have weapons, and if they're good weapons, so much the better. Thoughts came later about the operational justification for this medieval weapon in modern warfare as did thoughts about the history of this particular sword. It is slung from the left side for a right-handed swordsman, and the coloured cords attached to the pommel are the only mark of the rank of the officer. Blue for a captain. It would have been very interesting to know more about the captain and the career of the sword, but it seemed tactless to ask.

Other elements of traditional Japan in no danger at all of being superseded are the kimono, all kinds of local cuisine and produce, bathroom accessories which speak of the rural not-so-distant past, and the traditional routine of the *ryokan* (country inn) and above all the *onsen* (hot springs which were once balm to the aching limbs of a hard-working agrarian population and now soothers of the stressed souls of the average city-dwelling salaryman and his wife). I was slightly shocked on my last visit to Nikko hot springs (which is probably influenced by the huge tourist trade there) to be offered coffee rather than *ocha* (green tea) for breakfast, and more shocked to notice that that's what everyone, without exception, was drinking: *coffee.*

14 Room With A View

We were in contracting mode in 1997 because (negatively) our old lease was too expensive and (positively) we felt sufficiently confident to move a block uphill. Our most recent gallery, which we had until the year 2000, was at 15a Blythswood Square in Glasgow. Two huge weeping cherry trees stood in the garden opposite. In spring their blossoms were innumerable and after a fortnight's display the garden was covered by petals like pink snow. The Charles Rennie Mackintosh-designed door to the former Lady Artists' Club opposite tells of the Glasgow of a hundred years ago – elegant, confident and much given to clubs.

The Georgian square on Blythswood Hill dominates the city. The gallery was cabinet size and had one large room and a half compared with the greater space of its predecessor in nearby West Regent Street. It was rather quiet except at lunchtime in warm weather, when it was crowded. Our exhibition in Blythswood Square in April 1999 was our first. There was just room for ten of Steven Campbell's large pictures. Campbell had written illuminating catalogue notes for the 'Chesterfield Dreams' exhibition which commented on the paintings. As they originated in the sofa upon which the artist would dream his dreams, several of the paintings had button-backs like a chesterfield. They were couched, if you'll pardon the pun, in a new language. The art-historically minded could see traces of Beuys and of Jain art, and even more unexpectedly, of the potter Bernard Palissy. There were white ceramics modelled to fit the quilted background, which was often overlaid with one or two of these simple objects. As usual with Steven Campbell, everything down to the smallest detail was there for a reason. But gone was the carefree humour of his work three years earlier; these pictures were larger, more sombre, more elegiac. Quite apart from the exhibition itself, which Clare Henry wrote was Campbell's best yet, the ceramics, simple and assured, showed another aspect of his genius, and he later made the bigger ceramic plaques. They could be cast in bronze, as was suggested to the Royal Institute of British Architects (RIBA) in Edinburgh, but at the time of writing nothing has been done, and they still await their fate; which I think should be as splendid doors for a bank. Bankers used to concern themselves with nature and humankind, at least in the time of the Medici; it was not only a matter of 'products' and paper money.

Steven was exciting to work with because his haunted face was the façade, always, of the unexpected. 'Yes Steven, the boiling sap and the lightning-struck man are the subject of the painting.' 'No, the lightning strikes the tree which dies and releases its soul in the form of the man in a Victorian jacket who planted the tree.' There was no better expositor of Steven Campbell than the artist himself. He said it was his fault that it was raining heavily for the private view of his 1993 show and forgave a mistake on our card which misled visitors to the 1997 show. We sold one very large work to the Gallery of Modern Art in Glasgow and another to an Edinburgh collector.

My gallery became a sort of shop, because by this time we owned quite a lot of pictures and I was increasingly travelling in and out of the country. We sold Kathleen Turner's McTaggarts and her beautiful E.A. Walton to Ann Gloag, Stuart Park and to the Fleming Collection. But we were not going to go over the same ground again, to 'start over', and by this time I, being a restless soul, was more interested in Art Fairs. My mind was on other things, chiefly Japan: the Windyhill hall chair was sold to Toyota Municipal Museum of Art; R2D2 and a panel from the Willow Tea Rooms went to Hida-Takayama Museum of Art; and pots and a parcel-gilt tea service designed by Christopher Dresser to Koriyama City Museum of Art. All came from Blythswood Square.

Scotland and its painters though were still in my thoughts, and there were talks from me on the Scottish Colourists at Dundee University and at the Royal Academy, and on Mackintosh at Purdue University, Indiana, in whose landscape architecture department I felt especially at home, because our house in New Lanark, Scotland, was illustrated as a poster. 'Hey guys that's my house!' as I exclaimed to the academic party prior to our filing in to hear my paper.

Strathclyde University's Collins Gallery was the venue for a large exhibition 'A Scottish Colourist' which was a survey of the work of the Glasgow painter Donald Bain. His lively correspondence with J.D. Fergusson had recently come to light in Perth and I was able to publish quite a lot of it in the large catalogue, some of which has been quoted in previous pages. A surprise and delight of the show was that his sons, whom we had unsuccessfully tried to contact, appeared for the well-attended private view.

At Cambridge University's Summer School, my subject was Scottish Art, but soon I was focussing on Charles Rennie Mackintosh and this led me to develop the theme of modern design and buildings. I was intrigued by Arts and Crafts houses, like Mackintosh's Windyhill, Gibb Morton's Lintknowe at Darvel in Ayrshire, and in Glasgow John Ednie's house at 11 Whittinghame Drive and J. Gaff Gillespie's University Gardens house. They seemed all of a piece with houses of the same period in the garden cities in London, or in the Greek island of Leros where the occupying Italians had imported their own ideas of architecture, or in the early work of Le Corbusier, Josef Hoffmann and Adolf Loos. I went to Purkersdorf to see the Hoffmann Sanatorium, to Prague to see the Villa Müller, and to Utrecht for Gerrit Rietveld's Schröder House. Masters all. There were famous American examples like the Gamble House in Pasadena designed by Charles and Henry Greene or the Chicago houses of Frank Lloyd Wright. Radio City Music Hall and the Chrysler Building in Manhattan seem to me ideals of perfection.

The Minamisawa school buildings, including the library and campus, are by the architect Arata Endo, Frank Lloyd Wright's colleague and disciple in Tokyo. Arata Endo was also the architect of the house of the founder of Myonichikan (the original building complex of Jiyu Gakuen Girls' School which was Frank Lloyd Wright's chief private commission in Japan). Edmund Blunden, the English poet, and Gunta Stölzl had links to Minamisawa school; the latter's loom was kept there. Another Art Deco building in the neighbourhood is the Hitachi Company Club. It used to be the residence of Akio Watanabe.

I lectured on Hockney at Washington University, where the photographer Constance Stuart Larrabee (best known for her images of South Africa and her photo-journalism on Europe during World War II) portrayed me wearing a sort of harlequin suit acquired in Senegal. In Chestertown, Maryland, I drank juleps on her porch overlooking the Ohio River, on the Mason-Dixon line . Constance Stuart Larrabee donated her African images to the Smithsonian Institution's National Museum of African Art, her World War II pictures to the Corcoran Gallery (which was swallowed up by the National Gallery of Art in Washington in 2014) and her views of the Eastern Shore to the Chesapeake Bay Maritime Museum. I suppose I must be in there somewhere, along with the Kalahari bushmen and her famed portrait of Noel Coward with a smoking jacket and cigarette holder.

Since the time of the Hockney exhibition we had gone to annual Art Fairs at the Royal College of Art in Kensington Gore, where we marvelled at the newly restored Albert Memorial opposite the Royal Albert Hall. We made a feature of the long sight-line from the entrance to our stand straight ahead; paintings by David Hockney, John Bellany, Graham Munro and J.D. Fergusson succeeded each other in this special place each year, but there was no doubt that *The Bride* by Jenny Saville caused the greatest stir. Jenny had painted a Glasgow bride of lower-class origins and working-class occupation. But she was proudly female, holding a bouquet of withered flowers, and dressed in a veil and a Gossard corset (the white gown was nowhere to be seen). She was big and proud of it. The picture was beautifully painted; it was a masterpiece. It was bought by the late John Latsis. Where it is now, on a splendid yacht in the Mediterranean or in Switzerland, I know not.

In the Strathclyde University catalogue I was at pains to defend the artist Donald Bain from accusations of plagiarism, of J.D. Fergusson in particular, and I cited early examples of Bain's work which either were drawn from industrial Glasgow or from a kind of neo-romanticism, with neither of which Fergusson had anything to do. Later Bain did look rather like Fergusson for a while, but so did S.J. Peploe. Early David Hockney is like Jean Dubuffet – the artist is trying to see whether his own craft will produce the same aesthetic. And so we have Georges Rouault/William MacTaggart, Alberto Burri/Robert Cargill, Joan Miró/Tom Pow and so on. The later painters are seeing how the art of earlier painters they admired was achieved. Scottish painting is full of examples but it is common to all the schools; examples are countless. The Donald Bain show went on to the Paisnel Gallery in Mason's Yard in London where the pictures almost all found owners, including John Reid, who was then Elton John's manager. He acquired *The Five Sisters of Kintail* – a beautiful landscape of a highland village near the mountains of the same name.

I had etchings and lithographs which went to Japanese private collectors and helped fund my addiction to hopping on a plane to Tokyo. Maurice Denis, Fernand Léger, Auguste Renoir, Henri Matisse, Édouard Manet, Marc Chagall, Georges Rouault, Salvador Dali, Léonard Foujita, Pierre Bonnard and Emil Nolde – an impressive list – were all well recognized in Japan and are now in collections over there as printmakers. They supplement in miniature the many oil paintings by those masters brought to Japan before I arrived, in the excitement of the 'boom.'

In 2000 we moved back into the same tiny West Nile Street office in which I had begun. Then after seventeen years Fiona Robertson decided to return to her studio and brushes. I was often in Japan, and increasingly in Italy.

In August 2007 I had received news that Steven Campbell had died in Stirling Hospital when I myself was in Morioka Hospital in Japan. *Harry to Heaven* in his show ten years earlier in Blythswood Square came into my mind, and the Shelley picture on which Steven had inscribed 'Via Reggio', the place of the poet's drowning. His death was indeed the end of an era. In debunking mood, his *Family That Irons Together* shows dysfunctional people round an ironing table (instead of praying together). A painter of *Saint Sebastian*, although his model is appropriately riddled with arrows, is only painting himself. David Hockney thought that photography would have suited Campbell better, probably because the camera is more real and therefore is less shocking to the viewer, who accepts its imagery more readily. Campbell made performance art. But his roots were in picture-making and although he was proud of passages of painting an eye, or a flower, many details, well, he once when I asked him agreed that all such realism was a distraction. Each of his own paintings attempted vigorously to subvert the viewer's expectations.

Steven Campbell planned to live in Italy, and at the time of the 1997 show he had just returned from there with his family. I had to make do with short-stay bursts of the *bel paese*. A few notes I made there give a little of the flavour of Italy:

'The icy air of the tramontano reminds me it's still February as I look across the Val di Chiana below to Lake Trasimeno, but the day is blue to the east and in the south is a sheet of gold with the sun in its centre ...

' ... In Milan's Sforzesco Castello there is an amazing ceiling painted by Leonardo for the Duke of Milan, and a monochrome landscape by Leonardo in which he suggests some vast, mysterious geological formation. At Santa Maria della Grazia, Donato Bramante's church is impressive, with a vast Filippo Brunelleschi-like dome. Then the Brera Art Gallery with the wonderful Raphael *Sposalizio della Vergine*, and Piero della Francesca's enigmatic *Madonna and Child* under the suspended egg. *La Sposalizio* was originally in Citta di Castello, what a loss for them, and presumably the Piero was originally in a church miles away from Milan.

'The following morning's tour ends with *The Last Supper* where my opera glasses were effective in descrying Christ's face, shown on the point of dissolving into tears, a 'face so washed' being according to Shakespeare a sign of love or joy, not sorrow. This painting is based on perspective and illuminated by the windows onto a Tuscan landscape, behind the figures, all seated on one side like VIPs at the top table, which is on skinny trestles, with some of the disciples' feet appearing underneath. The effect is so light-suffused it is hard not to think that, despite the ravages of the salts in plaster and in pigments, Leonardo knew exactly what he was doing when he used his unconventional recipe.

'The lady guide wasn't a model of tact: Judas's dark skin had been linked with the idea of evil 'in those days' she hastily added, too late to make much amends to the Indian lady and Arab youth in the group. St John looked like a girl because he was the youngest disciple seated beside the oldest, St Peter, who consoles him.

'My apartment in Cortona is in the Vicola Rosa off the Via Guelfa, beside the Piazza Comunale with its clock tower and arcaded *pescheria* – there was a fish market up here, how did they manage that? – which leads to the Piazza Signorelli and the ancient museum and town hall with its walls covered in heraldic achievements carved in stone, and then the Museo Comunale with its Fra Angelico *Annunziazione* (which is all I knew of Cortona when I first visited) and its rooms of works by Luca Signorelli and his family, Giovanni Battista Piazzetta, and (another local boy) Gino Severini. I think the Fra Angelico was painted for Cortona because the town had come under Florentine influence. Would it once have been in the church in Urbino? As usual, the label says nothing about provenance.

'The Opera dell' Duomo in Florence is built above an ancient undercroft which is apparently still connected with the Knights of Malta. It is all laid out as if for a ceremony, with insignia discreetly visible. This interests me as I met the king of the Knights of Malta last year. The Museum of the Academy of Tuscany has rooms devoted to further displays on the Knights of Malta...

'In Bologna I park near a sexy underwear shop called 'busti' in the Via Mentana (useful landmark) and take the Via Guglielmo Oberdan to the museum where the antiquities include a very elaborate Etruscan chandelier and tablets of Etruscan script, as well as a beautiful old library to which an elderly gentleman directs me proudly. Bologna has seven churches, the two towers, the Museo Nazionale with a beautiful Frans Pourbus *Portrait of a Lady*, a Jean-Marc Morandi section, and a fascinating model of the old city with its forest of San Gimignano-like towers. Now it's all arcades and only two great towers are left – the Asinelli and the Garisenda Towers. Beside the Giambologna fountain, the town hall was covered with the photographs of the Bolognese resistance who had been brutally murdered by the Nazis over sixty years ago. This reminds me of the Italian war memorial in Argostoli – which I suppose is not that far away. Not to mention the tablet in Ithaca, or the Indian cemetery at Forli, near Bologna. Both have echoes of the brutalities of the last war.

'The Palazzo dei Priori in Perugia has a stupendous wall made of a few beautiful materials, the finest (palest pink marble) used most sparingly, windows and great doors appearing only where need arises, indeed nothing is regular, the piazza itself isn't flat. For the *Herald*, I reviewed the Pietro Perugino exhibition in the Palazzo dei Priori in Perugia and the Sandro Botticelli exhibition in the Palazzo Strozzi in Florence.'

Back in Scotland, in Harthill Castle in Aberdeenshire, I was valuing seventeenth-century oak furniture, glass illustrations of Shakespeare's sonnets ('They that have power to hurt, and will do none/ That do not do the thing they most do show'), and Japanese sculpture, all living cheerfully together.

I was no sooner back from this trip than I was called to another country house nearby. So I found myself taking the road which a week before I was travelling for the first time, past the Castle, and only a few miles further on to a slightly dilapidated Georgian mansion with a very long drive. There I found I was advising the descendants of the Reverend William Gunn, a Norfolk parson who went on the Grand Tour in 1786 and 1794. (On the sale of his diaries and papers, we and the auctioneers were astonished at the price reached. The entire collection was acquired by the Norfolk County Archive.) The Reverend Gunn had also brought back Etruscan artifacts and some pictures from his two lengthy sojourns in Rome.

Yet they gave no clue as to where the landscape paintings in his house came from. So I betook myself to Rome, to work in the Archive of the Palazzo Doria Pamphilj, because the Doria Pamphilj family papers could shed light on the mystery.

The famous landscape pair *The Marriage of Isaac and Rebecca ('The Mill')* and *A Procession with a View of Delphi* by Claude Lorrain, which are now in the Doria Pamphilj Palazzo Gallery were originally in the Bel Respiro villa in Rome on the Janiculum Hill, when it was lived in by the Pamphilj. In fact they were hung, as the inventories prove, in the Salon della Ringhiera (the Balcony Room) above the *giardino segreto* (the private garden) in the Bel Respiro, which is one of the most beautiful buildings in Rome and was the centre of what has been described as the most ambitious artistic programme of the Baroque.

It is fascinating to see how central Claude was to this programme, in the eyes of his patron the Prince Pamphilj, who placed his pictures in the most charming as well as the most important place in the Bel Respiro villa. Although the idea of building a house in the country came from Prince Pamphilj's uncle, (formerly papal nuncio in Madrid) before becoming Pope (his portrait painted by Velázquez), Bel Respiro in Rome seems to take its very name from the Buen Retiro in Madrid – the house is very Italian. Its surface has been encrusted by its architect, Alessandro Algardi, with classical statuary, and it has a fashionable *altana* (top balcony) on the highest point of the Janiculum Hill with a view across the intervening landscape to the Tiber beyond.

This is the view from the Salon della Ringhiera and *A Procession with a View of Delphi* – in case the point is missed *The Marriage of Isaac and Rebecca* painting by Claude shows the same view. The Baths of Caracalla and the old Appian Way are visible, and although the Tomb of Cecilia Metella and the Pyramid of Cestius are not in the finished work, Claude shows them in his preparatory sketches. I found the Pyramid with a final sweep of my father's wartime field glasses from near San Pietro in Montorio further down the Janiculum Hill, and as I punched the air, and as I was alone that day, people must have thought it rather strange. The monument to Cecilia Metella was visible from there. Claude had clearly painted the view from the front of the Prince's new villa Bel Respiro, and had been rewarded by having his two pictures hung in the room with the best view.

The Doria Pamphilj pair by Claude Lorrain and the pair in Aberdeenshire have near identical measurements. The overall effect of the two works is compelling.

The doyen of the works of Claude Lorrain and author of the catalogue raisonné is Professor Marcel Röthlisberger, a Swiss art historian and now retired professor from the University of Geneva. I travelled to Geneva to meet Marcel for the first time in November 2004 and he in turn came to Scotland to view the works. Marcel's initial opinion is that the pair of pictures are later, but still Roman. The paintings will, in due course, be subject to scientific examination. It is possible, in my opinion, that copies of the paintings were made later, by the family or their successors and taken perhaps to Nettuno where the Doria Pamphilj family had another residence, *en villegiatura*. Could these copies have found their way to England, then to Aberdeenshire?

I only turned the key finally on West Nile Street when the building was sold in 2008. We had been there, with a long gap, from 1984. Well, I get attached to places: my daily life goes on there.

Postscript

When a small party of us went round Henry Moore's studio and sculpture-filled garden at Much Hadham, although our excellent guide was the sculptor's son-in-law, Alan Bowness, I cherished an idea of forming my own views during the visit, which perhaps I would never repeat, and so I detached myself from the group to wander round on my own.

Music faintly audible far away, watching distant swallows wheeling and diving so far aloft they were barely visible, I thought, this is happiness. The Morocco sky – or a ceiling painted like the sky; Loch Laggan at sunrise when the frozen loch mirrored the mountains and the sky; the first sight of Invermark Castle; the Parthenon at night; a cyclone slowly turning at Nemphlar; the autumn moon in Kirkcudbright. Such moments go beyond what is visible. They often start with what is seen. Or heard. In *A Midsummer Night's Dream*, Theseus, Duke of Athens, replies to Hippolyta, Queen of the Amazons, who has spoken of the 'sweet thunder' of the hounds of her country, that *his* hounds, bell-like, cry in perfect pitch. These frissons draw us to art and are very like the principle that draws us to everything else pleasurable. They are the laughable dreams of the mind and the frissons of the body.

Art historians are looking at surfaces all the time. The landscape painting which results begins there. F.C.B. Cadell and S.J. Peploe saw the green water of the north shore of Iona, Henri Matisse and André Derain the vermillion of Collioure, Lyonel Feininger the shafts of light above Gelmeroda Church, Claude Lorrain the mists of the Roman Campagna, Piet Mondrian the flat countryside of Middelburg in Holland.

But there is always an obverse side of the coin. Adding insult to injury, I once stood on a sea urchin and then was promptly stung by a wasp. The British Embassy's Athens address was in a street named after four men who had been hanged. Graham Greene territory is there if one looks hard enough. I saw the wreckage of Famagusta abandoned by Greeks, and people-trafficking at Bogaz in Northern Cyprus. There was a marijuana-spotting helicopter at Malia in Crete, and subsequently a marijuana gun-battle in the hills near Heraklion. At Paxos there was prostitution and Lourdata in Kefallonia had been exploited by the travel industry, and before it by the Nazis, like Ithaca and Crete. In Paris there was a coven of ten-year-old pickpockets in the metro and in Rome and Naples no receipts or a few pages left blank for dubious purposes.

Idyll is sometimes close to nightmare.

If the art of painting lacks the element of time, music's power to move depends on the suggestion of an unfolding drama. The Quattrocento painters sometimes addressed this by showing several episodes of a story simultaneously. Victorian narrative painting had a hold on its nineteenth-century audience because it told a story, which implies the passage of time. Some paintings are incomprehensible without their titles. I wonder if art is ever able properly to move us unless it includes a narrative element along with abstraction, painterliness, design. The eighteenth-century painters like Sir Joshua Reynolds, nineteenth-century painters like David Wilkie, twentieth-century painters like Arthur Melville, Steven Campbell and David Hockney and architects like Charles Rennie Mackintosh concentrated on these qualities, and so did the artists I handled.

Art remembers our dreams when we wake up.

Index

Abercrombie, Douglas 20
Aberdeen Flowers 107
Abstract Expressionists 131
Acropolis 25
Adamson, Steve 58
Adler, Jankel 95
Agnew's 79
Akiko, Terada 172
Albert Institute 33, 54, 55
Albert Square, Dundee 33, 54
Aldrin, Buzz 124
Alexandria 8, 21
Alexandria Quartet 21
Alice in Wonderland 64
American Forces Network 18
A Midsummer Night's Dream
39, 185
Andrew Grant Gallery 81
Andrews, Keith 37
Annan, Thomas 149, 150,
Annand, Louise 95
Anne, HRH Princess, Princess
Royal 99
Antebi, Laura 133
Aoki-san 135, 137, 148
Arbuthnot, Peter 63
Archer, Jeffrey 64
Architecture of Glasgow, The
40, 41
Argyll, Duke of 84
Armstrong, Louis 16, 17, 19
Armstrong, Neil 124
'Art Across The Tay' 37
Art Institute of Chicago 149,
151
Artisans, The 8
Asaka, Prince 168
Ascherson, Neal 111
'The Secret Block for a Secret
Person in Ireland' 138, 139,
142
Ashbee, Charles Robert 145
Atkinson, Val 80
At the Edge of the Wood 145,
147
Auld, Alasdair 59
Avenue de L'Observatoire 60
Avignon 23, 25, 104
'Bad Penny Blues' 18
Baillie, Martin 114
Baillie, William 95, 111
Bain, Alice 116
Bain, Donald 38, 39, 44, 54, 55,
95, 104, 105, 106, 107, 113,
177, 178
Bain, Eunice 38
Baird, Edward 39
Balcarres House 35, 36
Balniel, Lord 36
Balthazar 21
Barnes, Albert 28
Barnes, Jefferson 155
Barrack Street Museum 53
Barrault, Jean-Louis 25
Batchelor, Professor Sir Ivor
43, 47, 66
Bathurst, David 60, 72
'Battery' 140

Bauhaus Museum 96
Bauhaus School of Art 96, 147
Baxter, Moira (Robertson) 11,
12, 21, 132, 148
Baxter, Stanley 12, 39, 85, 109,
121, 148
Baziotes, William 104
BBC 19, 30, 147
Bearsden 9, 18, 19, 96
Beatles 18, 79
Beaux Arts Gallery 107
'Be Bop a Lula' 18
Bechet, Sidney 17
Bell, Henry 7, 8
Bell, John Zephaniah 50
Bellany, John 76, 103, 106, 107,
126, 131, 132, 178
Belushi, John 125
Berdin, Christian 25
Berenson, Bernard 36
Berlin Philharmonic Orchestra
100
'Betjeman and Burton' 169
Beuys, Joseph 135, 136, 137,
138, 139, 140, 141, 142, 143,
165, 175
Beverley, Yorkshire 10
Beverly Hills 83
Beverly Hills Hotel 124
Billcliffe, Roger 42, 150
Biltmore Hotel 126
Birth of Venus, The 39
Bishop, Keiko 19
Bishop, Walter 19
Blackadder, Elizabeth 103
Blackie, Walter 150
Blain, William 49
Blairquhan Castle 70, 84
Blake, Peter 9, 60
Blaue Reiter Almanach, Der 97
Blowing Dandelions 83
Blue Note (jazz club), Tokyo
19
Blunden, Edmund 177
Blythswood Square, Glasgow
43, 45, 82, 175, 176, 179
Boase, Professor Alan 26
Boat Yard, The 59
Boccioni, Umberto 57
Bogliasco, north Italy 59
Bold, Alan 106
Bolden, Buddy 17
Bonnar, William 78
Book Soup, West Hollywood
132
Boots 84
Boswell, James 8, 55, 86, 120
Both, Jan 36
Boudin, Eugène 87
Boulevard, Le 56, 57
Bourne, Patrick 95
Bowness, Alan 44
Boyd, James D. 35, 53, 54, 112
Boyd, John 114
Boyd, William 37
Brady, James Campbell 109,
110
Brainin, Norbert 53

Brangwyn, Frank 53
Braque 20, 28, 105
Breton Peasant Woman 87
Brew, Muriel 156
Bride, The 178
Brigstocke, Hugh 120
British Museum 19, 35, 44,
66, 111
British Museum Print Room
111
Broadbent, Michael 63
Brodick Pier 121
Brookmeyer, Bob 18
Brooks, Bill 66, 68
Broughty Castle 53
Broughty Ferry 9, 34, 37, 50,
55, 60, 93
Brown, Bill 110
Brown, Clifford 17, 18
Brown, Dr David 93
Brown, Dr John 8
Brubeck, Dave 19
Brueggemann, Meister 99
Brüggemann, Bernd 20
Brunyate, Roger 26
Brymer, Miss 34
Buccleuch, Duke of 77
Buncho, Tani 161
Burlington House 36
Burning kelp 7
Burn-Murdoch, W.G. 50
Burri, Alberto 44, 178
Bute, Isle of 27
Bute, Jennifer 132
Bute, Lord 69
Bute, Dowager Marchioness
of 62
Byrne, John 84, 89, 106,107,
108
By the Bonnie Banks O' Fordie
87
Cabbages in an Orchard 13
Cadell, Francis 36, 43, 45,
70, 185
Cadell, John 36
Cadell, Simon 36
Caird Hall 103
Calder, Alexander 28, 104
Callendar, Red 18
Calvert, Eddie 18
Calvocoressi, Richard 101
Cambridge 120
Cambridge University's Sum-
mer School 177
Cameron, Dugald 152
Cameron, D.Y. 12
Campbell, Sir Ilay 61
Campbell, Sir James Callendar
120, 121
Campbell, Steven 79, 83, 84,
114, 115, 119, 126, 175, 176,
179, 186
Camperdown Collections
35, 54
Camperdown House 53, 54
*Camperdown, The Victory of
Admiral Viscount Duncan
at* 54

Cardazza, Gabriella 79
Cargill, Robert 39, 44, 112, 178
Carmichael, J.W. 83
Carracci, Annibale 62
Carron Works, Falkirk 121
Catalan School 104
Cathkin Braes 13
Cator, Charles 65
Cavendish, Sophie 64
Cézanne 28, 44, 45, 170
Chabaud, Auguste 44
Chagall, Marc 89, 179
Chapelle, Kenneth (Ken) 147
Chapman, Dave 39
Chardin, Jean-Siméon 84
Charles Heap Collection 81,
111, 133
Charonton, Enguerrand 24
Charlie Parker Quintet 19
Charlotte Square 43
Château des Enfants 106
Chateau Marmont 125, 126
Cheape, Hugh 154
'Cherry Pink and Apple Blos-
som White' 18
Chesapeake Bay Maritime
Museum 178
'Chesterfield Dreams' 119, 175
Children of Lyr, The 38
Christie's 6, 60–73, 75, 76, 77,
79, 115, 116, 117, 118, 120,
123, 161
*Christ in the House of Martha
and Mary* 37
Christo, Vladimirov Javacheff
124
Christ of St John of the Cross 15
Chrysler Building 177
Citizen's Theatre 12
City Art Gallery, Dundee 34
Clark, Alan 112
Clark, John 39
Clark, John Kenneth 113, 114
Clark, Lord 36, 47
Clayton, Michael 60, 61, 63,
66, 69, 70, 73, 77
Clea 21
Clements and Taggarts 113
Clifford Brown and his All
Stars 18
Clifford, Timothy (Tim) 87,
100, 117, 118, 133
Clyde, Bob 123
Clyde, River 7, 8, 9, 11, 166
Coats, W.A. 37
Cocktail, The 95
Coia, Emilio 77, 82, 107
Collier, Ken 18
Collins Gallery 177
Collins, Peter 39
Colombe d'Or (Hotel) 104, 105
Colonna and Doria Pamphilj
Collections 118
Colourists 20, 28, 43, 44, 45,
57, 60, 70, 78, 79, 176
Coltrane, Robbie 106
Comet (steamship) 8, 157
Conflict 59

Conholt Park 135, 136, 138, 143
Connolly, Billy 84, 100
Conran, Lady 109
Conroy, Stephen 83
Constable, John 15, 119
Conti, Tom and Kara 155
Contrabandista, The 60
Cook, David 83, 111
Cooper Hewitt Museum 156
Corinth 25
Cork, Richard 103
'Cosmas and Damian' 141
Cosmo Cinema 20
Cottage in Glencoe 12
Count Basie 19
Courbet, Gustave 27
Courier, The 60
Courtauld Institute 46
Coward, Noel 178
Cox, James 59
Cox, John 89, 90, 123, 124, 125, 126
Cox, Stephen 124
Cox's Stack, Dundee 60
Coyote 138, 139, 140
Crawford, Diane 86
Crawford, Hugh Adam 95
Crawford, John Gardiner 111, 112
Crawford, Cara 110
Crawford, Lance 81, 86
Crawford, Lord 34, 35, 36, 60
Crawford, William 63
Crawhall, Joseph 37, 40, 41, 42,
Crawhall Senior, Joseph 70
Creationists 119
Crick, Francis 101
Crosbie, William 103, 121
Crowd of Birds and Children, The 113
Cubism 56, 59, 129
Cuchet, Paul 25
Cumming, Carolyn 66
Cursiter, Stanley 28, 40, 56, 57, 58, 59, 81, 85, 87, 94, 103
Cutty Sark 8
Dada 54, 136
Daghani, Arnold 89
Dali, Salvador 15, 16, 19, 28, 138, 179
Dank in Farben 20, 96
Darwin, Charles 119
Davidson, George Dutch 40, 50, 51, 52, 53, 106
Davidson, Peter Wyllie 155
Davidson, William 148, 149
Davies, Graeme 152
Davison, Francis 89
D.C. Thomson 34
Deakins, Tom 111
de Chirico, Giorgio 62, 79
Degas, Edgar 11, 28, 46
de Hondecoeter, Gillis 36
Delaney, Eric 18
Delphi 25, 182, 183
Delvert, Carl 16
Demarco Foundation 135
Demarco, Richard 79, 80, 135, 136, 137, 138, 140, 143
de Mascarel, Evelyne 84
Denis, Maurice 88, 179
Denny, Elizabeth 10

Denny's (shipyard) 8, 10, 11
de Pisis, Filippo 38
Derain, André 20, 24, 186
Dethier, Jean 58
Deux Ouvrières dans le Salon de Couture 88, 90, 101
Diaghilev, Sergei 27, 41
Diaries (of Alan Clark) 112
Dictionary of Jazz (Panassié) 17
Dictionary of Modern Painting (Methuen) 16, 17
Die Drei Nurnen 118
Dior, Christian 38
'Dixon's Blazes' 13
DoCoMo Building 170, 171
Dodds, Johnny 17
d'Offay, Anthony 135, 137
Domino, Fats 18
Donald, David 76
Donaldson, David 82, 94, 103
Donaldson, Marysia 82
Don Giovanni 90
Double Helix, The 101
Douglas, Charles (Charlie) 69, 77
Dream on the Day of the Death of Beatrice 55
Dresser, Christopher 156, 157, 162, 176
Duccio di Buoninsegna 36
Duchamp, Marcel 54
Dudhope Castle 53
Duke's Antechamber, The 117
Dumbarton 7, 8, 9, 11, 75, 157
Dumbarton Castle 7
Dunbar, Alexander (Sandy) 54
Duncan Bequest of 1878 35, 36, 37
Duncan, George 36, 37
Duncan, John 34
Duncan of Jordanstone College of Art 39, 95
Dundee 33–60
Dundee Art Gallery 36, 57, 105, 112
Dundee Art Society 37, 38
Dundee Corporation 33, 53
Dundee Perth and London Shipping Company 37
Dundee Repertory Theatre 93
Dundee University 26, 37, 60, 95, 111, 176
Dunkirk 10
Dunvegan Castle 62
Durant, Margaret 18, 21
Durrell, Lawrence 21
Dutch, Helen 50, 51
Eardley, Joan 94
Edinburgh 20, 30, 35, 36, 43, 45, 46, 56, 57, 58, 61, 62, 66, 70, 73, 79, 80, 87, 88, 100, 106, 114, 116, 117, 118, 119, 121, 122, 124, 135, 138, 176
Edinburgh College of Art 80, 110, 136
Edinburgh Festival 20, 29, 80, 81, 85, 87, 136, 155
Edmiston's 61, 69
Ednie, John 119, 155, 177
Eighteenth VN Painting 130
Eldridge, Roy 17, 19
Ellington, Duke 19
Elliott, Patrick 59

Elwes, Christopher 66
Emmerich, André 126
Endo, Arata 169, 170, 177
Entwistle, Ray 87
Epidaurus, the Ancient Theatre of 25
Ernst & Young 95
Errington, Lindsay 83
Euclid 26
Evans, Gregory 126, 127
Evening Hour, The 87
Evergreen, The 87
Every good boy deserves favour 65
Expressionism 20, 97, 101
Faed, John 120
Faed, Thomas 8, 40
Falkirk Wheel 39, 93
Fallingwater 147
Family That Irons Together 179
Fantin-Latour 27, 47, 62, 72, 79
Farmar, Francis 66, 111, 115
Farr, Dennis 37
Fauconnier, Henri 20
Faulkner, Neil 126
Feininger, Lyonel 96, 97, 98, 118, 186
Ferguson, Niall 19
Fergusson, J.D. 9, 39, 40, 43, 44, 45, 55, 57, 60, 76, 95, 105, 177, 178
Fife 33, 34, 35, 51
Fife, Duke of 35
Fifteenth VN Painting 131
Figgess, Sir John 64
Fine Art Society, London 40, 41, 156
The First Cloud 46
First VN Painting 129
Fischer Fine Art 63
Fitzgerald, Ella 19
Fitzwilliam Museum, Cambridge 120
Five Sisters of Kintail, The 178
Flaubert, Gustave 132
Flaxman, John 182
Fleming, Ian 112
Fleming-Wyfold Foundation 95
Fleming's Bank 76, 109
Fleming Collection 146, 176
Fletcher, Alan 39
Flint, Russell 12, 83
Floors Castle 62, 70
Flowers at Bowling 146
Flowers on a Black Background 147
Foggie, David 50, 51
Foggie, Margaret 51
Forbes Collection 46
Foreman, Carol 192
Four Seasons 18
Four Tops 18
Fowberry Castle 70
Fowle, Frances 89
Fox, Iris 116
'France and Scotland' 107
Fraser, Douglas 123
Fraser, Sir Hugh 75
Frau ohne Schatten, Die 52, 124, 126–131

Frazer, Adrian 66
Freer Gallery 30
French School 31, 101
Frig Off Freddie You're Fired 107
'From a Family Collection' 95
Frood, Millie 76, 95
Fruitmarket Gallery 79, 84, 114
Fujisaki, Minae 170
Fuji Television 137, 164
Fuji Television Gallery 136, 137, 164
Funnell, Jenny 112
'Futurismo e Futuristi' 58
Gainsborough, Thomas 36, 124
Galloway Landscape, A 44
Galsworthy, John 39
Gardner, Ava 125
Garner, Erroll 16
Gates, Bill 82
'Gathering Mushroom' 7
'Gathering Mussels' 7
Gauguin, Paul 28, 41, 44, 62, 79, 87, 88, 89, 170
Gauld, David 42
Gauldie, Sinclair 39
Geldzahler, Henry 107
Gelmeroda 96, 97
Gelmeroda Church 186
Gelmeroda paintings 96, 97, 98, 118, 186
Gentleman Seated in his Study with Geological Specimens 119
Gere, John 35
German Expressionists 81, 95, 103
Gerry Mulligan Quartet 18
Giacometti, Diego 98
Gibbons, Carole 20, 39
Giles (cartoonist) 15
Gillespie, Dizzy 19
Gillies, W.G. 110
Girl and Tree 28
Girl in a Paisley Shawl, The 11, 21
Glasgow Academy 19
Glasgow Art Club 77
Glasgow Art Fair 81
Glasgow at a Glance 40
Glasgow Boys, the 28, 38, 42, 100, 103
Glasgow Corporation 15
Glasgow, European City of Culture 69, 93, 95
Glasgow Gallery of Modern Art 176
Glasgow High School 14
Glasgow Odeon 19
Glasgow Orchid Festival 1993 111
Glasgow Royal Concert Hall 99, 100, 101
Glasgow School, the 8, 11, 27, 28, 31, 40, 41, 42, 43, 44, 60, 83, 99, 103, 120
Glasgow School of Art 30, 53, 68, 83, 94, 145, 146, 147, 149, 151, 152, 153, 155, 171
Glasgow University 23, 26, 27, 30, 34, 37, 38, 40, 87, 90, 152
Glaspalast, Munich 41
Gloag, Ann 101, 102, 176

Index

golden section 151, 168
Goodison, Sir Nicholas 91
Good King Wenceslaus 42
Gottlieb, Adolph 44
Gould, John 63
Graham, W.S. 113
Grand Canal (Venice) 58
Granger, Dominique Moreau 84
Graves, Robert 119
Gray, Alasdair 20
Gray, Dorian 109
Green, Richard 117
Greene, Charles and Henry 177
Greene, Graham 186
Greengage Summer 21
Green Valley, The 60
Gregh, Eleanor 151
Grigor, Murray 30, 152
Grimshaw, Stewart 155
Grindea, Carola 89
Grindea, Myron 89
Gris, Juan 28
Grossart, Sir Angus 118
Grosvenor Gallery 41
Group of Seven 9, 73
Guardian, The 30, 136, 140
Gulbenkian Foundation 54
Gunn, William 182
Gunton, Philip 86
Guthrie, James 28, 41, 42
Hague School of art 12
Hague, The 35
Hahn, Kurt 101
Hamilton, Chico 18
Hamilton, Ontario 112
'Hankies' 107, 108
Hardie, Andrew 60
Hardie, Archie 26
Hardie, Gillian (Gillie) 36, 60, 77, 192
Hardie, Grandpa 13
Hardie, Marion 60
Hardie, Nell 111
Hardy, Thomas 15, 76, 120
Hare, Bill 103
Harlamoff, Alexei 72, 83, 117
Harris, Lawren 73
Harris, Martin 16
Harrison Collection 59
Harrison, Gabrielle 85
Harry to Heaven 179
Harte, Bret 102
Hartley, Marsden 59
Harvest Moon, The 146
Head of a Girl 101
'Heartbreak Hotel' 18
Heindel, Robert 102
Helenslee House 10
Hellier, Henry 30
Hemingway, Ernest 20
Hemmings, Peter 124, 126, 132
Henriques, Ben 111
Henry, Clare 82, 87, 94, 103, 107, 113, 176
Henry, George 41, 42, 44, 83
Henry Huntington Memorial Library, New York 55
Herald, J.W. 40
Heraldry 95
Herald (The Glasgow) 63,

82, 94, 100, 102, 103, 119, 123, 181
Herman, Josef 95
Herman, Woody 19
Hess, Hans 20, 96
Heuser-Mantell, Margret 97
Hida-Takayama Museum 147, 152, 154, 176
Highgate, London 12, 36
Hill House, The 145, 151, 157
'Hills of Dream Revisited' 52, 53
Hines, Earl 16
Hiroshige 161, 162
Historic Scotland 63
Hitchens, Ivon 28, 78
Hockney, David 11, 81, 107, 111, 118, 123–134, 135, 136, 138, 143, 177, 178, 179, 186
Hockney, Kenneth 133
Hodgkins, Frances 80
Hogarth, William 99
Holbein, Hans 109
Holiday, Billie 20
Honeyman, Grant 78, 90
Honeyman, Thomas John (Tom) 28, 43, 44, 45, 53, 56, 78, 90, 104, 106
Hope 20
Hopkinson, Martin 97
Hornel, E.A. 11, 28, 41, 42, 78, 88, 120
House of an Art Lover 153
House of Fraser 75
Howard, Paul 116
Howarth, Thomas (Tom) 30, 72, 113, 117, 145, 148
Howarth Collection 116, 118, 148
Howie, James 39
Howson, Peter 83, 85, 119, 126
Hukin and Heath 156
Hume, John 121
Hunter, Leslie 43, 45, 102, 104, 105, 106
Hunter, Margaret 59, 85, 86, 87
Hunter Blair, Jamie 70, 84
Hunterian Art Gallery 29, 87, 90, 96, 97, 118, 145, 148, 149, 152, 155
Huntington Library, Pasadena 124
Hutchison, Gemmell 12
Hutton, James 119
Ibrox Stadium 19
Ide Collar 72
Idomeneo 123, 124
Ikeuchi-san 167
Imperial Collection of Porcelain, Taiwan 65
Imperial Hotel 169
Imperial Regalia of Japan 172
Innes, James Dickson (J.D.) 70
In the Orchard 42
Inzievar House 70
Ipswich 14, 15, 18
Ipswich School 15, 16
Iris Fox Collection 116
Irwin, David 37
Isozaki, Arata 132
Italian Renaissance 26, 170
Jamesone, George 62
Japan 42, 137, 145, 149, 150,

152, 153, 157, 161–165, 169–173, 176, 177, 179
Jaurès, Jean 20
jazz 16, 17, 18, 19, 20, 29, 147
Jencks, Charles 171
Jervis, Simon 46
Jiyu Gakuen Girls' School 169, 177
John Brown's (shipyard) 8, 11
Johnson, Dr Samuel 14, 15, 55, 99, 120
Johnson, Ian 81
Johnson, J.J. 19
Johnstone, John 40, 115
Johnstone, Murray 95, 100, 111, 126, 133
Johnstone, Raymond 99, 126, 133
Johnstone, William 40, 47
Justine 21
'Kaiser Natron' 142
Kandinsky, Wassily 96
Kane, John 50
Kano School 161
Kathedrale des Sozialismus 97
Keil School 10
Keith Collection 76
Keith, David Barrogill 76
Keith, Mildred 76
Kelvingrove Art Gallery, Glasgow 15, 20, 28, 30, 38, 41, 59, 101, 119, 133, 155
Kelvingrove Park 155
Kemp, Martin 37
Kobayashi, Ken-Ichiro 170
Kennedy, Alexander 28
Kennedy, Eunice 82
Kennedy, John F. 82
Kennedy, William 41, 42
Kennington, Eric 147
Kenton, Stan 17
Kentuck Knob 83, 147
Kiefer, Anselm 118, 137, 138
King, Elspeth 121
King, Jessie Marion 18, 44, 52, 119, 155
Kinkell Castle 62
Kirchner, Ernst Ludwig 96
Kirkcudbright 11, 28, 42, 78, 88, 185
Kissell, Jennifer 102
Kitagawa, Tomio 148
Klee, Paul 20, 44, 51, 95, 96, 98, 109, 137
Knight Frank & Rutley 61
Knight, James 20, 21, 24
Knights of Malta 181
Knox, Jack 39
Knox, John 105
Knox, Liz 110
Kodály, Zoltán 27
Koriyama Museum of Art 156, 176
Lacey, Jackie 70
Ladnier, Tommy 17
Lady Artists' Club 45, 175
'Lady Madonna' 18
Lally, Pat 99
Landscape with Calves 12
Lane Sale 68
Lang, Blair 72
Lang, Daniel 81, 102
Lange, Josef 90

L'Année Dernière à Marienbad 20
Lannie, Lydia and Ernie 77
Larrabee, Constance Stuart 177
Las Meniñas 16
Last Dance, The 46, 47
Last of the Clan, The 8
László, Philip de 27
Latsis, John 178
Lauder, Robert Scott 37
Laurie, John 95
Laver, James 46
'La Ville: Visions Urbaines' 58
Lawson, Muriel 83
Leishman, Robert (Bob) 37
Lenaghan, Brenda 107
Lennon, John 18, 70
Lesaffre, Micheline 112
Les Nabis 88, 101
Lessing, Doris 58
Letter of Introduction, The 161
Leven, River 7, 8
Levin, Robert 98
Lewis, Wyndham 28, 59, 78, 90
L'Hermitte, Léon 83
Life of Johnson 120
Life on the Dniva 50
Lillie Art Gallery 95
Lindsay, Patrick 60, 67
Linnaean Society 111
Locke, Charles 98
Lomond, Loch 7, 143
London Symphony Orchestra 65
Lopresti, Liz 124
Lorrain, Claude 24, 26, 182, 183, 185
Los Angeles Art Fair 16, 126
Los Angeles Opera Company 124
Loteria Nacional: Buying the Tickets 53
Lothian Road, Edinburgh 57
Lowe, Poppy 57
Lumley, John 62, 66, 68, 79
Lutyens, Edwin 145
Lycée Mistral 23, 104
Lymon, Frankie 18
Lyttelton, Humphrey 18
Macchiaioli 120
Macdonald, Margaret 27
Macdonald, Margaret (wife of C.R.Mackintosh) 155
Macdonald, 'Spanish' 80
Macdonald-Wright, Stanton 59
Macfarlane, Norman 104
Macgregor, William York 41, 42, 100, 120
MacGregor, Neil 19
MacInnes Collection 20
Macke, August 96, 97
Mackie, Anne 88
Mackie, Charles 87, 88
Mackintosh, Charles Rennie 7, 13, 24, 27, 29, 30, 40, 50, 68, 76, 77, 81, 82, 83, 109, 116, 118, 135, 145–152, 154, 155, 162, 171, 175, 176, 177, 186
Maclaurin Art Gallery 78, 111
Maclean, Lady 62
Maclean, Will 112
Macleod, Fiona 52, 187
Macleod, Robert 30

189

Macmillan, Duncan 112
MacNair, Frances 155
MacNair, Herbert 155
MacNicol, Ian 28, 42, 72, 78
Macrae, Duncan 121
MacRae, Emma Fordyce 102
MacTaggart, Sir William 44, 70, 178
Magic Flute, The 131
Maison Carré 24
Malaisie 20
Manchester Art Gallery 84
Manchester University Press 132
Manet, Édouard 27, 179
Man in Harness 85
Man Walker 85
Marc, Franz 96
Marcoussis, Louis 28
Maris, Jacob 50
Marlborough Fine Art 84, 98, 119
Marquet, Albert 44
Marriage of Figaro, The 84, 89, 90
Marriage of Isaac and Rebecca, The 182, 183
Martin, Gregory 66
Martin, Sir Leslie 18, 99, 122
Maryhill Library, Glasgow 95
Mason, David 72
Mason's Yard 178
'Master Duck' 14
Matisse, Henri 20, 24, 28, 38, 44, 45, 57, 62, 101, 104, 106, 123, 179, 186
Maze, Paul 101
Macandrew, Hugh 37
McAndrew, Nick 133
McCance, Margaret 59
McCance, William 40, 44, 59, 87
McChlery, Morrison 95
McClure, David 39
McCracken, Francis 80, 81
McEwen, Dorothy 83
McGill, Harry 14
McGilvray, Bing 126, 127
McIlwraith, Averil 29
McInnes Collection 28
McLean, Ronnie 19
McLellan, William 113
McNicol, Cameron 101
McTaggart, William 8, 45, 47, 176
Mediterranean Hill Town 59
Meidner, Ludwig 96, 97
Meldrum, James 27
Mellis, Margaret 89
Mellon Foundation 83
Mellon, Paul 83
Melville, Arthur 41, 42, 60, 105, 186
Melville Exhibition 60
Menpes, Mortimer 169
Merzbild 72
Metamorphoses 79
Methlan Park 10
Metropolitan Museum, New York 107, 145
Michelangelo 55
Middleton family 62
Midsummer Night Race 27

Miles, Hamish 26, 37, 41, 54
Mills Observatory 53
Milne, Maclauchlan 76, 80
Ming Dynasty 72
Miró, Joan 104, 178
Mitchison, Naomi 101
Modern Jazz Quartet 19, 20
Modigliani 62, 109
Moltzau Collection 20
Mondrian, Piet 122, 125, 186
Mondrian Hotel 124, 125
Monet, Claude 101
Genji Monogatori 161
Monroe, Marilyn 125
Montgomerie, William 9, 55, 105
Montgomerie, Norah 55
Montgreenan House 69, 70
Harvest Moon, The 146
Moore, Henry 164, 185
Moore, Roger 104
Morel 83
Morin-Miller Gallery 97
Morning White 112
Morris, Margaret (Fergusson) 9, 38, 39, 43, 55, 95
Morrison, James 39, 76, 94
Morrocco, Alberto 39, 77, 78, 103
Morton, Alastair 122
Morton, Jelly Roll 16, 17
Morton, John Gibb 122, 177
Morton Sundour Fabrics Ltd 122
Mountolive 21
Mozart, Constanze 90
Mozart, Franz Xavier Wolfgang 90
Mozart, Wolfgang Amadeus 19, 90, 124, 131
Mrs Dalloway 58
Mukai Scholarship 152
Mukai, Tetsuya 152, 153
Mulholland Drive, Los Angeles 132
Mullen, Joe 69, 77
Mulligan, Gerry 17, 18
Munch, Edvard 51, 64
Munro, Graham 44, 79, 80, 123, 178
Munro, Ruth 80, 81
Musée Calvet 24
Musée Lapidaire 23
Museum of Contemporary Art, Los Angeles 132
Museum of Contemporary Art, Tokyo 156
Napoleon at St Helena 1816 47
Napoleon on Board the Bellerophon 47
National Art Collections Fund 90, 154
National Gallery, London 55
National Gallery of Art, Washington 178
National Gallery of Australia 46
National Gallery of Scotland 28, 37, 39, 42, 54, 57, 87, 88, 90, 100, 101, 117, 118, 121, 133, 161
National Galleries of Scotland 56, 98
National Library of Scotland

56, 88, 89
National Maritime Museum 47
National Museum in Tokyo 172
National Trust of Scotland 62
Nativity Angels 110
Naughton, Brigadier 35
Neat, Timothy 151
Neffe, Christian 101
Neffe-Degandt 101
Nelson, Admiral Lord 121
Nevinson, Christopher R.W. 28, 44, 59, 87
Newbery, Fra 147, 156
New Club, Edinburgh 57, 77
New Glasgow Group 95, 101
New Lanark 121, 176
New Mozartiana in Glasgow University 90
New Orleans 16, 17, 18
New York 17, 19, 31, 46, 55, 72, 81, 89, 96, 97, 98, 107, 110, 114, 118, 126, 131, 138, 145, 153, 156
New York School 131
Ngaisah 27
Nîmes 24
Nisbet, Edward 28
Nolde, Emil 96, 97, 98, 99, 179
Noone, Jimmie 17
Norfolk 15, 182
Nude – Reflections 70
Observer, The 80
Ogilvy-Wedderburn, Sir Andrew 49
Oliver, Cordelia 30
Oliver, Joe 'King' 17
On the Lagoon 47
On the Scheldt 50
Op Art 29
Orchardson, Sir William Quiller 46, 47, 54, 55, 70, 117, 136
Orchar, James Guthrie 34, 55
Orient Express 24
Origin of Species 119
Ory, Kid 17
Ospidale della Santa Cruz, Toledo 126
Ossian 38
Outerbridge Jr, Paul 72
'Outside Right At The Sunset Gate' 114
Paisnel Gallery 178
Palazzo Grassi 58
Palissy, Bernard 175
Palizzi, Filippo 120
Palumbo, Lord Peter 112, 147
Papal Palace 24
Park, Stuart 12, 42, 176
Parsifal 126
Parthenon, Greece 25, 185
Paterson, James 41
Patrick, Andrew McIntosh 40, 41, 43, 156
Patrick, James McIntosh 38, 39, 40
Paul Kovesdy Gallery 96
Paul Mellon Center for British Art (Yale) 83
Paul Mellon Centre for Studies in British Art (London) 83
Pechstein, Max 96

Pedlar, The 83
Pennell, Elizabeth 27
Pennell, Joseph 27
Penny, Nicholas 120
Peploe, Denis 44
Peploe, S.J. 43, 44, 45, 56, 59, 68, 70, 76, 89, 178, 185
Pepper, George 9
Pepper, Kathleen Daly 9, 73
Permeke, Constant 38, 44, 106
Perth Art Gallery 38, 95
Petitjean, Edith 89
Phillip, John 53
Picasso, Pablo 9, 16, 20, 28, 37, 41, 44, 45, 57, 72, 89, 104, 105, 137, 148, 164
Pier Arts Centre, Orkney 85, 87, 119
Piers Kettlewell Cabinetmakers 150, 153
Pinder, Carl 107
Piramide Cestia 183
Pissarro, Camille 28
Pompidou Centre 58
'Poor House Door' 139
Portrait of Constanze Mozart 90
Portrait of Harriet Dutens 120
Portrait of May 40
Portrait of Prince Charles Edward Stuart 120
Portrait of Sarah Malcolm 99
Portrait of the Artist's Son Titus 36
Portrait of the Composer Arcangelo Corelli 120
Portrait of the Kirkcudbright Bellringer Winefield Nellens 28
Post-Impressionist School 28, 37, 57
Post-Modernism 171
Pouncey, Philip 35
Pow, Tom 44, 178
Powell, Bud 16
Pre-Raphaelites 26, 44, 55, 66
Prévin, André 65
Princes Street, Edinburgh 57, 59
Pringle, John Quinton 27, 40
'Printmaking in Dundee' 52
Pritchard, Kathy 64
Procession with a View of Delphi, A 182, 183
Professor Young 40
Pulsford, Charles 44, 110, 111
Pyramid of Cestius 183
Queen Elizabeth 8
Queen Margaret's Medical College 146
Queen Mary 8
Queen's Park Synagogue 114
Giffnock and Newlands Synagogue 114
Quetta 10
Rachet, Pamela 24, 111
Rachet Frères 24
Radio City Music Hall 177
Raeburn, Sir Henry 56
Rain on Princes Street 57, 58, 59
Rake's Progress, The 123, 125
Ralston, Gladys 9
Ralston, Willie 9

Ramsay, Allan 36
Ranson, Paul 88
Rauschenberg, Robert 131
Rectitude of Chairs, The 150
Red and White Roses 12
Redpath, Anne 19
Regatta, The 57
Reid, A.J. McNeill 27
Reid, Alexander 27, 28, 44, 89
Reid & Lefevre 27, 28, 164
Reid, Sir George 106
Reid, John 178
Reith, Lord 19
Rembrandt 36, 70, 109
Resnais, Alain 20
Renfrew Ferry 95
Renoir, Auguste 101, 179
Reynolds, Sir Joshua 36, 76, 99, 120, 186
Rhône Valley 25
Ribbon Counter, The 57, 59, 85
Ribera, Jusepe de 72
Richard Gray Gallery 127
Richardson, Tony 132
Richmond, Sir John 87
Rietveld, Gerrit 177
Rijksbureau voor Kunsthistorische Documentatie 35
Rijksmuseum 36
Riley, Bridget 29
Ringhiera, Salon della 182, 183
Roach, Max 19
Robert Fleming & Co 95
Roberts, Alison 40
Roberts, Kenneth 40
Roberts, Sir Hugh 65
Robertson, Fiona 75, 179
Robertson, Giles 133
Robertson, Grandpa 14
Robertson, Jack 11
Robertson, James Downie 82, 83, 109, 110
Robertson, Moira see Baxter, Moira
Robertson, Rhoda 11
Robertson, William 9
Roche, Alexander 42
Rohlfs, Christian 96, 97
Rolfe, Ian 119
Roman Theatre of Orange 25
Romance 42
Romancecar 163, 164
Room de Luxe 68, 157
Black Gunpowder Factory at Roslin, The 121
Rossetti, Dante Gabriel 55
Röthlisberger, Professor Marcel 183
Rouault, Georges 44, 178, 179
Roux, Albert 104
Roux, Mademoiselle 104
Roux, Paul 104, 105
Royal Albert Hall 178
Royal Armouries 121
Royal College of Art 81, 107, 178
Royal Festival Hall 18
Royal Scottish Academy (RSA) 38, 47, 53, 136
Royal Scottish Academy's Diploma Galleries 47, 53
Royal Scottish Museum 119,

121, 154
Russell, Rachel 64
Russell, Richard 39, 93
Ryder, Albert Pinkham 50
Sabarsky, Serge 98
Sadanobu, Matsudaira 161, 165
Sailing of the Emigrant Ship, The 8
Sailing Vessels in a Calm 83
Salomon, Antoine 88
Saltwood Castle 47
Salvesen, Magda 36, 46, 72, 136
Samuel, Bill 82
Saenredam, Pieter 71
Sarraute, Nathalie 25
Saville, Jenny 103, 178
Sawallisch, Wolfgang 126
Schidlof, Peter 53
Schmidt, Richard 126
Schröder House 177
Schueler, Jon 46, 81, 102
Schwitters, Kurt 72, 96
Scotland Street School 151
Scotsman, The 77, 100, 107
Scott, Baillie 145
Scott, Colin 16
Scott, Mel 86, 147
Scottish Art Review, The 28
Scottish Arts Council 28, 36, 40, 43, 46, 55, 106, 109, 110
Scottish Ballet 102
Scottish Modern Arts Association 57
Scottish National Gallery of Modern Art 38, 57, 59, 95, 98, 101
Scottish Opera 84, 89, 123
Scottish Painting 30, 31, 41, 58, 93, 100, 146
Scottish Television 80
Scream, The 64
Scrutton, Hugh 76, 118
Sea Storm 31, 58
Seattle Art Museum 82
'Secrets Box' 140
Sekine, Mas 78
Seki, Taeko (Taeko-san) 2, 4, 19, 166
Sensation of Crossing the Street, The 57, 58, 59
Sergeant Pepper's Lonely Hearts Club Band 9, 60
Sérusier, Paul 87, 88
Seven Journeys, The 113
'Seven Painters in Dundee' 40, 94, 106
Seventeenth VN Painting 131
Severini, Gino 56, 57, 181
Sewell, Brian 54
sgraffito 130
Shafted 112, 113
Shamrockbank 7, 8, 9, 10, 11, 12, 13, 14, 21
Sharp, William 52
Shawlands 12, 13
Shepherd's Hill 12
Shikibu, Murasaki 161
Shriver, Eunice Kennedy 82
Shriver, Sargent 82
Sickert, Walter 83
Siebenbrodt, Michael 96
Simpson, Anne 63

Sinatra, Frank 38
Singer Factory, Clydebank 8, 13
Singleton, Alan 20
Singleton, George 106
Singleton, Hope 20
Singleton, Vincent 106
'Si Si' 18
Sisley, Alfred 62, 79
Skirving, Archibald 62
Smith, George 29, 145, 155
Smith, W. Gordon 94, 103, 107, 111
Smith, Thomas 120
Smith, William 119
Smollett, Tobias 8
Solitude 45
Solsgirth House 70
'Song of the Unborn' 131
Sonnenblumen und Mohn 96, 99
Sotheby's 55, 59, 86, 116
Spalding, Julian 84, 119, 133
Spencer, James 65
Spencer, Stanley 40
Square Table 29
St Andrew's University Library 51
St Giles Cathedral 124
St Kentigern 77
St Martin's School of Art 16
St Rémy 24
Stadt Hinter dem Strom, Die 96
Stanley Cursiter Centenary Exhibition 87
Starck, Philippe 155
Steer, John 37
Stölzl, Gunta 177
Stonegarthside Hall 13
Stone, Norman 19
Strauss, Richard 124, 131
Stirling Smith Art Gallery and Museum 120, 121
Studio Vista 31, 58
Sunflowers (Van Gogh) 170
Sunshine Building 171
Sutherland, Graham 17
Sutton, Denys 42
'Swallows' choker 155
Taffner, Donald 118, 145
Taffner, Eleanor 118, 145, 146
Takyo, Shiho 148, 149, 150
Tana, Andrea 102
Tanaka, Makiko 169
Tanguy, Père 107
Tàpies, Antoni 104
Tate, Buddy 19
Tate Gallery 36, 57, 93, 137
Tatum, Art 16, 17
Taylor, E.A. 44
Teien House 168
Terroristin, Die 58
Thomas, Gordon 18
Thomas, Roy 69, 70
Thompson, Ally 111
Thompson, Colin 37
Thompson, Emma 106
Thomson, Ann 84
Thomson, David 15, 72, 97, 98, 154
Thomson, Lord 77
Thomson, Michael 84
Thomson, Mike 78

'Three Scottish Colourists' 43, 44, 45
Tintock Cup, The 148
Tintoretto 62
Tisdall, Caroline 135, 136, 140, 141, 142, 143
Tisdall Collection 135, 142
Titian 62, 79
Toft at Elie, The 12
Toits Rouges, Les 95
Tokyo Metropolitan Government Building 170
Tokyo Tower 170, 171
Toll, Barbara 114
Toulouse-Lautrec 46, 47
Tourlamain, Gordon 78
Towie Barclay Castle 62
Toyota Museum 135, 136, 137, 148, 150, 176
Traill Collection 87
Traill, Isobel 87
'Tramstop' 142
Treatise on Metalwork 155
Tree of Influence, The Tree of Importance, The Sun of Cowardice 146
Tree of Personal Effort, The Sun of Indifference 146
Tremayne, Keith 86
Tristan and Isolde 130
Troup, Sir James and Lady 28
tuberculosis 17
Turner, Kathleen 176
Tutti Frutti 106
'Un Coeur Simple' 132
Uncle Stewart 21
Urban, Dr Martin 98, 99
Ure, Alan 148
Ure, Gudrun 148, 149, 155
Usher, Mrs Murray 76, 120
Usherwood, Nicholas 113
Van Beyeren, Abraham 36
Van Gogh, Vincent 24, 27, 29, 37, 41, 44, 62, 170
Van Vlissingen, Paul 135
Vatican Library 182
Vaughan, Sarah 19
Vegetable Stall, The 42, 100
Velázquez, Diego 16, 183
Venice 47, 58, 61, 62, 79, 89, 124, 142
Venice Biennale 142
Vermeer, Johannes 37
Vernet, Joseph 24
Very New Paintings 128, 130
Vettriano, Jack 11, 59, 113
Victoria and Albert Museum 30
Victoria Galleries, Dundee 53
View for the Curious at Salt's Mill, A 127
View of Crail 120
View of St Tropez 76
Vincent, Gene 18
Vine, The 37
Vorticism 59, 155
Voysey, Charles 122, 145
Vuillard, Édouard 28, 87, 88, 90, 91, 94, 101, 103, 109
Waagen, G.F. 35
Wada, Junko 170
Walker, David 40, 94
Wallace Collection 39

Wallace, William 7
Waller, Fats 16
Walmesley, Louise 78
Walton, E.A. 40, 42, 76, 176
Walton FRS, John 40
Walton, George 159
Warhol, Andy 81, 107
Wark, Kirsty 89
Washington Gallery 82, 83, 87
Watanabe, Akio 177
Watanabe, Shinichiro 172
Waterhouse, Ellis 36
Watson, James D. 101
Watson, Keith 111
Watt, Alison 103
Weatherill, Lord 172
Webb, Sir William 12
Weinberg 50
Wemyss Place 61, 79
Western Club 77
Whistler, James Abbott
    McNeill 27, 30, 31

Whitechapel Art Gallery 57
White Cockade Tea Room 155
White, Jenny 147
White Tulips 146
Whitfield, Paul 70
Whittinghame Drive 155, 177
Whitton, Mr 34
'Why Do Fools Fall in Love'
    18
Wilkie, Janet 121
Wilkie, Sir David 35, 41, 44,
    60, 66, 83, 161, 186
Wilkins, William 55
Williams, Sir Alwyn 90
Willow Tea Rooms 68, 145,
    152, 154, 157, 176
Wilson, Andrew 83, 93, 111,
    116, 119
Wilson Collection 83, 93,
    111, 116, 119
Wilson, Margaret 78
Wilson, Richard 106

Wilson, Teddy 16
Winding, Kai 19
Windyhill 145, 148, 149, 151,
    159, 176, 177
Wink, Johann Amandus 36
Winning, Thomas 121
Wishart, Ruth 100
Wiszniewski, Adrian 83, 84,
    112, 113
Witch's Blood 49
Wittrock, Wolfgang 97, 98
Wood, Flora 95
Woolford, Harry 71, 119
Woolf, Virginia 58
Wraxall, Lord 53
Wright, Frank Lloyd 83, 147,
    152, 168, 169, 177
Wright, Sir Michael 154
Wrythen Newel, The 151, 157
WyhowskiCollection 60
Wylie & Lochhead 155
Yasukuni Shrine 172, 173

Yeats, William Butler 51
Yellow Cigarette, The 84
Young, Andrew McLaren 26,
    27, 29, 31, 33, 37, 39, 40, 87
Young, Clara 40, 53
Young, Lester 16
Young Mariners, The 12
Your Cheatin' Heart 106, 107
Zavertal, Hugo 90
Zavertal, Vladislav 90
Zoffany, Johan 63, 72

Picture Acknowledgements

Bridgeman Images for *The White Piano* by Arthur Melville and *The Pedlar* by Sir David Wilkie.

Nolde Foundation for *Sonnenblumen und Mohn (Sunflowers and Poppies)* by Emil Nolde © Nolde Stiftung Seebüll.

National Galleries Scotland for *The Regatta* by Stanley Cursiter and *Deux ouvrières dans l'atelier de couture (Two Seamstresses in the Workroom)* by Édouard Vuillard.

Stirling Smith Art Gallery and Museum for *Harriet Dutens of Craigforth* by Sir Joshua Reynolds.

Culture Perth & Kinross Museums & Galleries and The John Laurie Estate for *The Cocktail Hour* by John Laurie, © The John Laurie Estate.

Deutsche Bank Collection for *Auf dem Friedhof in Thun (At Thun Cemetery)* by August Macke.

The Hunterian Museum and Art Gallery for *By the Bonnie Banks O' Fordie* by Charles H. Mackie. © The Hunterian, University of Glasgow 2017

A Procession with a View of Delphi and *The Marriage of Isaac and Rebecca* attributed to Claude Lorrain are held privately and we are grateful to the owners for their permission to reproduce these paintings.

William Hardie for the images: *William Hardie* by John Byrne, © John Byrne; *Chair with High-tapering-back for the Hall* by Charles Rennie Mackintosh; *Linthorpe Pottery vase and Tea Service* by Christopher Dresser; *Kathedrale, Titelholzschnitt zum Baiuhaus-Manifest und Programm* by Lyonel Feininger (print); *Gentleman Seated In His Study* (unknown); *William Hardie* by David Hockney (from *David Hockney New Drawings* © David Hockney); *With Cyril Gerber and Paul Howard; With Tom Howarth; With David Hockney; With Jamie Bruce and his daughter; Gallery Front, 141 West Regent Street; Car through railing; With Pat Lally, HRH The Princess Royal, Raymond Johnstone; With David Hockney; Steven Campbell; Peter Howson and Jill Gerber; Daniel Lang and Lady Orde; Blythswood Square; Gallery interior, West Regent Street; Taeko Seki; Arata Endo; The Piano House.*

We acknowledge the copyright holders of any copyright paintings in private collections.

All works in copyright are © copyright the artist or the artist's estate.